17985
L29
899

W9-BGB-076

THE
COSMO
REPORT

ALSO BY LINDA WOLFE:

PRIVATE PRACTICES

PLAYING AROUND: WOMEN AND
EXTRAMARITAL SEX

THE COSMO REPORT

by Linda Wolfe

ARBOR HOUSE
New York

Copyright © 1981 by *Cosmopolitan* magazine and Linda Wolfe

All rights reserved, including the right of reproduction in whole or in part in any form. Published in the United States of America by Arbor House Publishing Company and in Canada by Fitz-henry & Whiteside, Ltd.

Library of Congress Catalog Card Number: 80-70226

ISBN: 0-87795-315-5

Manufactured in the United States of America

10 9 8 7 6 5 4 3 2 1

To the 106,000 women who contributed the experiences on which this book is based

FOREWORD

Why would a magazine conduct a sex survey? The answer may
seem obvious: simply to find out about the sex-lives of its readers.
Something "obvious," however, frequently only seems obvious *later*
—after you've finished the job and it "works." The best magazine
ideas—like ours for the survey and the Burt Reynolds centerfold—
sometimes seem to "float" in, rather than arrive in a brilliant flash
because the magazine needs a "blockbuster" and the staff is ex-
horted to produce one. The sex-survey idea just "floated in" one
Tuesday afternoon at our regular staff meeting when editors, art
directors, production and copy people read article ideas out loud to
each other, this "winner" contributed by senior editor Myra Apple-
ton. Between the time Myra suggested it and the survey's appear-
ance in *Cosmo,* exactly six *years* went by. Why so long? Well, probably because *Cosmo*'s editor (me) just isn't very research-oriented and
the idea of compiling a questionnaire on *any* subject, even one as
fascinating as sex, binding it into the magazine, persuading readers
to cooperate by filling in answers and mailing these back to us, then
tabulating responses and trying to make sense of what everybody
said, seemed to me, on first hearing, about as do-able and interesting
as digging up Central Park. Nevertheless we went so far as to com-
pile a questionnaire. Everybody contributed questions, so we had
hundreds for Myra to work with. At that point I put the survey
away, to *ripen,* you might say, for six years, then in the summer of
1979 it seemed to me its time had come. How do you decide these
things? I don't know—you just have "feelings." So we got the
survey out again, perfected it . . . deciding whether to state the

7

multiple-choice questions first-person, second-person, whatever, adding new ones we hadn't thought of before and organizing them into categories. We also decided to run the survey as a regular *Cosmo* article (January 1980) rather than as a perforated tear-out with return postage guaranteed. That saved us money but required the reader not only to answer seventy-nine questions, scissor the pages out, put them in an envelope and address it, but add her *own* postage. I wrote a personal message exhorting her to do just *that,* telling her how wonderful it would be if she would share her sex-life with other *Cosmo* readers so we could see just how far the sexual revolution had brought us and if everybody was having more sex and enjoying it *more,* having more sex and enjoying it less, or whatever combination of frequency and reaction might become known.

What a response! For weeks the Simmons Market Research Bureau, the research organization *Cosmo* engaged to handle the survey, would call nearly daily to say, "You won't believe this . . . We've got a roomful of mail that looks like the blizzard of 'eighty-eight and it's still pouring in." I had my picture taken sitting on a stack of questionnaires that reached nine feet high. After eight weeks, when we finally stopped counting, more than 106,000 *Cosmo* readers had filled in and mailed their sex-survey questionnaires to us. Then came the task of interpreting the findings. Linda Wolfe, author, behavior and science writer and a fine writer *generally,* was engaged to study the results Simmons had compiled for us, plus read the hundreds of personal messages scrawled in the margins of many of the questionnaires and to prepare an article (an excellent one that we published October 1980). Everybody wanted to talk sex-survey on television. After all, this was the biggest response to *any* magazine survey in history and surely the largest sex survey ever conducted. Alfred Kinsey based his statistical calculations for *Sexual Behavior in the Human Female* on interviews with 5,940 women; Shere Hite, in her *Hite Report* on women, on about 3,000 responses; and Masters and Johnson's research for *Human Sexual Response* was conducted with only 382 females, 312 males. To continue comparisons, the Roper Poll samples only about 2,000 people, Harris 1,250. Qualitatively, surely it would be revealing and important to know about the sex-life of the *Cosmopolitan* reader, such a participator in the sexual revolution but also such an exemplary citizen (*Cosmo* women do not live *through* other people but achieve success by unrelenting hard work on their own). The *Today* show, *Tonight* show, Merv Griffin, Mike Douglas, John Davidson and dozens of others all investigated (and dissected) the *Cosmo* Sex Survey. One of my happiest memories is toasting in the sun in the Rose Garden Amphitheater in Portland, Oregon, being interviewed by Phil Donahue on his extraordinary television program and interrogated by that fantastic audience he draws. (*Why* would 68 percent of our readers have a sexual experience on a first date and not consider themselves promiscuous? *Why* would more than half of the *married* women have engaged in an extramarital affair? Biggest challenge: describing the "missionary position" to one perplexed audience member who swore she didn't understand it.)

So now the survey, comprehensively, clearly dealt with and interpreted in this excellent book by Linda Wolfe, is here for all of us to read and study. If *Cosmo* survey-participants are a little more active sexually than the country as a whole (and we don't *know* that to be true), it's somehow reassuring to know that a whopping 92 percent said they prefer sex *with* commitment (even though 55 percent have made love on their lunch hour). Read, enjoy . . . and, one hopes, profit with us from *The Cosmo Report.*

—**Helen Gurley Brown**

ACKNOWLEDGMENTS

I would like to acknowledge the assistance of Professor M. Pollack of the City University of New York, who served as psychological and statistical consultant on this book.

I would also like to thank Nancy McKeon and Paula Wiggins for their expert editorial services.

—L. W.

CONTENTS

INTRODUCTION

We have been living through turbulent times. We have had, as anyone can—and often relentlessly does—tell you, a "sexual revolution."

But what exactly does this mean? What exactly are people doing today that they didn't do yesterday? *(How different are those things, anyway?)* Has the revolution lived up to its promises, met people's hopes and fantasies? *(What are those hopes and fantasies?)* Has it disappointed them, made them yearn for yet a new sexual order? *(If so, what caused their disappointment?)* And for that matter, what about you and me? Are our sexual practices and feelings typical? *(Typical of whom?)* Are we in tune with the times, or woefully behind or eccentrically ahead of them? *(Where do we fit in? Is there some way we can measure ourselves?)*

As a writer who often explores contemporary behavior, I had for a long time been curious about questions like these. But they seemed impenetrable. There just wasn't enough solid information to allow for satisfying answers. It was not that there weren't plenty of books and articles purporting to measure America's sexual revolution. But they were invariably subjective accounts, or reports based on small, and usually homogeneous and highly special groups of individuals. No large-scale detailed survey of contemporary sexual practices and attitudes had been conducted on a vast group of diverse Americans. So although I was deeply interested in the sexual changes that had taken place in America since my college days in the fifties, I had more or less given up hope of ever being able to write about them.

17

Then, a year and a half ago, an editor from *Cosmopolitan* tele-phoned and asked me to report on and interpret the data from a survey on sexuality that had been published in the magazine in January 1980. I at first begged off. I had, as I've said, abandoned any expectation of investigating the sexual questions that most inter-ested me and, to be honest, I believed that the particular topic under consideration, women's sexual behavior and attitudes, had been written about to excess. They had been extensively reported on by Shere Hite in *The Hite Report;* Gay Talese had touched on them in *Thy Neighbor's Wife;* and scores of other lesser-known writers had been addressing them repetitively.

Then the *Cosmopolitan* editor told me that 106,000 women had responded to the survey and my interest picked up immediately. Hite, in *The Hite Report,* had studied 3,000 women. Talese had talked, at best, with a few hundred. And most of the other writers on whom I, and everyone else, relied when trying to understand contempo-rary eroticism, wrote about even smaller groups. My bookshelves were crowded with dense studies and thick volumes on sex based on a scholar's interviews with a hundred college women, or sixty urban teenagers, or a dozen patients in psychoanalytic counseling. Even Kinsey—although his work was more detailed, scrupulous and scientific than that of any other sex researcher before or since—had relied, for the famous "Kinsey Report" on women, *Sexual Behavior in the Human Female,* on a sample of only 5,940 people.

I told the editor I'd come and take a look. If nothing else, *Cosmopolitan*'s 106,000 responses might prove a never before equalled resource for sex research, a gargantuan body of information. Cer-tainly the respondents made up, by far, the largest group ever polled about sexuality.

Still, I didn't say yes to the notion of writing up the survey until sometime afterward. The editor had directed me to examine the survey at Simmons Market Research Bureau, a public-opinion re-search company in Manhattan that services many magazines and publishers. In the time that passed between speaking with the editor and visiting Simmons, I began to have doubts about the project. After all, I argued with myself, in a survey, size isn't everything. Variety is also important. And the women who had participated in the survey were probably all the same kind of women. I presumed to picture them . . . they all had sleek blonde hair, sensuous lips, a bold and unabashed gaze, and wore their blouses extravagantly unbuttoned. They were that image that pouts up at me from the stack of *Cosmopolitan* magazines at my corner newsstand every month. They were that famous *Cosmopolitan* girl, half fantasy, half dream. How much could a woman like this tell the world about sex in America?

Then, eventually, the day of my appointment with Simmons arrived. I was shown into a room where thousands of questionnaires lay heaped. They formed a mountain of mail, so high I couldn't reach the top. I began shuffling through the envelopes at the bottom of the hill, and picked up one at random. It was postmarked from the midwest. Inside was a meticulously filled-out questionnaire, and to my surprise, a letter. The woman who had written the letter explained that there were a few questions on which she had wanted to expand, and she went on to talk about her joy in her sexual responsiveness with her lover, a man with whom she had been living during the previous two years. Even his hug could sometimes bring her to the verge of orgasm, she said. She loved sex, she said. But then she went on to write, "The sexual revolution has been very enlightening to many women older than me. I'm 25. My mother has profited from it. But I grew up in the midst of it, and sometimes I wish the pendulum would sit where it is for a while instead of continuing to swing. Men have become so accustomed to a woman who says 'Yes,' with no thought other than of going to bed, that they assume every woman is like that. Especially men my own age. You can't say 'No' without their thinking you're weird, or a prude. So you have sex. The only problem is, VD runs rampant, no one knows last names, no one profits."

"No one profits." The phrase conveyed enormous sadness. And yet surely, in view of the woman's earlier remarks about her intense sensuality, she herself had profited. Or had she? What was it that was wrong? I wanted to know more about her. I wanted to know what previous sexual experiences she had had. I wanted to know *her.* Because one thing was clear to me. This woman was real. She wasn't "that *Cosmopolitan* girl." She wasn't a fabrication, an idealized version of what a contemporary woman should be.

Intrigued, I leafed through some of the other envelopes. Many of them contained comments, elaborations, reminiscences, scraps from diaries and journals. I met real women at every turn. They were concerned, thoughtful, idiosyncratic, ambivalent. I liked them, and admired their dedication to the project. But most of all, I was struck by how varied a sample of respondents the *Cosmo* survey had tapped. The women, I was informed by Val Appel, research director of Simmons, were between the ages of 14 and 80, hailed from every geographic region in the country, and ranged in occupation from corporate president and college professor to motel maid and telephone operator. So while all had in common the fact that they read *Cosmopolitan* magazine, or at least the issue in which the questionnaire appeared, their differences—particularly in such matters as educational backgrounds and economic levels—gave the sample a remarkable diversity.

This diversity thoroughly aroused my enthusiasm and, fascinated now, I examined the questionnaire closely. It had been devised by a panel of *Cosmopolitan* editors and covered an enormous number of sexual matters, from the familiar "How are your orgasms usually achieved?" to the rarely asked "Have you had sex with more than one person at the same time—in private, as opposed to group activity?" The questions were interesting and provocative.

As to the findings, I learned that they had not yet been subjected to computer processing, but that when they were, they would be available not just for married women, and single, separated, divorced or widowed women who live alone, but for women who live with lovers as well. In 1975 *Redbook* magazine had queried the sexual habits of married women, and received 100,000 answers, but what is news today is the hundreds of thousands of people who live together and, without benefit of marriage licenses, have intimate sexual relationships of long duration. According to the latest census, the number of couples living together has nearly tripled in the past decade. Yet the experiences of such couples have never been adequately reported.

I left Simmons, called *Cosmopolitan,* said yes, I *wanted* to write the article on their findings, and also that I thought the material warranted a book.

That was the genesis of both "The Sexual Profile of That *Cosmopolitan* Girl," which appeared in *Cosmopolitan* magazine in September 1980, and of *The Cosmo Report.* But the two are very different matters. For one thing, they concern two different groups of women. "The Sexual Profile of That *Cosmopolitan* Girl" analyzed the sexual habits and attitudes of only a portion of the sample, some 15,000 women who most resembled the magazine's typical reader: a woman between the ages of 18 and 34 who lives in a city of over one million in population and who earns her own living. The 106,000 women examined in *The Cosmo Report* of course *include* these but also comprise a much wider sector of American women. While most of them (85 percent) are between the ages of 18 and 34, some are as young as 14, and some are in their forties, fifties, sixties, and even seventies. While a fifth of *The Cosmo Report* women come from cities of more than one million, another two-fifths come from smaller cities, and the remainder from suburban and rural areas. And while the women in *The Cosmo Report* are primarily women who earn their own livings, chiefly as managers, administrators, professionals, technicians and office workers, there are also some homemakers and numerous students. So *The Cosmo Report* is more inclusive than "The Sexual Profile of That *Cosmopolitan* Girl." It describes the sexual patterns of a broader cross-section of American women.

That cross-section is, of course, what is called among survey-makers a "self-selected" sample. This means that the women who participated in the survey chose to do so, as opposed to their having been chosen at random by someone else. But then, all sex research in America, including Alfred Kinsey's *Sexual Behavior in the Human Male* and *Sexual Behavior in the Human Female,* has had to rely on self-selected samples. The reasons for this are obvious: if a surveyor calls or writes to people at random and asks them questions about their sex lives, most of them will refuse to answer. To pursue the method would be exceedingly costly, not very productive, and emphatically an invasion of privacy.

Consequently, investigators of sexual practices have traditionally relied on volunteers. Kinsey often used people who had come to hear him lecture on sex. Masters and Johnson, for *Human Sexual Response,* used medical students and hospital personnel. Shere Hite, for *The Hite Report on Women,* relied on volunteers from the National Organization of Women and from the readership of such magazines as *Bride's,* and the men's magazine, *Oui.* For *The Hite Report on Male Sexuality,* volunteers who read the Hite questionnaire in a men's magazine, or learned of it from some other source, were used. And an important sex survey sponsored by the Playboy Foundation and published in 1974 as *Sexual Behavior in the Nineteen Seventies* by Morton Hunt, used men and women who accepted invitations to attend private panel discussions on sex.

In each case, the participants in the research were people with an unusual amount of interest in sex, for otherwise they would not have attended the lectures, allowed themselves to be deflected from their studies or work, taken the time to fill out lengthy questionnaires, ventured forth to hear sex discussed at a panel.

Because they do their work among interested parties, some people feel that sex researchers are subject to coming up with findings that reflect exhibitionistic people rather than people as a whole. This charge was directed at Kinsey by those shocked—offended—at his findings. But actually, interest in sex flourishes among all kinds of people, among the repressed as well as the exhibitionistic, among the timorous as well as the adventurous, and among average and in every way moderate people. What is important is a survey drawn from all ends of the attitudinal and experiential scale. The Kinsey reports were based on such surveys. And so, in fact, is *The Cosmo Report.*

In the case of the Kinsey reports, criticism of his methods eventually died down and the findings ultimately came to be accepted as having indeed been representative of American sexual patterns as a whole in the period in which they had been examined. What of the *Cosmo* women? Are they representative of American women as a whole? I suspect that some of the findings in this book will shock sexual puritans, and that they will argue that the group must have been atypical, unusually uninhibited. But I would direct these critics to some of the academic surveys discussed in the book, recent investigations undertaken on small samples of Americans by university and foundation researchers. Often the behaviors of the *Cosmo* women turn out to be, if anything, more *inhibited* than the behaviors reported in some of the scholarly investigations. Having worked closely with the *Cosmo* data, I myself suspect that the sexual practices of this largely 18- to 34-year-old sample is not unusually extreme and that the *Cosmo* women may, in fact, be quite representative of young American women as a whole.

In any event, with *The Cosmo Report* it is at last possible to speak with a good degree of certainty about the extent of and effects on human happiness of the sexual revolution that has occurred in America as it has occurred, at least, among women. In addition, it gives those of us who want to place ourselves, to see where we fit into contemporary sexual patterns, a rather sturdy measuring rod. I say this because while *Cosmopolitan* magazine is thought by some people to attract only sexually excessive women, and is thought by others to attract only sexually repressed women, the fact of the matter is that its appeal is so vast and its readers so diverse that it is not possible—as any examination of the findings will reveal—to support any such generalization. Indeed, the readers who took the survey sounded every possible inflection in contemporary female sexuality, every imaginable tone from radicalism to conservatism, with all the pitches in between. And because of this range, no contemporary sexual ethic or experience has gone unrepresented. I suspect most readers will find themselves in the findings, as I did.

The Cosmo Report differs from "The Sexual Profile of That *Cosmopolitan* Girl" in another significant way. It is not simply a compilation of survey statistics, but the result of additional communications with some *Cosmopolitan* readers, chiefly women who took the survey.

I have mentioned that reading the unsolicited letters from women who had participated in the poll was a decisive factor in my desire to write the profile. I had been impressed, that afternoon at Simmons, by the enthusiasm of the respondents and their eagerness to share their thoughts about sex. I decided that when my article ran in *Cosmopolitan,* I would ask the readers of the article to write to me, hoping that I might in that way hear from a greater number of the original survey takers. If so many had communicated so helpfully without being asked, perhaps a request would elicit even greater assistance.

This is exactly what happened. There is a curious relationship that exists between certain magazines and their readers. The readers feel an attachment, a connection to the magazine, an involvement so intense that it is as if the magazine were a fellow being. They seek to guide it, chide it, praise it, scold it. *Cosmopolitan* is such a magazine. Thus the response of its readers was phenomenal.

Letters blizzarded the magazine. But no, they were not just letters. They were documents, chronicles. There were twenty-page handwritten memoirs, lengthy essays neatly typed on bond paper, short, poignant paragraphs on pink and green and blossom-decorated stationery, tersely written autobiographical accounts on business stationery that bore the letterheads of some of America's most famous corporations, a number of "Fortune 500" companies among them. Some women sent thick sections from their diaries. Some sent photographs of themselves with their lovers, husbands and children. One woman, a graduate student of psychology, sent a thesis she had written for a course in human sexuality. And hundreds upon hundreds of women enclosed their return addresses, expressing their willingness to be interviewed on the subjects they had written about. In all, more than 2,500 letters were received. A remarkable response.

I have been immensely moved by these communications.

Working in the midst of a major metropolis, lulled by the sophisticated and often blasé atmosphere of journalism and publishing, I had been under the impression, as mentioned, that women's sexuality had been overly explored, that everybody knew all they needed to know about it. But the women who wrote to *Cosmopolitan* taught me otherwise. Hundreds of letters began with, "Thank you for the opportunity to discuss my sex life. I have never been able to tell anyone else this, but . . ." And hundreds of others began with, "Thank you for the survey. I never before realized that I was just like other women. I always thought I was peculiar because . . ."

I learned that there was still a tremendous amount of inhibition, ignorance and confusion surrounding sex, and that women needed, *required* more forums in which to address one another. But if I learned about shame and misinformation, I also learned that there had indeed been a loosening up, an end to repression for many women.

When it comes to sex, as in most things, America is far from homogeneous. Indeed, as Masters and Johnson have observed, "the strength with which individual cultures continue to exist in this country precludes the emergence of any dominant influence." To get at the variety and richness of the individual sexual cultures that exist in our land I have, wherever possible, used the *Cosmo* women's own words to enliven and clarify the statistics. The book is filled with individual voices, with women explaining what they enjoy, and what they deplore about sex. In addition, the stories of certain women are continued from chapter to chapter, their histories unfolding from the day they discovered masturbation or decided to relinquish their virginity to the lovemaking techniques and triumphs they experienced only yesterday. Thus the *Report* is more than a collection of statistics. It is, I suggest, a book of *lives.*

During the time I have been working on *The Cosmo Report,* I have been asked repeatedly by numerous friends and colleagues what the major findings are. Like any collector, I am fascinated by all my finds. But there is, I suppose, one that ought to be mentioned here because it is particularly important, particularly challenging to think about.

It concerns how the women polled assessed the sexual revolution. It turned out that there was a neat, almost exact split in the sample on this matter, with close to 50 percent of the women feeling content about today's more sexually free atmosphere, and a little more than 50 percent feeling that things had gone too far. This latter group of women believed that sex today had become too casual and too difficult to avoid, and that they themselves, and perhaps all women, had become pawns in a revolution chiefly engineered by men.

This finding would not be especially significant if the *Cosmo* women were prudish, inexperienced. But the fact is that taken as a whole, they are perhaps the most sexually experienced and experimental group of women in western history. A majority had had between two and ten sexual partners; many had had far more; and most had participated in a considerable variety of sexual practices.

But sexual discontent is still rife among them. This discontent made itself apparent in many ways other than the mere answer to a multiple-choice question. The women wrote about it repeatedly, and even *admirers* of the sexual revolution expressed it. Many complained that they often went to bed with men on first dates not out of choice but necessity: a man would not ask to see them again if they did not have sex the first time. Many explained that they had had numerous lovers not because sexual variety appealed to them but because they couldn't find men willing to form steady relationships, which they emphatically preferred. Many described participating in seemingly liberated sexual activities like masturbation in front of a partner, group sex and orgies, not because these activities gave them physical satisfaction but because they enabled them to hold on to lovers. And most spoke of having had early sex because of peer pressure (just as Kinsey's women, three decades ago, spoke of *not* having early sex because of peer pressure). Indeed, it turned out that a great deal of what today passes as uninhibited sexual behavior is in fact the result of new inhibitions, is in fact conformity to new sorts of sexual tyranny. No wonder then that so many of the *Cosmo* women were disillusioned with sexual freedom.

The statistical finding about the sexual revolution, and the complaints lodged against that revolution, merit attention and concern; they tell us not what some old guard has to say, but what women right now on the ramparts, so to speak, of social change are experiencing. They are women chiefly aged 18 to 34, the very people whose lives have been most affected by the sexual revolution, who have most thrived on its benefits, and most suffered its excesses.

One effect on me of contemplating the beleaguered situation of such women was that I decided that *The Cosmo Report* ought to be more than a report on the state of the sexual revolution in America. It ought also to be something of a handbook, a trustworthy source of useful sexual information for any woman who needed such information. And really, that is all of us today. All of us have more or less been thrown into the waters of the sexual revolution and simply told to swim. There are many among us who are ignorant of the motions that will best keep us afloat, and others who, while paddling along quite successfully, often seem to lose sight of the shore. What should we be doing? Where are we heading?

Both situations are important. Certainly a woman may founder sexually today because she doesn't know certain erotic techniques. But she may also founder because, although knowing and using all of them, she doesn't receive from her sexual encounters the kind of happiness she imagines they should bring. Perhaps she doesn't understand the limitations of sex, what she can expect from it and what she cannot. Or perhaps she doesn't credit the role of her upbringing and individual emotional biases in sexual pleasure. Or, to take another example, certainly a woman may founder sexually because she has never received the least pleasure from intercourse. But she may also founder because she enjoys intercourse, yet has been constantly barraged by voices telling her that that activity is somehow exploitative and retrogressive. From the responses and letters of the *Cosmo* women, it was clear that for many women today, psychological and social confusions were standing in the way of erotic security as much as was poor technique.

So I decided to try to make *The Cosmo Report* offer direction as well as report, direction about psychosexual and sociosexual questions as well as about sexual technique. Whether a woman wants to learn how to have a first orgasm or how to have multiple orgasms, how best to select a first lover to ensure the best possible sexual initiation, or how best to refuse an old lover to ensure the least amount of recrimination, how to conquer shyness about fellatio or cunnilingus, or how quickly or how slowly to go to bed with a new man, how directly or indirectly her clitoris should be touched after orgasm, under what circumstances to masturbate in front of a partner, whether to permit herself to have sexual fantasies in the midst of intercourse, how to say yes to new and unfamiliar sexual experiences, and even how to say no to them . . . I hope she will find some good answers here. The answers may well prove unusually useful, because they come not from academic authorities, experts and propagandists distant from the problems that women today face, but from peers, people who have arrived after trial and error at sensible answers to the same questions, and from whose replies I have tried to distill the most timely and wise advice.

What I hope I have done, then, in *The Cosmo Report* is: to report on the sexual climate in America today; to make that climate come alive through individual stories and adventures; and to offer balanced, realistic help to anyone with questions about weathering sexual storms, squalls, or just plain sprinkles.

Linda Wolfe
Croton-on-Hudson, New York
June 1981

THE COSMO SEX SURVEY

For each question, please check the box for the answer that seems most appropriate for you.

PERSONAL BACKGROUND

1. How old are you?

   Under 18 . . . . ☐
   18–24 . . . . ☐
   25–29 . . . . ☐
   30–34 . . . . ☐
   35 or over . . . . ☐

2. Do you live in a . . . (check only one)

   City of more than 1
   million . . . . ☐
   City of 10,000–1 million ☐
   City of less than 10,000 ☐
   Suburb . . . . ☐
   Rural area . . . . ☐

3. Location:

   Please write in your zip code. (If you are not in the U. S., write in the country.)

ZIP CODE: _ _ _ _ _

   Outside U. S. (specify country):

   _____

4. Marital status:

   Living with your lover . ☐
   Married . . . . ☐
   Single and living alone or
   with a platonic
   roommate (skip to Q.
   6) . . . . ☐
   Separated (skip to Q. 6) ☐
   Divorced (skip to Q. 6) . ☐
   Widowed (skip to Q. 6) ☐

5. How long have you been married or living with your lover?

   _____ ☐

29

6. Education completed:

Elementary school or less
. . . . □
Some high school . . . . □
High-school graduate . . □
Some college . . . . □
Some graduate school or
more . . . . □

7. Occupation:

Creative arts . . . . . . □
Management/
Administrative . . . . . . □
Professional/Technical . □
Secretary/Clerk . . . . . □
Sales . . . . □
Homemaker . . . . □
Other . . . . □

8. Household earnings per year of all members of your household combined:

Under $10,000 . . . . . . □
$10,000 to $14,999 . . . □
$15,000 to $19,999 . . . □
$20,000 to $24,999 . . . □
$25,000 or more . . . . . □

9. Your earnings personally:

None . . . . □
Under $10,000 . . . . . . □
$10,000 to $14,999 . . . □
$15,000 to $19,999 . . . □
$20,000 to $24,999 . . . □
$25,000 or more . . . . . □

SEXUAL EXPERIENCE

10. How old were you when you first had sex with a man?

Under 10 . . . . □
10 to 15 . . . . □

16 to 20 . . . . □
21 to 25 . . . . □
26 to 30 . . . . □
31 or over . . . . □
Never have (skip to
Q.35) . . . . □

11. Did you have an orgasm the first time?

Yes . . . . □
No . . . . □

12. How would you describe your reaction the first time?

It was a thrilling
experience . . . . □
It was moderately
pleasant . . . . □
I had no particular
reaction . . . . □
It was somewhat
disagreeable . . . . . . □
It was painful and
upsetting . . . . □

13. How long had you known your partner?

Less than a week . . . . □
At least a week but less
than a few months . . □
A few months . . . . . . □
Almost a year or longer □

14. Was he . . . (check only one)

Your husband? . . . . . □
Your fiancé? . . . . □
A steady boyfriend? . . □
A casual acquaintance? . □
Other _____ □
(Please explain)

15. With about how many men have you made love?

None . . . . ☐
Only one . . . . ☐
2 to 5 . . . . ☐
6 to 10 . . . . ☐
11 to 25 . . . . ☐
More than 25 . . . . . . ☐
How many? _____ ☐
(Write in)

16. How many years in age do you prefer between you and your lovers?

More than 5 years
    younger than you . . . ☐
1 to 5 years younger . . ☐
Same age . . . . ☐
1 to 5 years older . . . . ☐
5 to 10 years older . . . ☐
11 or more years older . ☐

17. How often do you usually make love?

At least once a day . . . ☐
Three to five times a
    week . . . . ☐
Once or twice a week . ☐
Once or twice a month . ☐
Less than once a month ☐

18. Would you like to make love more frequently or less?

More . . . . ☐
Less . . . . ☐
About the same . . . . . ☐

19. Do you prefer to make love . . .

In the morning? . . . . . ☐
During the day? . . . . . ☐
At night? . . . . ☐

20. Which is your favorite position to make love?

Male dominant/female
    underneath . . . . . ☐
Female dominant/male
    underneath . . . . . ☐
Side by side . . . . . . ☐
Posterior . . . . ☐
Standing . . . . ☐
Other _____ ☐
(Please explain)

21. Aside from in bed, what is your favorite setting to make love? (check only one)

Couch . . . . ☐
Floor . . . . ☐
Beach . . . . ☐
Grass . . . . ☐
Car . . . . ☐
Shower or bath . . . . . ☐
Other _____ ☐
(Please explain)
No other setting . . . . . ☐

22. Which, if any, of these do you find pleasant accompaniments or preliminaries to sex? (check as many as apply)

Food . . . . ☐
Drink . . . . ☐
Music . . . . ☐
Smells (perfume, body
    odor, etc.) . . . . . . ☐
Drugs (pot, "uppers,"
    etc.) . . . . ☐
Sexy talk . . . . ☐
Pornography . . . . . . ☐
Other _____ ☐
(Please explain)

23. Do you like to make love . . .

    In daylight or bright
    light . . . . ☐
    With the lights on dimly
    . . . . ☐
    In the dark . . . . ☐

24. How long do you usually like foreplay to last?

    Less than 5 minutes . . . ☐
    5 to 15 minutes . . . . . ☐
    Up to half an hour . . . ☐
    Up to an hour or more . ☐

25. How long do you usually take to reach orgasm after the onset of foreplay?

    Less than 5 minutes . . . ☐
    5 to 10 minutes . . . . . ☐
    Up to 20 minutes . . . . ☐
    Up to half an hour . . . ☐
    Up to an hour or more . ☐

26. When making love, which of the following do you like? (check all that apply)

    Have your man undress
    you . . . . ☐
    Pinch, bite, slap him . . ☐
    Be pinched, bitten,
    slapped . . . . ☐
    Have someone beat you ☐
    Pretend to fight
    physically with the
    man or try to get away
    . . . . ☐

27. How frequently do you have an orgasm?

    Always . . . . ☐
    Usually . . . . ☐

Sometimes . . . . ☐
Seldom . . . . ☐
Never . . . . ☐

28. Do you have multiple orgasms?

    Always . . . . ☐
    Sometimes . . . . ☐
    Never . . . . ☐

29. What is the greatest number of orgasms you have had in one love-making session?

    1 . . . . ☐
    2 to 5 . . . . ☐
    6 to 10 . . . . ☐
    11 or more . . . . ☐

30. Do your orgasms vary in intensity?

    Often . . . . ☐
    Sometimes . . . . ☐
    Never . . . . ☐

31. Are they usually achieved as a result of . . .

    Vaginal entry . . . . . . ☐
    Clitoral manipulation . . ☐
    Other stimulation?
    _____☐
    (Please explain)

32. In which of the following do you regularly participate? (check as many as apply)

    Cunnilingus . . . . ☐
    Fellatio . . . . ☐
    Anal sex . . . . ☐
    Fetishes . . . . ☐
    Flagellation or other
    sadomasochistic
    behavior . . . . ☐

33. What areas of your body other than the clitoris respond erotically to stimulation? (check as many as apply)

Mouth . . . . □
Ears . . . . □
Breast, nipples . . . . . . □
Anus . . . . □
Other _____ □
     (Please explain)
None . . . . □

34. Do you take the aggressive role in lovemaking?

Always . . . . □
Often . . . . □
Sometimes . . . . □
Never . . . . □

35. How old were you when you first masturbated?

Younger than 5 . . . . . □
5 to 9 . . . . □
10 to 15 . . . . □
16 to 20 . . . . □
Over 20 . . . . □
Never have (skip to Q. 39) . . . . □

36. Do you still masturbate?

Yes . . . . □
Yes, but only in the absence of a sexual partner . . . . □
No (skip to Q. 39) . . . □

37. How often do you masturbate?

Every day . . . . □
Several times a week . . □

Several times a month . □
Rarely . . . . □

38. When you masturbate what means do you use? (check as many as apply)

Hand . . . . □
Vibrator . . . . □
Water spray . . . . □
Other
_____ □

39. When do you have sexual fantasies? (check as many as apply)

During intercourse . . . □
While masturbating . . . □
Other times when I am not active sexually . . □
In dreams . . . . □
Never (skip to Q. 41) . . □

40. Which of the following do your fantasies involve? (check as many as apply)

Your partner . . . . □
Someone else you know □
A celebrity . . . . □
A stranger . . . . □
Animals . . . . □
Other _____ □
     (Please explain)

41. During what stage of your monthly cycle is your sexual appetite strongest?

Immediately before your period . . . . □
During your period . . . □
Just after your period . . □
Midcycle . . . . □
It is about the same all month . . . . □

42. What type of birth control do you use? (check as many as apply)

     The Pill . . . . ☐
     An IUD . . . . ☐
     A diaphragm . . . . ☐
     Condoms . . . . ☐
     Foam . . . . ☐
     The rhythm method . . ☐
     Withdrawal . . . . ☐
     Nothing . . . . ☐

43. How do you feel about abortion on demand, that is abortion any time a woman wants one?

     Approve . . . . ☐
     Disapprove . . . . ☐
     No opinion . . . . ☐

44. Have you ever had an abortion?

     Yes . . . . ☐
     No . . . . ☐

45. Have you ever felt unpleasantly pressured into sex and finally gave in against your better judgment?

     Yes . . . . ☐
     No . . . . ☐

46. Have you ever been raped or sexually molested?

     Yes . . . . ☐
     No (skip to Q. 48) . . . ☐

47. By whom?

     Your husband . . . . . . ☐
     A relative . . . . ☐
     A friend . . . . ☐
     A stranger . . . . ☐

48. Have you ever had a lesbian experience?

     Yes . . . . ☐
     No (skip to Q. 51) . . . ☐

49. How old were you?

     Under 10 . . . . ☐
     10 to 15 . . . . ☐
     16 to 20 . . . . ☐
     21 to 25 . . . . ☐
     26 or older . . . . ☐

50. Do you still have such relationships?

     Occasionally . . . . ☐
     Regularly . . . . ☐
     Exclusively . . . . ☐
     Never . . . . ☐

51. Have you ever been to bed with a male homosexual?

     Yes . . . . ☐
     No . . . . ☐

52. Have you ever had an incestuous experience?

     Yes . . . . ☐
     No (skip to Q. 54) . . . ☐

53. With whom?

     Father . . . . ☐
     Brother . . . . ☐
     Uncle . . . . ☐

54. Have you ever been to an orgy, sex club, or partner-swapping party?

     Often . . . . ☐
     Occasionally . . . . ☐

One time only . . . . . . ☐
Never (skip to Q. 56) . . ☐

55. Did you participate?

Yes . . . . ☐
No . . . . ☐

56. Have you had sex with more than one person at the same time (in private, as opposed to group activity)?

Often . . . . ☐
Occasionally . . . . ☐
One time only . . . . . . ☐
Never (skip to Q. 58) . . ☐

57. Were these partners . . .

A man and a woman . . ☐
Two or more men . . . . ☐
Two or more women . . ☐
Some other combination
of men and women . ☐

58. Do you like group sex . . .

Better than a one-to-one
relationship . . . . . . ☐
As a change of pace . . ☐
Not at all . . . . ☐

SEXUAL MANNERS AND MORALS

59. Do you believe good sex is possible without love?

Yes . . . . ☐
No . . . . ☐

60. If you are single and engaged in a long-standing affair, do you feel free to have sex outside the relationship?

Yes . . . . ☐
No (skip to Q. 65) . . . ☐

61. How might you best describe your experience with having sex outside of a long-standing relationship?

A once-in-a-while
occurrence . . . . . . ☐
On a continuing basis
with one other person ☐
Frequent, almost regular
events with new
people and/or one or
more old friends . . . ☐

If you are married—Go
to Q. 62
If you are single—Go to
Q. 65

62. If married, have you had an affair outside marriage?

Yes . . . . ☐
No (skip to Q. 65) . . . ☐

63. How might you best describe your experience with an extramarital affair?

It helped your marriage ☐
It hurt your marriage . . ☐
It had no effect on your
marriage . . . . ☐

64. Did your husband know you were having an affair?

Yes . . . . ☐
No . . . . ☐
He suspected but never
knew for sure . . . . . ☐

65. Does your partner or husband feel free to have other sexual contacts?

Yes . . . . □
No . . . . □
Don't know . . . . □

66. Do you . . .

Think he should and
would not mind
particularly . . . . . . □
Wish he wouldn't . . . . □

67. Have you ever slept with a man on the first date?

Frequently . . . . □
Occasionally . . . . □
Only once or twice . . . □
Never . . . . □

68. Have you ever gone to bed with more than one man in the same day?

Frequently . . . . □
Occasionally . . . . □
Only once or twice . . . □
Never . . . . □

69. How frequently have you spent the night with the man with whom you have just made love?

Always . . . . □
Usually . . . . □
Occasionally . . . . □
Once or twice . . . . . . □
Never . . . . □

70. Have you made love on your lunch hour?

Frequently . . . . □
Occasionally . . . . □

Only once or twice . . . □
Never . . . . □

71. Have you ever seduced a man?

Once or twice . . . . . . □
Occasionally . . . . □
Often . . . . □
Never . . . . □

72. Have you ever had an affair with a married man?

Yes, only once . . . . . . □
Yes, more than once . . □
No (skip to Q. 75) . . . □

73. Do you feel the experience was . . . (check only one)

More rewarding than
painful . . . . □
More painful than
rewarding . . . . □

74. Is it something you would be likely to do again?

Yes . . . . □
No . . . . □
Don't know . . . . □

75. Do you enjoy making love?

Always . . . . □
Usually . . . . □
Occasionally . . . . □
Never . . . . □

76. Are you good at it?

Yes . . . . □
Not sure . . . . □
No . . . . □

77. Is your sex life satisfactory?

Yes . . . . □
No . . . . □

78. In your own words, what would make your sex life better? _____

    _____

    _____

79. Do you think the sexual revolution has . . .

    Caused sex to be too casual. You still feel

sex should be saved for a "meaningful" relationship . . . . . . ☐

Made it hard for you to find acceptable reasons to say no to a man sexually . . . . ☐

Had a good effect on most of us . . . . ☐

Other comments

_____ ☐

After you have completed this questionnaire please mail it to the address below, where it will be tabulated along with other completed questionnaires. There is no need to sign your name, and all results will be left anonymous. The tabulated results will be reported in a soon-to-be-published issue of *Cosmopolitan*.

Cosmopolitan Research Center—7th Floor
212 East 43rd Street
New York, N.Y. 10017

PART ONE
Sexuality with Partners

Chapter One
The First Time

1. Someday He'll Come Along, the Man I Love

While not exactly your typical "Cosmo girl," being 61 years old, I do have this evening free from any frantic sexual activities—or any others, for that matter—and am thus responding to your invitation to send you a letter. The first time? It was all so long ago. I think I was 15, but I might have been 14. It hurt, and I was young enough not quite to understand what was going on. My partner— blond, with silky hair and ears that stuck out and made me laugh—was an older man—of 17. I hadn't understood until that night why my parents hadn't wanted me to go out with him. They kept saying he was too old for me. Too old in experience was what they meant. These assignations weren't as easy as they are now. But as you can see, we managed. And I still remember it.

—a woman from a small city in Michigan

One doubts that there is a woman alive who doesn't remember the first man with whom she had sexual intercourse. That goes for the woman who has had one lover—just that very first—and stuck with him ever since, as well as for the woman who has since had a hundred lovers. There seems to be something about the first time that makes the event an unforgettable episode in a woman's devel-

---

NOTE: While letters were edited for fluency, every effort was made to retain individual styles of expression.

41

opment and causes the first man to put an indelible imprint on her consciousness.

It isn't just because he's first. Some people claim they can remember all their big "firsts"—first love, first movie, first job, first pair of high heels. But if you prod them, they stumble. Details grow hazy as time unstitches the seams of their reminiscences. This is true even when you question them about first love. But when it comes to the first sexual partner, memory flows. Perhaps the reason this is so is that the first time really isn't the first time. It is an event that has been previewed over and over in the imagination—worried about, considered, yearned for, fled from—for years, sometimes a decade or more, before it ever occurs. In a sense, it is a culmination rather than a beginning. Few women go to bed with a man for the first time without having long wondered and daydreamed about just what might be involved, how they would feel, and who their first partner would be.

Many women begin their wondering and daydreaming when they are very young, often by the time they are ten or eleven. Girls that age are highly romantic, if not erotic. They are endlessly intrigued by certain male movie and TV stars, collecting their photos, memorizing their histories, knowing their every idiosyncrasy and habit. And it is not uncommon to hear them, their faces intent, their hearts full, humming the lyrics of popular songs with an intensity that suggests that the songs already have profound meaning to them. "Someday he'll come along, the man I love," little girls sing, and "Some enchanted evening, I will meet a stranger," and "Who's gonna be my love?" By the time she enters her teens, the typical American girl has already been considering for some time, if still in a pre-physical way, the choosing of a sexual partner.

Once she is a teenager, her daydreams about love become sexualized. This is true not just in modern-day America where sexually explicit movies, television shows, books and magazines are all around us, from the time we are tots. In fact, teen-age girls everywhere and in every era have always thought sexual thoughts. Remember Juliet, as Shakespeare imagined her in the sixteenth century, a 14-year-old impatient to go to bed with Romeo:

> Come, gentle night; come, loving black-browed night:
> Give me my Romeo; and, when he shall die,
> Take him and cut him out in little stars,
> And he will make the face of heaven so fine
> That all the world will be in love with night,

And pay no worship to the garish sun.
O, I have bought the mansion of a love,
But not possessed it; and though I am sold,
Not yet enjoyed. So tedious is this day
As is the night before some festival
To an impatient child that hath new robes
And may not wear them.

One needn't look only to Shakespeare. Young girls daydreaming about sex during early adolescence exist in literature from all periods and cultures.

By the time a girl actually has her first sexual encounter, she has, generally speaking, been anticipating it and preparing for it for years. So her first full-fledged sexual encounter, unless it occurs as a result of early rape, has been played out in her head, albeit sometimes without the crucial details, a hundred times over.

No wonder, then, it is always so memorable.

But there is a sad fact about first sexual encounters. Historically, most girls have been dismally unprepared for their sexual initiation. A hundred years ago, a mother was expected to offer her daughter at least a little bit of information and guidance concerning her first time—which, of course, usually occurred on her wedding night—but many mothers, inhibited and uncomfortable about sex, reneged. Girls had sex for the first time in ignorance and dismay.

Here is the great American novelist Edith Wharton writing of what happened to her in the 1880s. She begged her mother, shortly before her wedding night, to tell her "what marriage was really like." Her mother answered disapprovingly, "I never heard such a ridiculous question!" Young Edith persisted. "I'm afraid, Mama," she said. "I want to know what will happen to me." But her mother was silent, and a look of disgust crossed her face. "You've seen enough pictures and statues in your life," she managed to explain at last. "Haven't you noticed that men are . . . made differently from women?" Then Edith's mother, too embarrassed to continue, terminated the conversation with a gruff, "Well, then . . . for heaven's sake don't ask me any more silly questions."

Edith Wharton's marriage was not consummated for three weeks, and for long afterward sex remained a problematic, distressing experience for her. Years later she was to blame this on the inadequacy of her mother's advice and to chide the inhibited matrons of her day for failing to provide their daughters with useful information concerning first sex.

Well, one might say, that was in the latter part of the nineteenth century. Girls have easy access to sexual information nowadays.

Yet, oddly enough, in spite of the sexual revolution, there is still an unpleasant air of secrecy and silence regarding first sex. It's well known that young girls in America today have intercourse at very early ages, that it is the rare one indeed who waits until her wedding night to have sex for the first time. And yet there is precious little information available for girls concerning that initial and crucial sex encounter. Preparation for that first time seems to come after the fact, whether the girl was young a hundred years ago or is young today, and whether she is 14 or 18 or 21.

This is not to say that library and bookstore shelves are not full of books that explain sex explicitly, or that today's adolescent does not know what the sex act is like, and who does what to whom. But the books do not seem to go to the heart of the matter. Sexual initiation today is still often being conducted in ignorance and with dismay.

This is one of the themes explored in this chapter. The chapter also investigates not just the ages at which the first time most commonly occurs, but who a young girl's first partner is likely to be, what kinds of first sex are more likely than other kinds to be emotionally and sexually fulfilling, and what effect the first time is likely to have on a woman's future sexual development. But, above all, the chapter by, delving into the social role of first sex, attempts to explore what is making the experience come about earlier and earlier.

We live in an advanced society, one that has long ceased to honor the importance of commemorating, as our more primitive ancestors did, the transition from youth to maturity. In fact we are in general a society short on celebrations, rituals, the honoring of life's passages. Sexual initiation seems almost to have been chosen by today's adolescents themselves to fill a need, to serve as a commemorative rite of passage.

They undertake it with all the fear and unease that, say, Carib youths experienced when they had to prove their adulthood by running through rows of sharp-toothed pineapple fronds. They mostly derive little physical joy from the event. And often it scars them, if only psychically. But wounded as they are, they are ready now to join their elders. And generally the wounds and psychic injuries of first sex seem far less significant to them than the fact that they have, at last, made the passage.

2. How Old Were You?

MAJOR FINDINGS:

Twenty-one percent of the women surveyed first had sexual intercourse by the age of 15.

Sixty-nine percent first had sexual intercourse between the ages of 16 and 20.

Nine percent first had sexual intercourse between the ages of 21 and 25.

It should come as no surprise to anyone that American females are today having their first experiences with sexual intercourse premaritally and at much earlier ages than girls used to have them. Yes, there *has* been a sexual revolution in America. Compare the results of the *Cosmo* survey about the ages at which very young girls first have sex with what Kinsey found out back in 1953.

Among Kinsey's sample of close to 6,000 females, 3 percent had had intercourse by the age of 15. It was a statistic that some conservative Americans did not want to accept. Or at least they wanted to believe that Kinsey had interviewed such a unique sample of women, such an uninhibited group, that his findings could not be said to reflect what was happening with American girls as a whole. Today it is now believed by most scholars and researchers that Kinsey's sample was indeed representative of American women as a whole and so his findings could be said to have reflected national habits.

It has been nearly thirty years since the Kinsey report. *Cosmopolitan* discovered that 21 percent of those who responded to its survey had had sex by the age of 15. Does this mean that across the nation, one out of every five women has had sexual intercourse before the age of 15? Perhaps the *Cosmopolitan* sample was a unique one? A particularly sexually uninhibited one? There are people who would like to believe this is so, sexual puritans who would prefer to assume

NOTE: Percentages greater than 2 percent have been rounded off to the nearest whole number.

that while one out of every five of the kinds of women who read *Cosmopolitan* may have had sex by 15, the figure would be much lower for American women as a whole.

The author is reasonably certain it wouldn't be—or at least that it wouldn't be appreciably lower for American women who are today, like most of the *Cosmopolitan* women, under the age of 34. In fact, if anything, one suspects the figure might be considerably *higher.* This is because the age of first sex has been shown to be going down and down in numerous surveys of adolescent sex, not just in the *Cosmo* study.

In 1979, for example, clinical psychologist Aaron Hass published the results of a small but much publicized survey of adolescent sexual behavior, *Teenage Sexuality.* Hass' sample was tiny: he studied only 318 girls. But he had, he asserted, drawn them from a variety of American ethnic backgrounds and geographic regions and had avoided choosing only girls whose families were exceedingly liberal about sex. Hass found that in his sample, 41 percent of the girls had had sexual intercourse by the age of 16.

More significantly, in 1973, a more authoritative survey, *Adolescent Sexuality in Contemporary America,* was published, this one by social psychologist Robert C. Sorenson. Sorenson too studied only a small number of teenagers—411 of them—but he chose them by scrupulous scientific methods in the hope that they would be representative of America's entire adolescent population. Sorenson found that one out of every *two* girls in his sample had had sexual intercourse by the age of 15.

It seems reasonable to conclude, in view of the findings of Sorenson and Hass, as well as that of *Cosmo,* that *today at least one out of every four young women in America has had sex before 15.*

In any event, without question, the percentage is very far from Kinsey's 3 percent. And there is no doubt that the trend toward having sex early is deepening. While only 15 percent of the *Cosmo* women who were over 25 had had sex before 15, among the women who were under 25, a fourth, or 25 percent, had had sex by 15.

Having sex early is, indisputably, increasingly frequent in American society.

Still, most girls do not have sex as young as 15, even today. Most girls first have sex when they are between the ages of 16 and 20. This was the time of sexual initiation for more than two-thirds of *all* the *Cosmo* women, and even for more than two-thirds of the women *under* 25. And according to a major 1980 national survey on adolescent sex conducted by two Johns Hopkins School of Public Health sociologists, the year between 19 and 20 may be the crucial one. The Johns Hopkins team—Melvin Zelnick and John F. Kantner —found that at 19, half of the 1,700 girls they queried had not yet had sex.

Having sex early is more and more frequent in American society, but having it during the last years of high school or the first years of college or employment is the norm.

3. Who Was the First Man?

Major Findings:

The vast majority of the women surveyed—64 percent—had their first sexual experience with a steady boyfriend. Another 16 percent had it with a casual acquaintance. Only 6 percent went to bed for the first time with a fiancé; only 5 percent with a husband. Nine percent went to bed with men who were in none of these categories—presumably family members (see Incest), strangers or men they had known only briefly.

As these major findings show, it is rare for a woman to choose for her first time a man with whom she does not have some degree of intimacy. The intimacy isn't based on permanent commitment, as it was in Kinsey's day when some 50 percent of women had their first sexual intercourse after marrying. Rather, the steady boyfriend, instead of the husband, is the man with whom most of today's women opt to lose their virginity.

This may have more to do with changes in our attitude toward marriage and premarital sex than with our attitude toward intimacy. People marry later these days, and there is little social stigma attached to premarital sex. (If anything it is the reverse; see page 51.) But while later in life many women will frequently have sex with casual acquaintances, their first time is, for the most part, experienced within the confines of an established steady relationship.

How steady? Some of the women's relationships were quite

long in the making before sexual intercourse was attempted. A large number—44 percent—knew their first partners almost a year, or longer than a year. Later in life these same women, typically, entered into sexual relationships with men they knew only very briefly. Later, many of them had sex on first dates. But, for first sex, they mainly chose familiar partners, boys and men to whom they felt some measure of real attachment.

Prior intimacy prevails in first sex.

4. Why Did You Decide to Have Sex for the First Time?

I answered only a few of the questions in your survey. I filled out what I could, but it wasn't much, because I haven't yet had sex with a man. I've had lots of boyfriends but so far I've always said no when one of them suggested intercourse. You could say I've done the whole alphabet of sex, but I've always stopped short before the last letter. I've gone from "A" to "Y," but I've never reached "Z." What I'd like to know is, what makes necking and petting stop seeming like going far enough? *When* does this happen? What makes people decide to go from X and Y to Z?

—*a 17-year-old girl from Connecticut*

Very few of the *Cosmo* women cited physical passion as the spur for their first experience with sexual intercourse. Whatever their reasons for having intercourse might be later in life, their initial reasons were definitely more social than physical.

For the majority, the first time is a kind of initiation rite— something we do in our society to indicate we have come of age. Like the 26-year-old woman, a legal secretary from California, who wrote the account below, we may have sex for the first time just because it is the "right time":

I look back on my first time as a funny, enjoyable, glad-to-have-it-over-with experience. I refer to my first lover as "Pencil Dick," as I don't believe I felt much of his presence inside me. It happened quickly, and it came about at just the right time for me. I was 17 and I felt it was high time for me to lose my virginity. My first lover had also decided it was time for me to lose it, and so he prepared for the event by priming me with vodka and orange juice. Still, he seemed to have overlooked the most important ingredient, birth control. But happily, luck was on my side, and a baby didn't enter the scene at that time in my life. . . . It happened in the vacant parking lot of an elementary school (an appropriate place, I must admit). We were necking and petting heavily in the back of his carpeted camper truck. We got drunk, and he led me to think he was quite experienced with sex, although afterward I was to find out it had been his first time also. The cad! Before the fateful act, he assured me that he would not come inside me, and would pull out before nature took its natural course. It didn't happen that way. He was on top, and inside me (or so I figured—as I've mentioned, I couldn't really feel him) and after about five minutes of moving around on top of my body, he fell by the wayside exclaiming in a horrified voice that he had lost control and spilled his manhood (unbeknownst to me) inside my young, no longer virgin, body. To show how inexperienced he was, he suggested that I go outside and urinate to get rid of the possibility of an unwanted pregnancy. I explained that I didn't think that would work, and went about pulling on my clothes and preparing for the ride home. When we got back to my house he stopped the truck to let me out and made the audacious statement that he thought we shouldn't see each other for a while. We should sort of let things cool off for a while. It didn't really bother me, as I'd just been through a milestone event, and so I agreed that we should keep distance between us for a while. One other memory sticks out in my mind. It happened the very next morning while I was washing the family car. The following thought kept going through my mind: "I'm a woman!" Finally!

"Pencil Dick" and his fumbling didn't bother this woman. In fact, she found humor in the experience. It served her purpose. Other women were less amused by their first times, but their experiences served the same purpose, a rite-of-passage:

I was 18 years old when I had my first encounter with intercourse. It happened with someone I'd known for seven years. We weren't even dating, though. In retrospect, this sounds pretty funny. But at the time, it didn't. I just felt it was about time I found out about sex, and so I deliberately chose this guy for my virgin (no pun intended) attempt.

—a 23-year-old from Ohio

I'm 17 years old. I had my first sexual experience about a half-year ago. It was with my steady boyfriend, but at the time I'd known him only two weeks. I had turned down many young men before him, but he was very convincing, and it was probably my time for it.

—a New Jersey teenager

I was 17. We were in the woods, a few feet from a running creek. I'd known the guy two years. We'd discussed having sex often before. Once it was in exactly this place, and I'd jumped up and said, "Screw? Who me? Not on your life." In October '77, it was "Yes, me."

—a 21-year-old from Massachusetts

I lost my virginity when I was 17 and a senior in high school. The boy was a good friend of my brother's. He was always at our house with a bunch of other guys who were all one year older than me. He was an all-around superjock, playing varsity football, basketball, and track, and he was extremely good-looking. Tall, blond, blue-eyed. He could charm the pants off me. He did. It happened one night after one of our frequent parties. I had to drive him home. We had never been out on a date but we'd flirted quite often whenever we saw each other. That night was just the right time. We drove to a nicely secluded place and got in the famous back seat. Although it was my first time, it sure wasn't his. He was so used to girls falling all over him that he had developed an incredibly lazy streak. He lay there and just wanted me, this little inexperienced virgin, to do everything. I did my best, but he finally had to help out. My first thought afterwards was, "Is that it?!" We drove home and never said a word to anybody. But at last I felt free.

—a 24-year-old from Wisconsin

But within the rite-of-passage pattern there are other whorls, other reasons that make a girl decide it's time to say "Yes." The fear of losing a boyfriend may tip the scale:

I was 15. The guy was "Mr. Everything" at school—a senior. And I was just a soph. It was a true case of hero worship. Within five months of dating I felt I had to give in to keep him. I was very insecure and felt I was in constant competition with the prom-queen types. He definitely took advantage of the situation. And I let him.

—a 20-year-old from Virginia

I was 16. It was a total waste. The reason I did it was to make boys like me. I'm overweight. But the whole thing was the pits.

—a 20-year-old from Illinois

Sometimes it is the fear of losing girlfriends, or of being different from the rest of the people in one's crowd. Here *The Cosmo Report* shows a dramatic change from the past. Kinsey wrote in 1953 that there was "public condemnation" of youthful premarital sex. The *Cosmopolitan* survey-takers described the opposite. They felt publicly condemned when they postponed having sex. One suburban high-school girl wrote, "I am 15. The girls in my school give one another parties when they lose their virginity. They don't invite me, because I once told Thelma, my friend, I didn't think it was right to have sex until you're a junior. She said I was the only 15-year-old girl in the whole sophomore class who hadn't and I was a freak and maybe she wouldn't even be my friend anymore."

Keeping up with the crowd accounts for many decisions to have sex for the first time. The woman below wanted to be like everyone else in her Michigan crowd:

The first time was when I was 13. My parents had separated. My mother was working at two jobs to support us. I was lonely. Most of my friends were at least five years

older than me, and had been sexually active. I felt left out.
I wanted to lose my virginity so I could be one of the gang.
The guy was 16. I had known him for three weeks. During
one session of necking we got further than ever before. He
was rubbing my clitoris and I was very close to orgasm.
That day I was afraid, and continued to say no. But after
thinking about it the rest of the night, the next day I said
yes.

This young woman wanted to be like everyone in New York City
—at least as she perceived them:

> I was 14½, and it was with a 14-year-old boy. We had
> several beers each. And it just happened. It was in 1964.
> It was in New York City and no one seemed to be a virgin
> there.

And this woman, from New York City, wanted to be like everyone
in California:

> The first time I had sexual intercourse was when I was
> almost 21. It was only because I was moving from con-
> servative New York to California. I didn't want to be a
> virgin when I got to California because I figured I'd be the
> only one, so I asked a former boyfriend to make love to
> me before I moved.

Of course, there are all kinds of decisions. Not every decision
is a conscious choice, and some women seem not so much to choose
to have sex as to have it accidentally. They are drinking, or smoking
pot, and they relinquish their inhibitions. Here are some of the
semi-accidental first times recounted by *Cosmo* women:

> I was 16. It wasn't supposed to happen, but it did. I got
> kind of high, so I don't really remember it much.
>
> *—a 17-year-old from Delaware*

> The first time for me was a year ago, at my boyfriend's
> birthday party. It was a twenty-keg party, outdoors, with
> over five hundred people. I was taking birth control pills,
> just in case I ever wanted to have sex. But it didn't happen

with my boyfriend. I was drunk and stoned and I met this guy named Ron and he was a year older than me and we started talking and we walked away from the party and did it in the mountains. I didn't get much from it. We went out after that, but we never did it again. I felt ashamed of myself because I didn't really want to do it. It just happened.

—a 17-year-old from New Mexico

The first time that I had intercourse I was 15 years old. My boyfriend (at the time) and I were high and so we did it. It just happened. I didn't get anything out of it and I felt nothing for him.

—a 17-year-old from New York

Some women decide to have sex for the first time, some women happen to have it. But today, as the *Cosmo* survey-takers volunteered, it is more likely for first sex to be undertaken for reasons of social acceptance than because of a compelling physical urge.

5. Was It Emotionally Satisfying?

MAJOR FINDINGS:

Only 18 percent of the women found the first time "thrilling." Thirty-one percent found it "moderately pleasant." Seventeen percent found it "somewhat disagreeable." Eighteen percent found it "painful and upsetting." Sixteen percent said they'd had "no particular reaction."

What makes first sex disagreeable, upsetting, emotionally bland, or exhilarating? Some authorities on the subject of adolescent sex say that, to a large extent, the first time is the result of self-fulfilling prophecies. If one expects it to hurt, it will. If one expects it to feel good, it will. If one expects to feel guilty, one will. If one expects to feel proud, one will.

But while expectation certainly plays a role, the major factor in whether a first sex encounter is pleasant or distressing seems to be the same factor that always affects the pleasurableness of sex: the quality of the relationship between the lovers.

Women who didn't know their partners well, or who were prompted to have first sex because the time seemed right, whether or not the partner did, tended to have the worst reactions to first sex. The woman who wrote the following letter is typical. Her first time was at a party with someone she had met that very night. She was 20.

> I believe the only reason I had sex the first time was that I was determined not to be a virgin when I reached my next birthday, that important-sounding one of 21. So at a party one night, I had intercourse with a guy I met at the party who showed very little concern with the fact that I was still a virgin. He didn't use any type of birth control and was insensitive to my feelings, both physically and emotionally. He took his time about having intercourse, and went on with it longer than I wanted him to. I wanted to ask him to stop, but I just couldn't. When he finally quit and left me alone, I was bleeding, and extremely emotionally upset by what had happened.

The woman who wrote the next letter had her initiation with someone she had dated for two weeks. She was 19:

> My first time was with a guy I'd known very superficially in high school. I ran into him a year after graduation, in a drugstore. I was dying to relinquish my virginity by then. I'd been fooling around but not going all the way since I was 15, and I was really anxious and ready. And he was available. After two weeks of dating we did it. It was awful, mainly because I couldn't talk to him. I didn't even like him. I just wanted to lose my virginity. Anyway, it hurt to the point of nausea.

Sometimes the fact that one doesn't know a first lover well is not because of brevity of acquaintance but because one really isn't fully equipped yet to know someone well. One is just too young, and consequently imperceptive. The girl who told the story below had just turned 13:

My first time was on a friend's farm. He was 17. We were talking together, talking dirty, but we always did that and I didn't think it could ever lead to anything. He was saying things like, "I'd love to pop your cherry," and I was saying things like, "Well, I've had my eyes on you too." But then he said, "Well, since we both agree, why don't we do something about it." After that, he took his pants off so quickly I didn't have time to figure out what was coming next. Then he jumped on me and literally shoved himself inside me. It was the worst pain I'd ever experienced in my life. I screamed bloody murder while trying to push him off me. He just wouldn't quit. He said, "It's okay. Just relax and loosen up." I cursed him and called him every name I could think of, while the tears just rolled down my cheeks. When it was over he said, "Wasn't that good, baby?" I ran home, took a bubble bath and soaked myself for about three hours. I felt so dirty, and I hurt, and I thought I'd never have sex again.

Of course, sometimes one knows a person a long time, and is old enough to be able to understand him and to communicate one's feelings, but is too ashamed or inhibited to do so. Such a story was told by a 21-year-old California woman:

The first time? I am sure I will never forget it. It happened about six months ago. One night, after four and a half months of dating, I came back from a party with my boyfriend and we parked at the beach and got into the back seat, and then I don't know what got into him, maybe he just couldn't wait any longer, but I kept saying no and he kept saying yes and all of a sudden he grabbed at me and held onto my blouse, and he ripped it right off me, and, oh, I was mad, it was a brand new blouse, I had gotten really dressed up for our date. I held on to the blouse, and he tugged on it, and the seam split in two, and he tore my nylons, oh, they were still on me, but there were huge holes, not runs, all through them. He pulled them down and my underwear came down with them and my beautiful straight skirt with slit really got slit, he tore the whole slit open, and meanwhile, I was crying and fighting. But it was an already lost battle. I have no idea how, but he had me where I couldn't move and when he went in, I screamed, I was in pain, and there was blood all over him. I didn't feel any excitement at all. All I did was cry and cry. Afterwards, I told him I never wanted to see him again, but I still am seeing him, we are still together. I don't think it will last much longer. He's still always pressuring me into sex, I wish I'd never met him, but I don't know how to say goodbye now that all this has happened between us.

These women's stories contrast sharply with those of women who knew their first sexual partners well enough to have formed a trusting attachment to them:

My first time was with my steady, and first, boyfriend. We were both 17, and I was madly in love and he cared a lot for me. We dated for five months beforehand, and it was the first time for each of us. The attraction was the strongest I've ever felt, before or since, and I'm sure it was mutual. Even after fourteen years I can still vividly remember much of what we did, from the first kiss on our first date to the big event five months later. The experience was fantastic with this man, and I'm eternally grateful to have had such a wonderful start.

—*a 31-year-old from Arkansas*

I had just turned 15. My boyfriend was three years older than me, and I loved him. We enjoyed foreplay for many months, and never once did he pressure me into having intercourse. My curiosity and my body became aroused. One day we were at a party at the house of a friend whose parents had gone away for the weekend. We wound up in a spare room in the basement of the house with me pleading with my boyfriend to go all the way. He warned me that it might hurt, and said that he'd be as careful as possible, and I remember saying, "Just be quiet and do it already." I was very surprised that it didn't hurt. I bled a little, but I was having such a great time that I don't recall any pain.

—*a 22-year-old from Connecticut*

I was 15. It was with my boyfriend, whom I'd been going out with for one year. We had been petting for a long time, but we never expected it to go any further than that. Neither of us did. I really didn't know what I was doing or what was going on. But he was very kind and gentle and it was a great experience.

—a 20-year-old from Michigan

Those women who trusted their first partner enough to discuss the sex act *in advance*—to plan it, rather than just let it happen— tended to sound the *most* emotionally satisfied by their sexual initiation. Their ages made less difference than did their ability to talk to their lover before the event and work out the details. The letter that follows is from a woman who was only 14 when her first time occurred:

I had been going steady with a boy the same age as myself for about six months before we decided to do it. When I think about how we planned and discussed it, I'm amazed at how mature we were about the whole thing. I knew very little about birth control and had no one to educate me about it, so we decided to use the "withdrawal" method. It was the most beautiful experience for me because I really cared for this boy and he really cared for me. It was the first time for both of us and we cried together.

This woman experienced no pain at first intercourse, but even those who did, yet trusted their partners enough to plan with them their sexual initiation, tended to find their first times emotionally satisfying. Here is what a woman, now 28 and an employment agency director, remembers about her first sexual encounter, which occurred twelve years ago:

The first time that I had intercourse I was naive sweet 16. I was still wearing braces on my teeth. I had had several boyfriends before, but I was always afraid to go the limit. But then—with a boy I'll call Jim—I did. He was tall and skinny and sweet, and he was my friend first, and so our relationship grew. He and I used to have long kissing sessions, on a beach near where we lived, and during these sessions we petted lightly at first, then gradually more heavily. It was in one of these romantic sessions that we decided to go to his house for more privacy. We continued our kissing and petting in his room, and we began undressing each other. I remember that he wanted very much to enter me, and that I wanted him to. But I was also tense and scared, so it was difficult for him, and painful for me. He tried for a long time before he could get in. When he finally did, the shock of his penetrating my hymen was like being numbed by ice water. That was the way it was for me. Not much fun, really. And yet, while I'm now 28 and there have been many men since Jim, my relationship with him will never be forgotten. And what's more, I've been attracted to tall skinny men ever since.

Here's the story of another 28-year-old, a woman studying for a graduate degree in a human sexuality program given at a northeastern university. She wrote about her first time in a thesis on personal sexual development:

> I'd been brought up very strictly. There was really only one aspect of sex that my parents, especially my father, would discuss with me and my sisters—the great responsibility of keeping our virginity intact. My father was adamant in his constant warnings that "nice girls don't do it" and "guys are only after one thing" and "no one will ever respect you afterwards."
>
> Still, when I was 20 I developed a deep, meaningful relationship with a guy and we had sex. It came about slowly. This guy was easy to talk to and never made me feel uptight. He was considerate and caring. He was my friend. He was also patient and understanding about my not wanting to "go all the way." I could see that our heavy petting sessions always left him very anxious and frustrated, but he never complained or tried to pressure me.
>
> After six months the high morals with which I'd been conditioned gave way to my love for him and to my own pressing needs for sexual expression. After lots of soul-searching and deliberation I finally decided I was ready for it. He bought condoms and foam and, thank God, he knew what he was doing. He had to help me insert the foam—I was a wreck! I was so nervous and tense that I tightened up, which hindered intromission. Still, I think

my first time was under ideal conditions: we loved each other, we were old enough to handle it, we had complete privacy, and we shared the responsibility for contraception.

There is no doubt that first sex can hurt, even when the participants don't expect that it will. A good deal depends on a woman's hymen—that thin membrane that usually covers part of the vaginal opening until it has been stretched by intercourse. Some hymens obstruct the vaginal opening more than others do. Some are shorter, taller, wider, narrower, thicker, than others. Some are taut and some have already been stretched by a woman's athletic activities or her use of tampons. If a woman has a sizable amount of taut hymen tissue when she first has intercourse, the stretching that occurs during the initial thrusting can be uncomfortable indeed. So trusting a partner and planning the event with him won't ensure an absence of pain. But it may ensure a woman's being able to take the pain lightly, as in the first letter below, or being able to work out with her first lover an imaginative solution to the pain problem, as in the second letter:

> The first time for me was this past February. I was in love with the guy. It hurt, but I didn't care. Some people make it sound so painful, and tell you you'll want to scream. It isn't true. It just hurts a little.
>
> —*a 16-year-old from Maryland*

> My first time was when I was 17½. I had just graduated from high school and I was going off to college in the fall and I didn't want to start college while still being virginal. I had a boyfriend I'd been seeing for six months and we decided to try intercourse. We planned it all for weeks in advance. He borrowed a friend's apartment. I told my parents I was sleeping over at a girlfriend's. Everything was set. But then, it didn't work. It hurt every time he tried to enter me, and he didn't want to hurt me. We didn't know what to do. Finally, we just gave up. But the next week he asked around among his friends and got the name of a doctor—a woman gynecologist—and she cut my hymen. She just went snip. No pain. No

fuss. After that, my boyfriend and I made love all the time.

—*a 29-year-old from New York*

6. Was It Sexually Satisfying?

MAJOR FINDINGS:

Ninety percent of the women did not have an orgasm the first time.

Even when a woman comes away from the experience feeling glad that she made love with the specific man she chose, or just glad that she got the event out of the way—it's extremely rare for her to find her first time sexually satisfying. Among the *Cosmo* women, first sex resulted in orgasm only 10 percent of the time. It would appear that it makes no difference whether a woman has had orgasms during early petting sessions with her first intercourse partner. The first time that intercourse becomes part of the couple's sexual repertoire, the woman usually does not climax. And it makes no difference whether her first intercourse occurred back in the "dark ages" of the fifties, or in the supposedly enlightened seventies. The low orgasm rate during first intercourse was exactly the same for those who gave up their virginity in the past decade as it was for those who had given it up twenty or even thirty years ago.

So the permissive atmosphere surrounding sex today does not seem to have improved the sexual quality of the first experience. Here is a letter from an articulate 23-year-old who had sex for the first time just five years ago. Today, according to her letter, she works as a "telecommunications analyst." Five years ago she was a freshman at a southwestern engineering college:

> I started out, that first year, living with three other girls in a two-bedroom apartment. About two-thirds of the students at my school had to live off-campus, due to lack of student housing. Two months after school started, I met the four guys living upstairs from me and my roommates and I fell in love with one of them.

We had hardly any privacy, neither of us had a car, we each had three other "roomies," and we each shared a bedroom. But one weekend two of my roommates went home, and one was spending the weekend on campus. I asked my boyfriend if he would stay the night with me because I was "afraid to be alone." He agreed. I guess we both had the same idea about what we wanted to happen, but neither of us could admit it. (He was a very strict Southern Baptist, and also a virgin; I'd been brought up to "save myself" for marriage.)

We started out sleeping in separate beds, and then I crawled in with him. We started some heavy petting, but he stopped just short of intercourse. I remember feeling so frustrated and thinking there had to be more. I was sure that intercourse would be wonderful, that I would finally get the great feelings I had when I masturbated, if only we "went all the way." So I pushed him into it.

When he went ahead, however, I was probably the most amazed girl on earth at that particular moment. I didn't feel anything! I didn't bleed. It didn't hurt. And it didn't feel good. I couldn't even feel him inside of me.

The most surprising thing of all was that he moved in and out. My mother had dutifully told me the "facts of life" when I was about 10. But she had neglected to tell me any of the mechanics of sex.

I also had not realized how *wet* sex was. When we were finished, I felt so sticky that what I really wanted to do was take a bath. But he fell asleep immediately, and I spent a miserable night: sticky, uncomfortable, and stuck in the wet spot.

Many other women also reported feeling uninformed about sexual intercourse, no matter their age or schooling, and no matter how recently their first time occurred:

It was three years ago. I was nearly 22. It was with a man I like and had been dating a long time. But it wasn't a smooth experience. My mother had never discussed sex with me and although I knew all my girl friends were having sex, they didn't talk about the details either. I ended up feeling angry with my boyfriend because it hurt, and left out because he enjoyed it, and when it was over I went into the bathroom and cried.

—a 25-year-old from Pennsylvania

I had just turned 18 and graduated from high school. I was very eager to try intercourse, but at the particular moment it happened I felt confused and, to a certain degree, violated and invaded. I thought to myself, "Is this all there is?" I'd had no sex education at all and was totally bewildered. It took place four years ago.

—a 22-year-old from Wisconsin

I am 18 years old. My boyfriend and I tried having sex a few weeks ago. We really tried but he was so big and I was so little and tight, it was impossible. I felt like a failure. I still do. He tried to soothe and comfort me, but I still feel bad. I wish I knew what's wrong with my body.

—an 18-year-old from Indiana

The fact that first sex is so sexually unsatisfying may be because—as so many of the letters indicate—few first-timers know very much about the mechanics of sex. The unknown is always somewhat scary, no matter how much one longs to venture out into it. Even women who declare that they were in love with their first partners sometimes also report sexually disastrous initiations. It is difficult to experience pleasure while contending with tension and ignorance:

I was almost 18 years old at the time and it was with a steady boyfriend. We were both virgins, and the whole thing was pretty close to a disaster. I felt just about nothing at all, and it surprised me because I loved the guy. I loved him so much, and I thought love was supposed to make it perfect.

But if tension and ignorance make it difficult to experience pleasure the first time around, even when one is in love, imagine how much more destructive they can be for those who feel no attachment to their partners, or for those who have first sex because a boyfriend pressures them to do so, or for those who have it because they are afraid they will be social outcasts if they don't. When sex is undertaken for these reasons the goal of sexual pleasure is subordinated to other concerns. And this being so, it is hardly surprising that sexual pleasure is not the end product of the experience.

Here is a letter from a Long Island woman who had her first time because she had turned 18:

> On my 18th birthday, the summer before I started college, I celebrated by drinking in a bar with a bunch of my girlfriends. We had phony IDs. I saw a guy I thought was good-looking and approached him! It was quite daring for a young girl who had barely done any petting, had spent all of her high-school years at an all girls prep school, and who was literally scared to death of sex. It was because it was my birthday that I got up the nerve. People used to worry about being old maids if they didn't marry by a certain age. Now they worry about being old maids if they don't have sex by a certain age. I was worried about this. So I picked up this man, dated him twice, and on our third date went to bed with him. But unbeknownst to me, he'd taken some form of barbiturate. I didn't know. I was trying *so* hard. I even decided to perform fellatio. But he had no reaction to anything I did. In fact, he fell asleep. I was devastated.

Similar to the Long Island woman, the New Jersey woman whose letter follows had her first time because she felt obligated to do so:

> Recalling my first true sexual experience just brings back bad memories. I was a freshman in high school, dating a senior for about a month and a half when he started discussing having sex with me. I just laughed, not believing what I was hearing. He didn't bring up the subject again for about a month. Then he came to me on bended knee with a pre-engagement ring. It was a fad in my school at the time. Feeling obligated, I agreed. What a mistake. Between the pain and the lack of knowledge of my body, I was petrified.

But there is still another reason for the sexual disappointments of the first time. It goes beyond a woman's guilt or fear or lack of

attachment, beyond whether she has concrete sexual knowledge. It
has to do, of course, with the man. For intercourse to be enjoyable
to the female, she needs to be well-aroused and well-lubricated.
This is particularly true for first sex. Yet unfortunately, all too often,
first sex occurs without sufficient foreplay to accomplish lubrication, for unfortunately, a young girl's first sexual partner is usually
as inexperienced as she is and doesn't understand the mechanics of
sex.

Typically among the *Cosmo* women their first time occurred
with a boy who was their age-mate or just a year or two older. A
20-year-old from California told a representative story:

> At the ripe old age of 16 I lost my virginity to a boy of the
> same age who I'd been dating for about four months.
> Three out of those four months I'd heard a constant
> stream of "Please let me do it" and "I'll be gentle" and
> "Everyone else is doing it." So I thought, well, maybe.
> Maybe this is the person I've been waiting for. Maybe my
> dreams and fantasies will be fulfilled. Oh, brother, what
> a mistake! He was gentle, but I think it was because he was
> just about as afraid as I was, and not much more ex-
> perienced. To say the least, I experienced no orgasm, no
> joy, no nothing.

Young and inexperienced males notoriously tend to hurry the
sex act. Among the *Cosmo* women it was those whose introductions
to sex had occurred with older partners, trusted older partners, who
most often reported having found first sex physically satisfying:

> My first affair was when I was 16. The man was 41,
> married, a respected professional in the health field, and
> the father of a 17-year-old boy I knew. I guess some
> people would find our relationship shocking, but I am an
> advocate of these "May-December" relationships. My in-
> troduction to sex was as positive as it could be: warm,
> affectionate, gentle and loving. I had a combination boy-
> friend, husband and father all rolled into one.
>
> —*a 35-year-old woman from Massachusetts*

> I was 19 when I had intercourse for the first time. The man
> was separated and 32 years old. I'd known him for over

a year. I made him wait before we made love, even though he had left his wife for me, because I wanted to be the exact age my mother was when she got married. She said she'd waited, so I should too. (Thank heavens she married relatively young!) It was the most perfect first time I could have imagined. It was just before Christmas. He came up to visit me at school and we made love in a friend's apartment. I'll never forget the way my friend's Christmas tree looked. I'll never forget those colored lights and the way the tinsel glittered.

—a 27-year-old woman from Virginia

But even if her partner is older, if a woman is feeling uneasy about him or if their relationship isn't one that fosters emotional equality, first sex is not likely to satisfy her, no matter the man's sexual experience. Or her own, for that matter, as this letter from a high-school girl who only recently had sex for the first time shows. Her partner was her English teacher:

I am 18 and I recently had intercourse for the first time. It was with my English teacher. I'd been having oral sex with him all semester. We'd get together during free periods. First it was just to talk about sex. He said he wanted to help me. Teach me the right way of looking at things. Then he asked me to go down on him, and he did it to me, too. This was in the classroom. I felt flattered. I felt special. Then a few weeks ago he said, "Why don't you come over to my apartment?" I went there. I was excited. I'd liked his going down on me, and how it made me feel. I'd liked his talking to me. But when I went to his apartment it was all different. There wasn't any conversation or even any foreplay. He just wanted to get right down to business. It hurt, and I cried, and I felt sad, and I still do.

Tension, fear, guilt, the absence of care between the partners, the absence of mechanical knowledge—any one of these factors can keep sex from feeling pleasurable. And since frequently *all* these factors are combined in the first experience with sex, it is small wonder that the experience is usually less than sexually satisfying.

7. Remembering the First Time

Although for 90 percent of the *Cosmo* women, the first time did not result in sexual satisfaction, it did tend with the passage of time to become a crucial and often consoling memory.

Some women are highly philosophical about this. "I don't regret the first time at all," wrote one woman, whose first lover had been, like so many, insensitive and inept. "It takes a while to get used to sex. And how would you ever get used to it if you just waited and waited for Mr. Perfect to come along? He mightn't arrive on the scene until you were 30. And somehow I suspect that by that time a girl would be feeling so peculiar about herself for not having tried sex that even Mr. Perfect wouldn't be able to make her enjoy it."

Another wrote: "I wish I could have skipped over the first time and leaped right into the second—with my current lover, a man who is absolutely a genius in bed. But I suppose if he'd been first, it would have been just as bad."

Most women who described their first experiences had somewhat less perspective than these two. They didn't actually *see* the connection between the poor marks they gave their first lovers and the higher grades they assigned to subsequent lovers. And yet, invariably, they did rate Lover Number Two more highly than Lover Number One. It made no difference whether Lover Number One was a casual acquaintance or a husband. He hardly stood a chance.

Why not? Probably because of the fearful, angry or guilty feelings that so often accompany the first time. But there is little fear or guilt—and not much anger—associated with the second man. As the following letters show, while the first lover may be a man a woman remembers all her life, her second lover is more often the man she credits for making her enjoy sex.

> I had my first sexual experience at the age of 17 with a steady boyfriend who happened to be my first boyfriend and who I eventually married. During sex with him, I experienced no joy. Not the first time nor any of the times afterwards. I would have preferred to end sexual relationships for good until, four years ago, I met a man whose personality intrigued me and toward whom I felt a strong

sexual attraction. I left my husband and started seeing this man, and recently he and I married. I would never have believed that sex could be so good!

—a 28-year-old from Florida

My first time was awful. As my ex-boyfriend used to say, "It's a crummy job but somebody has to do it." He was rough and didn't care about me. He just wanted to get his rocks off. I made him stop before he could really get in, but he broke my hymen and I bled and later I cried for hours. I was sore for a week and sure I'd never let him—or any other man—touch me again. I broke up with him. But thank heavens I didn't give up on all men. I soon discovered my current lover, and I've been seeing him—and enjoying sex—for the past seven years.

—a 24-year-old from Nevada

My first sexual experience was with a boy from my neighborhood, when I was 16. He was a year older than me, and I'd dated him two months. It wasn't great. I wasn't really turned on by the sex. I did enjoy being beside him, though. But it was only after we parted that I met my first real love, a guy I am living with right now. The first sexual experience with him was different—much more exciting. I knew him five months before I had sex with him, because after the first one I wasn't so sure I wanted another one. But it was altogether different. I felt warm and excited and happy.

—an 18-year-old from Illinois

I was 17 and beginning to feel sexual urges. I fell in love with a man four years older than me. Our first sexual experience wasn't what sex was cracked up to be. I bled and felt uncomfortable for a day or two afterwards. It took a while before sex became enjoyable, a good couple of years. I married that first man, but it wasn't until after we divorced and I had other lovers that I was truly able to enjoy sex.

—a 24-year-old from Rhode Island

Clearly, in sexual numerology, being Number One isn't everything.

8. Waiting for the First Time

Kinsey found that young girls in his day avoided premarital sex because of social pressure against it. Today, as we have seen, an opposite situation prevails. There seems to be social pressure to have intercourse early, to get it out of the way. As a result many girls who do not have sex while still in their teens report being under considerable social stress and psychological strain. They wonder constantly if they are "old-fashioned" or "prudish," begin to doubt their values or attractiveness, and ask perpetually, "What's wrong with me?"

Their query represents a misconception about what is really happening on the teenage sex scene. To look back at the results of the Johns Hopkins sociologists' national survey on adolescent sex: The survey involved nearly two thousand urban girls. It found that exactly half of them were sexually active by the age of 19. Exactly half were not. (The figures cannot be *precisely* compared with *Cosmo*'s figures, since the *Cosmo* survey established how many girls were sexually active by age 20.) In view of the Johns Hopkins study, a teenage girl who has not had sex should not feel there is anything at all wrong with her. She is, after all, just like half her peers.

Despite this fact, anxiety about delaying first sex seems endemic among teenagers, even the younger ones.

> I am sure I am much older than most girls who haven't had sex. I don't really want to have sex. It scares me. But I hate feeling like I'm the only one in the world who hasn't tried it.
>
> *—a 16-year-old from Connecticut*

> I am less than three weeks from being 17 and am still a virgin. I've had a few boyfriends—no one special—and I've necked and petted a bit. But that's all I've done. I

always say "No" when one of my boyfriends wants to go further. Is something wrong with me?

—a 16-year-old from Maryland

I am a college freshman and better than average-looking. In fact, I have been encouraged by many people to start a modeling career. But boys don't seem to like me. I think it's because I give off signals that tell them I'm still a virgin and boys today just don't want to bother with you if you're a virgin. Is there any hope for me?

—a 17-year-old from West Virginia

9. Effects of the First Time on Future Sexual Happiness

MAJOR FINDINGS:

Although fully half of all the *Cosmo* women didn't particularly enjoy their first time in bed, by the time they were more experienced, 97 percent were enjoying making love.

There is an extraordinary range of emotions, settings, levels of intimacy with partners, and degrees of physical knowledge or psychological maturity connected with the first time. There are women who experience pain, women who have no physical trauma at all. There are 14-year-olds who consider themselves emotionally well-equipped to handle a first time, 22-year-olds who report feeling childlike and unready. There are women who are the aggressors in sex, suggesting intercourse to reluctant boyfriends, and women who are pressured and even forced into first sex. There are women whose first sexual intercourse follows after many months of sexual experimentation with a partner, after necking, petting, oral sex, and even anal sex. And there are women for whom the first sexual intercourse is a first experience with sex of any kind whatsoever. Above all, there are women who fondly remember their first sexual experiences, and women who deeply regret them.

What most of these women have in common is that they eventually become decidedly enthusiastic about sex. A resounding 97 percent of the *Cosmo* women said they enjoy the emotional aspects of making love, and 70 percent of them said they always or usually have orgasms. These are rather dramatic findings when viewed in relation to the fact that more than half of them did not enjoy making love the first time, and nine-tenths of them found first sex physically unsatisfying.

Why and how such a marked change in sexual attitudes and response comes about forms the subject of chapters 4 and 5, which explore sexual practices and orgasm with a partner as developmental processes. But before I leave the subject of the sexual novice and turn to more mature sexuality, I want to say to any reader who has just had, or who has not yet had, her sexual initiation, that with the possible exception of initiation by rape (which does seem to leave a lasting anxiety over sex) there is apparently no correlation whatsoever between a boring, discouraging, or downright disastrous first time in bed and future sexual happiness.

Chapter Two
Turn-Ons

1. He's in the Mood for Sex (She Isn't)

What stimulates women? What preliminaries put them in the mood for sex? Largely because of scientific studies by Masters and Johnson, what excites—and satisfies—women in bed began to receive wide public attention in the 1970s. As a result many women were able to become less shy about stating their sexual preferences and many men became aware of their misconceptions about women's orgasms. But less attention was paid to a matter of almost equal importance: the kinds of stimuli that make a woman desire sex in the first place.

According to sex therapists, the inability or reluctance to feel desire is far more prevalent than any other sexual problem (such as impotence or the failure to have orgasms). It's not news that the inability or reluctance can be deep-rooted—caused by prohibitions laid down in earliest childhood by parental attitudes explicitly or implicitly equating sexuality with vulgarity or vulnerability. But it can also result simply from the fact that a person just is not in the mood for sex. He or she is not, as the expression goes, turned on.

A large number of turn-on problems occur because of the different ways men and women are stimulated to desire sex. For example, a man knows that seeing an X-rated film excites him. He takes his partner to one. She not only doesn't get excited but seems actually put off by the experience. When he says, "Let's go to bed,"

71

she says, "I'm not in the mood." Or she knows that an intimate talk after a leisurely candlelit dinner will excite her. She serves dinner, pours the wine and asks him to tell her about his childhood or his job, his friends or his colleagues. He not only doesn't feel excited, but seems actually put off by having to dawdle and discourse. When she says, "Let's go to bed," he says, "I'm not in the mood."

These are classic scenarios for *not* getting into the bedroom. But turn-on problems can occur even when a couple has agreed to have sex and is already in the bedroom.

For example: They have just returned from, say, an afternoon swim date. The man is eager. The sight of the woman's sun-tinged body in her bikini was enough stimulation for him to be already keen for sex. The woman, though agreeable to sex in theory, still needs to be turned on: the sight of him in trunks—however well-built and tanned he may be—was not enough for her. For the man, the sunlight flooding the apartment with warmth and brilliance promises to make their lovemaking session particularly delightful, allowing him to observe her body in all its provocative details. For the woman, the light has just the opposite effect. Their failure to understand each other's differences will lead to stressful sex, if any at all.

Women are not turned on by the same things that turn men on —at least many women are not. Certainly visual stimuli excite them far less than they excite men. Among the *Cosmopolitan* women, only 22 percent were stimulated by pornography. Only 9 percent liked to make love in a brightly lit room (see page 129).

Is this reluctance to look boldly on the acts of love a matter of cultural conditioning or physiology? No one really knows. Nor does it really matter. What does matter is that this difference between men and women presently exists. What does matter is that couples need to adjust to this reality.

It need not, though, be a hardship. Women are turned on by a wide variety of things, from sounds and smells and tastes to fantasies of meetings to come and remembrances of encounters past. Some of the things that turn women on are unsurprising—such things as a kiss or the sound of a lover's voice over the telephone. But other female turn-ons are more curious. Women are so sound-oriented that various aural stimuli can put them in the mood—rain on the roof, wind rattling against windowpanes and even, as one woman wrote in her letter, the hum of a certain refrigerator. Some of the preliminaries that put women in the mood for sex today are quite up-to-the-minute—such as marijuana or the music of, say, Neil Diamond or Bruce Springsteen. Others are remarkably old-fashioned: the *Cosmo* respondents—for all their wide experience of sex—still overwhelmingly like having their lovers undress them.

Men and women may be turned on by different things, but women's turn-ons are every bit as potent as men's. Both sexes are well-advised to keep this in mind.

2. Favorite Turn-Ons

MAJOR FINDINGS:

Pornography was far less likely to excite the women than was music or the sound of their lover's voice telling them what sexy things he wanted to do in bed. Drinks or even smells like cologne or perspiration were far more likely to excite them than drugs or a carefully planned dinner of favorite foods. But all these excited *some* of the women:

Music is a turn-on for 78 percent.

Drinks are a turn-on for 66 percent.

Sexy talk is a turn-on for 49 percent.

Drugs are a turn-on for 30 percent.

Pornography is a turn-on for 22 percent.

Food is a turn-on for 17 percent.

Turn-ons are matters of individual as well as gender preference. Most women did not find pornography a turn-on, but some did. Most did not find food a turn-on, but a few did. It is important to know and understand one's own preferences. It won't profit a woman to know that nearly 80 percent of her sisters prefer music in bed. If she is excited by mystery or the sounds of silence, music will just annoy her.

There are, of course, some women who have never stopped to

discover what puts them in the mood for sex. When asked about turn-ons they talk about foreplay. "Having him play with his fingers on my clitoris," they say. Or, "having him kiss the lips of my vagina."

Genital activities are not turn-ons. Turn-ons are accompaniments or preliminaries to genital sex. They can be conceptual—matters of thought, such as anticipation or fantasy. Or they can be perceptual—matters of the senses. When they are perceptual they involve physical stimuli. But a turn-on touch, for example, is only indirectly sexual—a kiss on the mouth, a stroke on the thighs, a handshake.

The *Cosmo* survey's women described being turned on by both conceptual and perceptual stimuli. Many of their favorite conceptual turn-ons involved anticipation. (Sexy talk—that turn-on for nearly half of all those polled—is really an anticipation turn-on, not an aural or sound turn-on.) Others involved having a secret that no one else knows, or taking a risk, or breaking a rule.

Here are some of the anticipatory, risk-taking and rule-breaking things that were listed as turn-ons in the letters of some of the women:

"Wearing sexy lingerie under business attire."

"Talking about sex in unlikely situations—for example, at business meetings or formal receptions."

"Posing for nude pictures for my boyfriend."

"Having my husband talk to me on the phone about wanting to be in bed with me."

"Having a man tell me that he is going to please me first and I can't do anything for him until he says I can."

"Telling a man that I am going to stimulate him all over but he can't touch me, or come inside me, until I give him permission."

"Reading sexy novels."

"Watching soap operas."

"Thinking all week about what my boyfriend and I are going to do in bed on the weekend."

Love can be a conceptual turn-on too. As can the feeling of being loved, or of being special to a particular man. Letter-writers described being turned on by such things as:

"Talking with a man I admire."

"Receiving flowers."

"Having a man say that he cares for me."

"Buying my lover a gift that's personal."

"Having a man reveal his feelings. Feelings about me are best. But about his work or his life is okay too."

"Having an intimate conversation. It doesn't have to be sexual in nature. The man just has to be saying to me the kinds of things I figure he doesn't say often to anybody, or maybe never said."

"Having my lover mention a little private joke, or enough of it—sometimes just a word will do—while we're in company."

And a 24-year-old senior staff accountant from Colorado mentioned a conceptual turn-on not cited by any of the other women but long known to romantic poets:

> I am turned on by a sense of mortality. What I mean by this is that whenever I've faced danger and come through it safely, or had some other reminder of how brief the human lifespan is, I feel as if I've been given a tremendous aphrodisiac.

Conceptual turn-ons aren't always effective by themselves, and so some women get in the mood by combining a conceptual turn on with broad sense-stimulation. What excites them is being touched *while* they're in risk-taking, rule-breaking or loving situations:

"Fooling around in places where you might get caught, like in the office late in the evening."

"Petting in places that are public, like movie theaters."

"Fooling around with a man while he's nude and I'm fully clothed. Or the other way around."

"Having a man put his hand under my skirt and panties and stroke my thighs while he's driving."

"Having my lover touch my arm when we enter a crowded party, as if to let everyone there know I'm his."

Being turned on through the senses alone is also common. Some women reported being turned on by smells. "Paco Rabanne after-shave lotion," one specified. "British Sterling deodorant," said another. "Incense," said quite a few.

Others talked about sound turn-ons:

"Having my lover talk to me during sex. He doesn't have to tell me what he's going to do to me, or what he enjoys. Just hearing the sound or feeling the sensation of his voice in my ear excites me."

"Once I worked in a fast-food place, and every time the refrigerator turned on, I'd get a sexual rush. It was the sound that did it."

"Neil Diamond's 'The Grass Won't Pay No Mind.' "

"Bruce Springsteen."

"Only Bach."

"Early Beatles."

Taste turn-ons were rare. "Chili," one woman wrote. "Spicy Chinese food," wrote another. "Oysters," wrote a third. Several said, "Caviar"—though it seems not unlikely that a caviar turn-on is conceptual rather than perceptual—it betokens the wealth of the man who buys it, and money is sexy, although it was rarely stated as a turn-on. Instead, it made its presence known in the reports of women who were stimulated by such things as "champagne in bed" and "riding in my lover's limousine."

Among the visual turn-ons some women cited were:

"Having a man give me a deep passionate look of unabashed love."

"Looking at men's tight asses, broad shoulders, long legs, and curly chest hair."

"Making love in a room with lots of mirrors so I can see the sexual ballet in progress."

"Looking at men when their ties are loosened, their top shirt buttons are undone, and they have five-o'clock shadows."

"Being with a man who can flirt with his eyes."

"Seeing softcore porn, like the two *Emanuelle* movies."

"Watching my boyfriend walk around nude with an erection."

But perhaps the most unusual report of a visual turn-on is this one, sent in by a long-married California woman:

> I am 34 years old and my husband is 38. We've been married fifteen and a half years. After all those years we thought we each knew everything that turned the other on. But just a few months ago we discovered something new, quite by accident, and it still brings a smile to our lips whenever we think about it.
>
> It happened on a Sunday afternoon. We were on our way to pick up our two children from the movies. As we drove down our residential street in our average suburban neighborhood I saw a couple lying on the front lawn of a nearby house. The man was lying on his back and the woman was straddling him. I told my husband that it looked as if they were making love. He said that I must be mistaken, but quickly turned the car around and parked in a spot where we could see them but they couldn't see us. As we watched it became obvious that this couple was, indeed, getting it off. The woman was wearing a skirt with a slit on the side, but the skirt had gotten turned around so that the slit was in the back. Every time she raised up, her bare rear showed. The man was raising her up, reaching around her and lifting her up and down slowly. Then he reached up and under her blouse and stroked her breasts. Even though an occasional car passed by close to them, and they had to stop their movements, they didn't end their lovemaking.
>
> I knew I was intruding on their private moment but I couldn't stop looking at them and being very turned on. After what seemed to be a very long time, the woman started to speed up her movements. As she arched her back and threw her head back, I remembered how many times I had done that very same thing. Was that how I

looked? Finally she collapsed on the man. When she did, her skirt was up around her waist and she was completely exposed.

At this point, both my husband and I were so sexually stimulated that I couldn't breathe and my husband couldn't start the car fast enough. As we pulled away he honked the horn and I gave the couple the "okay" sign. We drove to get the kids, and all the way we kept talking about how exciting what we had seen had been. We had seen some porno movies in our time, but this was very different.

When we got home, neither of us could wait for the kids to go to bed, so we told them we were going to take a nap. Since they are old enough to take care of themselves, we didn't worry about leaving them alone downstairs while we went up to the bedroom. We were so excited that not much foreplay was needed. In fact, we couldn't wait just to simulate our young couple's experience. It was a glorious afternoon and evening.

But the best part of the experience was finding out that you can still find new turn-ons even after you've been married a long time. We have always been very open to each other's needs, but this experience showed us that the future always has something new and different in store, as long as you open your minds. And your eyes.

Even short of seeing two neighbors copulating on a suburban lawn, it would seem the world is full of turn-ons for those whose minds are sufficiently open to receive them. Preliminaries, as in most well-staged events, not only serve to set up the main event but have a life of their own.

3. Drinks and Drugs as Turn-Ons

What of alcohol—a reported turn-on for nearly two-thirds of the women? And drugs, for nearly one-third? Are these turn-ons conceptual or perceptual; do they act mainly by exciting the mind or by stimulating the senses? The verdict was mixed: "For me, alcohol is definitely an aphrodisiac." wrote one woman. "So is pot," suggesting that alcohol and pot stimulated her body. "They make me feel uninhibited," wrote another, suggesting they worked on her mind, "and after I've smoked pot or gotten high on beer, vodka or rum, I am not very choosy about sex."

Most medical authorities would agree with the second woman. They would say that drinks and drugs work as turn-ons by affecting the mind rather than the body. Taken in small doses, they relax inhibitions in people who are sexually repressed, and sometimes stimulate the kind of personal talk that in turn stimulates intimacy, permitting such people to experience the pleasurable anticipatory feelings about sex that come more easily to the less repressed. But drinks and drugs are not aphrodisiacs—not substances that actually sexually arouse the body or make it more capable of sex. It is widely known that too much alcohol can cause impotence in men and a lack of sexual desire in women, and that cocaine—even in small doses —can numb sexual response.

But marijuana too can be sexually anesthetizing to a degree, can produce a feeling of depersonalization. For the more inhibited this may be a desirable feeling; without it sexual responses are more difficult. For others, depersonalization is disappointing; it makes sex feel as though it is happening to someone else.

A reasonable conclusion is that drinks and drugs are turn-ons chiefly for people who *expect* them to be, and not for those who have no such expectations.

3. Turn-Ons and Aggression

MAJOR FINDINGS:

A dramatically high number of the respondents—95 percent—like their partners to undress them before sex.

A decidedly small number—8 percent—enjoy being pinched, bitten or slapped.

Only a statistically insignificant number—less than 1 percent—like to be beaten.

These findings should put an end to a widespread misconception about female masochism. While there is no question that some women enjoy masochistic sexual fantasies (see Chapter Seven), they clearly do not enjoy pain. Fantasy and reality are entirely separate matters. The gulf between them is apparent not just from the fact that less than 1 percent of the *Cosmo* women reported that they liked being beaten, but also from the fact that even slightly painful experiences—being pinched, bitten or slapped—appealed to but a fraction of them.

A curious fact about this female distaste for pain during sex is that for years the writers of sex manuals failed to credit it. Instead, they frequently saw fit to suggest that mild violence could enhance sexual pleasure, and consistently recommended that men pinch, bite or slap their partners. One can only assume that these writers must have canvassed men only, and neglected to ask females what pleased them. Had they done so, they would have found that when they recommended male aggression in bed, they were recommending ways for a man to turn off, not turn on, the majority of his sexual partners.

What, though, about aggression on the female's part? Do women like to pinch, bite, or slap their partners? Not if they are like the *Cosmo* women. The survey-takers liked giving this kind of "punishment" even less than they liked getting it. Only 7 percent expressed any fondness for being physically rough toward their partners.

They did like mock fights, however. A fifth said they enjoyed pretending to struggle with their partners, or play-acting at trying to get away from their embraces.

And they did like the mild aggression inherent in a man's undressing them. One woman wrote:

> I'm very free sexually. I often seduce a man by flirting with him and physically stimulating him during necking and petting. But when it comes right down to the final moment I just need that extra added little something that comes of having a man take off my clothes. I need his undressing me. I don't know exactly why. Maybe it's flattery. Or maybe it's courtesy. It's something old-fashioned, of that I'm sure.

Certainly the fondness for wanting to be undressed does suggest an old-fashioned female need. It implies the desire to be *courted,* persuaded to have sex. To have a man undress a woman—as opposed to her taking off her own clothes—is to have a man be the sexual aggressor. When a man undresses a woman, she perceives him as her pursuer, a being more impatient, ardent and curious than herself. This form of mild aggression in bed seemed to be the only aggressive activity that had appeal for a majority of the women.

Chapter Three
The Whens, Wheres and How-Oftens of Sex

1. The Uses and Abuses of Sexual Measuring Scales

There seems to be something almost inherently anxiety-producing about the whens, wheres and how-oftens of other people's sexual habits. On hearing that their neighbors or sisters or girlfriends make love five times a week, or three, or only just once, too many people worry that their own sexual frequency is abnormally low or extraordinarily high. On hearing that their neighbors or sisters or girlfriends make love only at night, or only by dawn's early light, or only in bed, or only in romantic outdoor settings, too many people decide that their own sexual habits are prissy or overly bold, that their sexual habits are somehow, in fact, either *right* or *wrong.*

Of *course* it is foolish. Of *course* no woman should measure herself against her neighbors, sisters or girlfriends. Of *course* when it comes to sex it is what we do and how we feel about it that counts, not when or where or how often we do it. Yet it is almost unavoidable to compare ourselves with others, to weigh ourselves and find ourselves wanting. This makes sexual measuring scales seem of dubious value.

Still, knowing when, where, and how often—on the average—people make love is not all for nothing. From the statistics about frequency and sexual expectations one can learn not only how often a typical married woman makes love, and how often she wishes she were making love, but also, by comparing the two, gain some insight into the widespread marital discontent among women. From the statistics about the best times and places for sex one can learn not only what most women in our society prefer but also project how couples whose lovemaking is unsatisfactory to the female might improve their relationship. In addition, from statistics about lunch-hour sex, one can venture a thought-provoking interpretation of the familiar but long-unexamined sexual myth.

These miscellaneous whens, wheres, and how-oftens of sex are offered up in the spirit of inquiry. They are not strict criteria; they should be viewed as patterns, not used as tests of one's individual performance.

2. Sexual Frequencies: How Often Do You Make Love?

MAJOR FINDINGS:

Thirty-six percent usually make love three to five times a week.

Thirty-two percent usually make love once or twice a week.

Fifteen percent usually make love once or twice a month.

Nine percent usually make love less than once a month.

Eight percent usually make love once a day or more often.

As the findings above show, the most typical lovemaking frequency of the *Cosmo* women is three to five times a week. The next most common pattern is once or twice a week.

Should a woman worry if she makes love more or less often than this? Of course not. There is no such thing as a right or wrong amount of lovemaking. Appetites for sex vary and are as individual as appetites for food, water and companionship. They can of course be affected by the nature of an individual's relationship, but even when a relationship is excellent some will want, and have, more sex in *their* excellent relationship than others will in theirs.

Regardless of individual differences, however, having a high frequency is clearly related to having a partner who is regularly available. The *Cosmo-*survey women who are married or who have live-in lovers make frequent love more often than those who are less attached. They are nearly one and a half times as likely to make love three to five times a week. Indeed, some 90 percent of them make love at least once a week, whereas this is true of only some 66 percent of those whose sexual partners do not live with them.

As for daily sex, while only 5 percent of the women with out-of-house partners have it, 9 percent of those with husbands or live-in lovers do.

But there is a curious sidelight to daily sex. It is three times more common among singles with live-in partners than it is among married women who live with husbands.

Why the discrepancy? Is a marriage license an inhibitor of sexuality? Not demonstrably. But many marriages today are not undertaken until after a couple has lived together for some time, and sad though it may seem, familiarity does tend, eventually, to breed restraint. Not, though, contempt, or even boredom. Sex researchers such as Masters and Johnson have often asserted that if a sexual relationship is a good one for both partners, pleasure may actually *grow,* even though a couple makes love less frequently.

3. Sexual Expectations: How Much Sex Is Enough?

Major Findings:

Sixty-three percent wished they were making love more frequently.

One point five percent wished they were making love less frequently.

Thirty-six percent were content with their sexual frequencies.

There's an old riddle that asks, "What's better than sex?" The answer goes, "More sex."

To some extent *The Cosmo Report* bears out this riddle. The desire to have more frequent sex was expressed by close to two-thirds of the women taking the survey. It was expressed by women who had sex rarely and by women who had it frequently. Certainly it was expressed more often by those for whom sex was rare: an overwhelming 92 percent of women who made love only once a month longed for more frequent sex, as compared to 42 percent of those who made love three to five times a week. But more sex is desired even by some women who make love daily; among such women, a third wanted more.

Still, if the survey indicates that *some* women always want more sex, it also provides clues to how much sex is enough *usually*—or enough for *most* women. A majority of those having sex three to five times a week said they were content with their sexual frequency. But once the frequency slipped below that figure, the numbers of the discontented increased dramatically. Among women having sex once or twice a week, less than a third were content. It would appear that, at least from the *Cosmo* sample most women would like to make love at least three to five times a week.

4. When Is the Best Time for Sex?

MAJOR FINDINGS:

Nighttime lovemaking is preferred over morning or daytime lovemaking by 71 percent of the women.

If one asks a man when the best time for sex is, chances are he'll say "anytime" or "all the time." The *Cosmo* women don't agree. While males often express a penchant for daytime sex—and, particularly, morning sex—*Cosmopolitan*'s respondents voted overwhelmingly in favor of making love at night.

Why this preference? A clue lies in the answer to another question *Cosmopolitan* asked in its survey. "Do you like to make love in daylight or bright light, with the lights on dimly, or in the dark?" In responding, a huge majority indicated that they preferred darkness or dim lights. Only a small group—9 percent—opted for daylight or bright lights. The letters and comments sent in by survey respondents illuminated this matter even further. Among the thousands of communications received, only a handful mentioned sunshine or bright light as an enhancement to sexual pleasure. Those women who did like bright lights sometimes also said they considered themselves—not necessarily unhappily—exhibitionists. One such woman wrote: "I like sex outdoors, indoors, it doesn't matter where. I've done it on a bus, standing up in a bathroom, bending over a hassock so my lover could enter me from the rear, on my lover's desk. And I like bright lights. As I write this, I can see just how much of an exhibitionist I am. Ain't it great."

But the majority of women wrote with pleasure chiefly of sexual experiences that had occurred in semi-darkness. Typical were:

"My current lover and I make love by firelight, and nothing was ever so exciting to me."

"I get really turned on when we make love by candlelight."

"The best sexual experience I ever had with Nick, the man I'm seeing now, was on a camping trip last summer. It was pitch-black out, and we made love in front of the embers of our cooking fire."

"I like a bed lamp on, but nothing brighter. Too much light kills the romance of sex."

Why women have such a strong preference for sex at night and in darkened rooms or settings is a matter of debate. The preference could be a cultural one caused by inhibitions that prompt women to shy away from seeing sex too clearly. Or from wanting their lovers to see them too clearly. (Many letters from the *Cosmo* women indicated a self-consciousness that somehow seems more female than male, an anxiety about not measuring up physically to a partner's ideals.) But preferring dimness to brightness during sex could also have something to do with female physiological requirements. Perhaps in order to be turned on a woman actually *needs* dimness, with its resulting opportunity to focus on private sensation rather than be distracted by external stimuli. Perhaps there are biological as well as cultural factors at work in the marked preference for dimness.

5. Lunch-Hour Sex

MAJOR FINDINGS:

Forty-five percent have never made love on their lunch hours. Twenty-six percent have done it occasionally. Twenty-four percent have done it once or twice. Five percent have done it frequently.

There was a time when married women shivered at the phrase "lunch-hour sex." It made them worry about the sexual opportunities available to their husbands when, off at work, they were surrounded by attractive, available, single female colleagues. Lunch-hour sex suggested adultery and, specifically, the infidelities of married men with single women who had no steady lovers.

The facts about lunch-hour sex hint at a different story. Lunch-hour sex is simply not a common experience for single women who live alone. In fact, lunch-hour sex seems to be the privilege of married women or of those who live with their lovers. It was twice as common for the survey women who were married, or who lived with their lovers, to have sex in the middle of the day *frequently*, than it was for those who were single to do so. It was also much more common even on an *occasional* basis for the married woman or the woman living with her lover.

I suspect that lunch-hour sex—rarely reported by women who live alone—is primarily the prerogative of those who occupy the same quarters as their sex partners. I suggest that while it is certainly practiced sometimes by adulterous husbands and wives, it is more often practiced by the nonadulterous. Does this seem a bit anti-climactic? That's the risk of statistics: They make us contend with facts, instead of fantasies.

6. Where Are the Best Places for Sex?

MAJOR FINDINGS:

The *Cosmo* survey respondents' favorite setting for lovemaking—aside from bed—was the floor. Their least favorite was the car.

The survey asked, "What is your favorite setting in which to make love—aside from in bed—among the following: the couch, the floor, the beach, the grass, the car, the shower or bath?" Over a third voted for the floor.

Why the floor? Several letters said because it allowed for spontaneity in sex. "I adore making love on the floor," one woman wrote. "My lover and I often start caressing each other while we're watching television on his couch. After that there's something incredible about just sinking down onto the floor and going right on with the fun, right there, instead of spoiling the spontaneity by having to trek to the bedroom." Said another woman, "My lover and I frequently get excited while we're working together making dinner, or doing the dishes afterwards. Next thing I know, we're slipping down onto the floor. I love it when we do this. It's as if we want each other so badly that we don't need to rely on all the superficial things—on pretty sheets and sexy nightgowns—and that's a real turn-on."

The floor was also considered a comfortable place for sex. Indeed, comfort was the chief consideration in evaluating settings: "It's roomy, you can stretch out in any position, move around and not worry about getting close to an edge and falling off."

Among the outdoor settings favored were:

In the forest by a stream under a starry sky.

In the leafy woods.

Late at night on a deserted beach.

Outdoors in a tent in front of a roaring fire at the beach. Watch out for the sand, though! Better get on top, and let him worry about the sand grains.

In our pool, early in the morning.

In the ocean, on a moonlit night.

Outside, on a blanket, at night.

Bur for the most part outdoor settings—although they *seemed* romantic—had appeal for only a few, perhaps because privacy is difficult to ensure outdoors. Only 18 percent favored lovemaking on the beach, 13 percent on the grass.

Lovemaking in the shower or bath was preferred by 16 percent . . . "I love the feeling of water spraying over my body while I'm making love; it's an extra bit of stimulation on the skin."

But another letter-writer fumed against watery settings for sex, indoors or outdoors: "Whenever I hear about people liking to make love in the ocean or the shower or any other watery place, I know they haven't tried it. They're just fantasizing. I *have* tried it, however, and I can tell you such places are my least favorite ones. First, it's hard to achieve a comfortable position in water. You can't get your balance, and if you try to wrap your legs around your partner so he can thrust up inside you, he usually loses his balance and you both go under. That's what happens in ponds or the sea. In the tub it's just as bad. Because the other thing about water and sex is that water and women's lubrication just don't mix. When water gets inside you it seems to dissolve your secretions. So the thrusting rubs and hurts. In the shower it's also terrible. You can't get comfortable. I hate sex-by-water."

Indoors, 18 percent favored couches. Some other favored pieces of household furniture were hammocks and deep armchairs, and one "bottom line" respondent advised, "My favorite setting for sex is on the huge pillows we have on our living-room floor. A lot of times my husband and I will be lying on them listening to music and the next thing I know we're undressing each other. We've been married a year and we've bought a living-room set with a sectional couch and matching chairs, a dinette set and color TV, but those pillows are the best investment we've made."

Some of the more unusual settings enjoyed were:

"My lover and I have this special little hotel we go to a lot, and we always rent a room there that's called The Love Suite. It has an eight-and-a-half-foot round bed with satin sheets, a fireplace, lots of mirrors, stereo, a bar and a Jacuzzi."

"In my lover's boat, out in the middle of the ocean where there are only seagulls and fish to know, and while my lover moves in and out of me we're being rocked by small waves."

"I had an experience in the mountains off the beaten path that was extraordinary. Feeling the cool soft mountain breeze as my lover pulled passionately in and out was a very satisfying experience."

"Some of the places I've enjoyed making love were: on a rock in the Colorado River while kayaking, and last year in the second-floor men's room at the Denver airport, because where do you do it if you're going one way and your lover is going another?" (Incidentally, this woman said she was a forty-five-year-old education consultant who found the *Cosmo* survey "disappointing" because the young women of today were "unappreciative" of sexual freedom.)

Interestingly the car, *the* setting for lovemaking during the repressed fifties, was not at all popular with the *Cosmo* survey women. Only 4 percent liked making love in cars:

"I've had sex in every place imaginable, and the only place I didn't like was in a car. I'm six feet tall and need all the room I can get."

"My least favorite place is in a car. I find it exceedingly difficult to get comfortable in one, and being physically comfortable during sex is just as important as being mentally comfortable."

If cars were out, beds were in. Even though the survey specifically asked for favorite sexual settings *aside* from bed, many could not refrain from indicating—after they had checked a favorite—that it was really second best to bed. "A big soft bed with feather pillows and comforters," one woman wrote. "A waterbed," said a few. "A firm-mattressed bed," specified others. One bed enthusiast more or less rhymed:

> You can keep your couch
> It makes me say ouch
> And also your floor
> It rubs me raw
> In the woods
> You get bit
> The beach is the pits
> Tubs are too damp
> Cars are too cramped
> Enough hemming and hawing
> It's time it was said
> Be it ever so boring
> There's no place like bed.

Chapter Four
Sexual Practices

1. The Expansion of Sexual Repertoires

Hundreds of changes have been wrought in the sexual and social lives of Americans as a result of the sexual revolution, but none is more striking than the fact that most men and women today employ an extraordinary variety of sexual practices in the course of their day-to-day lovemaking. Many take sexual variety for granted, so accustomed to it have they become, but in fact it is a remarkable, and recent, development. Not so very long ago in the United States, having sex with a partner meant, for a sizable majority of people, having coital sex—intercourse—only, and having it in only one position—with the man on top. Kinsey estimated that in his day, as many as 70 percent of Americans had never even attempted intercourse in any but this fashion.

Today, as all recent sex surveys have shown, and the *Cosmo* survey will be no exception, a repertoire of sexual practices is customary. When having intercourse, contemporary couples make use of many different positions. Before, after, or as a substitute for intercourse they experiment widely with manual, oral and other types of sexual activity. In the past, sexual experimentation, when it occurred at all, did so chiefly among the upper and educated classes. Today, a cornucopia of sexual pleasures is within the grasp of every man and every woman.

Men have profited profoundly from the change. Far less inhib-

91

ited than women in earlier decades of this century, they often felt
sexually thwarted by wives who denied them fellatio, or who
refused them intercourse of any duration or in any way but in the
most uninspired of positions. As psychotherapeutic literature of the
fifties and early sixties attests, while some husbands went to prosti-
tutes, many simply went into despair.

But women have profited even more. Brief sexual intercourse
in the missionary position is without doubt the sexual activity least
likely to produce orgasm for a woman. With the change in erotic
custom brought about by the sexual revolution, it at last became
possible for legions of women to experience a full range of sexual
activities and, as a result, to discover the joys of climaxing during
partner sex.

For society as a whole the expansion of sexual acts has been a
sudden phenomenon, a change that has occurred virtually overnight. But for the individual, expanding the sexual repertoire is
nearly always a gradual process. The occasional man or woman will
explore the full gamut of sexual practices in the first days of his or
her very first relationship. But for most, erotic diversification is a
matter of the passage of time.

In the letters of the *Cosmo* women, this fact stood out above all
others. "My life has been formed of chapters," wrote a 35-year-old
woman from the midwest. "Not just mentally, but professionally
and sexually." She is a twice-divorced woman with two children
who, alone and in need of finding a way to support her family and
herself in the future, returned to college after she was 30, completed
her degree, and enrolled in law school. On the night she wrote to
Cosmopolitan, she was nervously awaiting the results of the bar examination in her state. To distract herself, she explored her life in
detail, concluding:

> I've gone through all the experiences usually written
> about—a too-young first marriage, boredom, outgrowing
> him, leaving, loneliness, poverty at the edges, a too-quick
> second marriage to a non-boring but thoroughly irrespon-
> sible drinking woman-chaser, a decision to go it alone,
> and then a period in which I realized I had to provide for
> my own future, and that of my two sons. Hence the edu-
> cation. But if I've learned about the law over these years,
> I've also learned about sex. In this area too, my story will
> be familiar. Like many women I have read about, I had

difficulties about sex in my earlier years. I was raised by a strict southern Baptist mother, and it was hard to accept that it was okay to have sex once I married when it had been a taboo subject before. The defense mechanisms of my brain almost refused to permit me to enjoy sex. (Or maybe it was that at a young age—I was 20—no woman really appreciates sex the way she will ten or fifteen years later. At least that was my experience.) I had sex, but I didn't really enjoy it. There were parts of foreplay I used to consider improper, and positions I thought vulgar. Only later on did I change. Then I realized that sexual taboos are not set in stone. People can change, if their minds remain open. People can start new chapters.

There was a P.S. at the end of the letter. It read, "I have my bar results! I passed. I'm legal now!" The woman who wrote the letter was about to enter yet another chapter of her life. But while her late-in-life academic progress was unusual, her sexual progress was similar to that of many other *Cosmo* women. Hundreds and hundreds of them reported that they had had to unlearn inhibitions and school themselves in expanding their sexual practices.

Many factors influenced this educational process. "I used to view certain sexual practices with disgust," wrote another woman who had changed as a result of reading about sex, "until I began learning that many people engaged in them."

But perhaps the single most important factor in a woman's learning to be sexually expressive was establishing a relationship with a trusted partner.

The young girl whose letter follows found such a partner quite early in life and began her odyssey through sexuality with a wide range of sexual pleasures:

> I guess I should start out by telling you that I am 16 years old and I live with my mother, who is separated. Her job requires her to be out of town regularly for two weeks out of every month. I wouldn't say my mother is exactly liberal, but she does trust me a lot, and when she is out of town I take on the responsibilities of our house and home. Undoubtedly this has given me a lot of freedom and maturity. I first had sex this past June. I'd been dating for two years and almost all those dates led to necking and

petting. But it always ended there—with clothes on—
until I met T, who was 21 and a sophomore in college. We
dated for three weeks, and ended up in bed.

I know I was lucky to have T. He had a real infatua-
tion with my breasts and fondling them was always a part
of our foreplay. So was oral sex. I liked it when he did it
to me though at first I didn't like doing it to him. I didn't
know *what* to do. Even *Playgirl* isn't very explicit about
fellatio. But I figured it out and got better at it. We also
tried anal sex twice, although I didn't like it and we decided to drop it. And we made love in a lot of positions,
and also on the floor and the davenport, because I didn't
like the after-bounce of his waterbed. I loved the feel of
him inside me and there is nothing I've seen in this world
so far that can compare with the look of ecstasy he got on
his face when he came.

This young girl was exceptional and fortunate. For most women,
finding a trusted partner is a matter of trial and error and so they
may not develop a full range of sexual activities for years. That is
what happened to the 32-year-old woman from Kentucky who tells
the story below:

When I was married my husband and I never did anything
but have intercourse. We did it often, at least three or four
times a week. It never lasted more than five minutes, and
I never came once. Our sex life was pitiful. But I don't
want to blame it all on my husband. We had married
without either of us having much experience, and we were
embarrassed with each other. We never tried anything
new. We broke up after eight years and one child, and I
started dating again. I had a lot of lovers, and with them
I started doing a lot of things I'd never done with my
husband. But I still didn't have orgasms, and I never ever
suggested ways of making love that might help me to have
them. Then at last I met my present lover, a very special
man. With him I can say what I want, or he just knows.
With him I always have orgasms and sex is an adventure.
It's different every time.

We have oral sex, and anal sex, and we make love in
every conceivable position. I like them all, especially the
man on top, or the woman on top. I also like him to enter

me from behind, while I am on my knees. I like foreplay, and want it to last at least fifteen minutes. But sometimes I don't mind starting right out with intercourse. My lover will put his penis inside me to begin with, and he'll play around with my clitoris while he's maintaining a really relaxed kind of screwing. After a few minutes of that, I'm ready to come. And even after I do, if he just keeps on, I can come again. Sometimes I can come four or five times. My lover is gentle, considerate and expert. And I am in every way different from the way I was with my husband.

Sometimes I wonder if he's got someone he can be different with too. I hope so!

Having a variety of sexual pleasures means sharing them. Time, social habits, psychological factors and even luck may influence whether or not, or how soon or how late, one finds a partner with whom to share the cornucopia. But one thing is certain. Women do not express themselves sexually in a fashion that is set and unchangeable throughout their lives. They will be one creature with one man, and a different—and altogether freer one—with another.

2. Foreplay

Major Findings:

Forty-eight percent of the women liked foreplay to last up to half an hour. Thirty-six percent liked foreplay to last up to fifteen minutes. Two percent were content with brief foreplay, of up to five minutes in duration, and 14 percent preferred extended foreplay, of an hour or more.

The word "foreplay" is inherently problematic. It refers to sexual activities that precede intercourse—among them, manual or oral stimulation of nongenital parts of the body and manual or oral stimulation of the genitals. What makes the word problematic is that it suggests that these activities are somehow less significant than intercourse. They come *before;* they are *preliminaries;* presumably, what follows is more substantial. But to women, foreplay is often the most substantial part of sex. Some women simply cannot have orgasms during intercourse; many others find having orgasms during intercourse exceedingly difficult unless they have been thoroughly stimulated, manually or orally, prior to the start of intercourse. So "foreplay," despite its trivializing sound, is exceedingly important to women.

The *Cosmo* women were united in their praise of it:

> To me, foreplay is more pleasing than intercourse.
>
> —*a 27-year-old from Minnesota*

> Foreplay is great! I wish it could go on forever. The more the better.
>
> —*a 20-year-old from Texas*

> I can spend hours—literally—in foreplay, and still not want to stop.
>
> —*a 22-year-old from Florida*

> I adore foreplay. I don't think of it as a prelude to intercourse but as a part of sex.
>
> —*a 23-year-old from Wisconsin*

> I enjoy foreplay more than intercourse. I'm having a hard time putting this into words, but when I've had foreplay and enjoyed it, I can't wait for intercourse. When I haven't had it, I hate intercourse.
>
> —*a 39-year-old from Virginia*

> Foreplay is the greatest. Only orgasms top it.
>
> —*a 24-year-old from Connecticut*

> Foreplay is better than orgasm. Why? Becuse it lasts longer.
>
> —*a 23-year-old from Texas*

> I couldn't live, or love, without foreplay. I can spend hours just caressing a lover and never get tired of it. I love the

feel of a man's body, and the hard muscled areas, and the correspondingly soft spots, thrill me every time. And I love being caressed, from my face to my feet. I'm somewhat overweight and all my lovers have told me how much they enjoyed touching me because my body is soft and well-rounded. "You're something to hold onto," they've said.

—*a 25-year-old from New Jersey*

Men today presumably know how women feel about foreplay. Yet to read some of the *Cosmo* women's complaints, it would appear that men often ignore or overlook what they know. A Nebraska woman wrote:

A lot of the men I meet are into marathon screwing. They think the longer they can do it, the better they are and the better I like them. They're so wrong. I like them when they're into marathon foreplay. When it comes to intercourse, for me, twenty good strokes is plenty! But give me up to an hour of foreplay at least!

And the young California woman who lost her virginity to the fumbling "Pencil Dick," and who has had numerous lovers since that night, found that quite a few of them were just as callous and inept as her first lover:

I cannot stress enough how important foreplay is. I wish men could get it through their thick skulls that foreplay is essential to women if they're to pass through the gateways to ecstasy. My own orgasms are only as strong as the amount of foreplay involved. Getting my body primed to a maximum during foreplay can produce earth-shattering orgasms, and exciting sexual memories. Not getting it primed wastes everybody's time.

What kinds of foreplay did the *Cosmo* women particularly enjoy? Their number-one favorite was clitoral stimulation, whether manual or oral. But there were other foreplay activities that they relished and, in fact, expected or hoped for as precedents to clitoral stimulation. As one woman wrote, "It doesn't really feel good when a man goes right for your clitoris the minute you're in bed. That can hurt. The clitoris has to be coaxed out. Intercourse is best when it begins with clitoral stimulation, but clitoral stimulation is best when it begins with breast or skin or lip stimulation. I'm talking about petting and hugging and kissing, those old-fashioned things. Some guys act like those things went out with the horse and buggy. They think they're really something, just because they've finally discovered the clitoris. They still don't understand what makes us women tick."

Some of the non-clitoral foreplay activities that *Cosmo* women preferred were:

Being bathed and then put to bed. I'm primed for most anything afterwards.

—a dental technician from New Mexico

Having my ears kissed, also my armpits. These are absolutely excruciating pre-intercourse pleasures for me.

—a high-school student from Alaska

Kissing and heavy petting. Exploring my partner's body. Hugging and squeezing. Talking and listening and looking at each other.

—a factory worker from Wisconsin

I like a man to rub my body all over with a tickling, teasing touch before he goes near my clitoris. If he rubs my clitoris too soon, it hurts. But if he rubs and strokes my body, and then sort of teases my pubic hairs, and doesn't stop, I'll soon be pushing my clit into his hand.

—a bartender from California

One of the loveliest things about my lover is his immense tenderness. He will stroke my arm or cheek, making me feel cherished, or give me a gentle kiss that suddenly becomes demanding. Two or three minutes of tongue-kissing is almost all the foreplay I need. After that, I'm extremely well-lubricated.

—a writer from California

I like starting with soft little kisses and nibbles, undressing each other, savoring every part of each other's bodies.
I like men who spend a lot of time on my breasts, because
my breasts are very sensitive (not painfully sensitive, sensually sensitive) and because I feel they are beautiful, and
I am quite self-conscious about the rest of my body.

—the telecommunications analyst from Texas

Foreplay means a great deal to me and does a great deal
for me. Just having a man fondle my breasts, or having
him lick or suck them, drives me wild.

—a housewife from Alaska

For me, foreplay begins when my man calls me for a date.
I find the ritual of getting dressed up sexually stimulating,
and it's exciting to see him all dressed up when he arrives.
We usually have a very light supper (too much food
makes even the most amorous lover sleepy) and several
drinks. Then we go out, and when we return home the
foreplay begins in earnest. What pleases me most is light,
wet kisses from my feet, up to the backs of my legs with
the emphasis on the backs and fronts of the knees and the
insides of the thighs. Having my lover suck gently on my
toes is fantastic also! So are back and entire body massages. I like doing these things to my lover, not just having
them done to me.

—an accountant from Colorado

Like these women, most of the women who took the survey
found various parts of their bodies capable of erotic response. The
most erotically susceptible, non-genital areas of the body were the
breasts and nipples; 88 percent of the respondents said they were
aroused by stimulation of these areas. The next most erotically
susceptible area was the mouth, with 65 percent of the respondents
reporting themselves aroused by kissing. Fifty-seven percent could
be aroused by stimulation of their ears, and 27 percent by stimulation of their anuses.

But if these body areas—as well as arms, backs, legs, necks and
even fingers and toes—are capable of erotic response, none of them
is as responsive and as central to female arousal as the clitoris. As

a 23-year-old housewife from Oklahoma wrote, "My husband has this one technique where he will touch only my arms, inner thighs, neck, stomach, small of my back—anywhere except the place that is throbbing to be touched. When he moves down to that, to my clitoris, then we're really in *business.*"

The *Cosmo* women enjoyed many different *kinds* of clitoral stimulation. Oral stimulation is discussed on pages 101–106. But even in the realm of manual clitoral stimulation, different types of stimulation were discussed. There were, for example, distinctly individual preferences when it came to how continuously or discontinuously a woman liked her clitoris to be touched:

> I like a man to start and stop, start and stop. This excites me so much that I want to beg him to keep on doing it. But when men *do* keep on doing it, it isn't as effective. So I warn my lovers, "Whatever I say when we're in the middle of it, even if I say, 'Don't stop!'—just keep on stopping and starting."
>
> —*a chemist from Oklahoma*

> I hate when a man teases my clitoris and then stops. I want a long, slow, drawn-out period of clitoral manipulation.
>
> —*a nursery schoolteacher from Michigan*

There were also distinctly individual preferences concerning how vigorously the clitoral area should be stimulated, with some women opting for strenuous stroking and pressure, and others for light stroking and relatively little pressure:

> So many men hurt me when they rub my clitoris. I can come with the slightest amount of clitoral pressure, but when a man starts to rub me hard there, the way *they* like to be rubbed hard, I want to scream with pain, not pleasure.
>
> —*a factory worker from Georgia*

> I get excited by light feathery touches on my clitoris, but after a little bit of that, I want a man to rub hard, and even harder, and even harder yet.
>
> —*a college student from Massachusetts*

Once clitoral stimulation, whether manual or oral, is added to the roster of foreplay activities, foreplay can lead to orgasm with a fair degree of predictability. More than 75 percent of the *Cosmo* women have usually had an orgasm by the time they have had twenty minutes of foreplay—with 11 percent of them climaxing in less than five minutes of foreplay; another 17 percent have usually had an orgasm by the time they have had a half-hour of foreplay. But there is a small group, 5 percent, who require an hour or more of foreplay to reach orgasm.

3. Oral Sex

Major Findings:

Eighty-four percent of the women regularly participate in cunnilingus.

Eighty-four percent of the women regularly participate in fellatio.

The change in western society's attitude toward oral sex has been one of extraordinary dimension. Only a hundred years ago it was considered a perversion. In America, there were stern laws against it. In Europe, sex researcher Krafft-Ebing concluded that men who indulged in it, or who required their partners to indulge in it, were sexual psychopaths.

All of that now seems difficult to believe. With each sex survey that has been conducted in America, it has become more and more apparent that a majority of adults practice oral sex.

In the fifties, Kinsey found that some 50 percent of women engaged in fellatio, and some 54 percent in cunnilingus. By 1972, when the Playboy Foundation study was done, the practice had become even more popular. Some 60 percent of the women studied engaged in fellatio, and some 65 percent in cunnilingus. By the mid-1970s, when *Redbook* investigated 100,000 married women, 85 percent were occasionally or often practicing fellatio, and 87 percent were occasionally or often practicing cunnilingus.

Among the *Cosmo* women, oral sex is regularly participated in not just by more than four-fifths of the married women, but by more than four-fifths of the single women.

Many women thoroughly enjoyed both activities. Typical were such comments as:

My husband and I didn't try oral sex until we'd been married three years. Once we did, it was as if we'd discovered sex itself. Nothing could be better. We spend hours pleasuring each other with oral caresses. We were both shy about it at first but we worked out how we felt about it and how to do it. I don't like swallowing his ejaculation so I only suck him until he's close to coming. He likes me to have an orgasm while we're having intercourse, so he just sucks me before intercourse until I'm very excited (although sometimes I can't predict my orgasms, and I come a little too soon). It's made us both so close and so happy that I can't imagine why we didn't make love this way in our first few years.

—a 26-year-old from Idaho

Oral sex is gorgeous! I love putting my boyfriend's penis in between my lips and pulling and pulling at it with my mouth and making it grow bigger and bigger and imagining how it's going to feel when he puts it inside me. And I love his going down on me and flicking his tongue back and forth on my clitoris, and then taking it between his lips and making it all moist and ready. How did people ever get excited before there was oral sex?

—a 22-year-old from West Virginia

Getting and giving head are the best parts of sex.

—a 30-year-old from Nevada

Despite this enthusiasm, however, there were some women who enjoyed receiving oral sex but not giving it:

I know I'm supposed to like sucking my boyfriend. He likes sucking me. But whereas he gets all horny when he's doing it to me, I don't feel anything when I'm doing it to him.

—an 18-year-old from South Dakota

> I don't like giving head. I'm always afraid the man will come in my mouth and even the ones who say they won't often do.
>
> —*a 30-year-old from Arizona*

And, interestingly, there were some women who enjoyed giving oral sex but not receiving it:

> My lovers always want to go down on me. But I don't like it. It seems so impersonal. They're so far away. I don't mind doing it to a man, but I don't like it when they do it to me and I get excited and there's no one to hold in my arms.
>
> —*a 29-year-old from New York*

> I like giving head a lot. But I hate getting head. I tell men this before we even start to fool around. But they always say it's because nobody gives as good head as they do. So they try and my blood runs cold.
>
> —*a 24-year-old from California*

Apparently, despite the widespread practice of oral sex, there are people who have deep-seated conflicts about the practice. According to psychiatrist Dr. Helen S. Kaplan, the noted sex therapist who has written frequently about the matter, such people should not automatically engage in oral sex but should, rather, "explore their negative feelings, either alone or with a lover with whom they feel comfortable" beforehand.

There are also some people who, although they generally like oral sex, do not like to have it in *all* their relationships. Writes Dr. Kaplan of males who do not always want to offer cunnilingus: "Vaginal odor varies enormously from woman to woman. Some women have a normal, clean, but strong and pungent odor; some women have a very light, mild, barely perceptible odor. And men vary enormously in their preferences: Some men are disappointed if a woman's odor is too light or too pungent. Olfactory cues are very exciting sexual stimulants, and genital odors are an important, but usually unconscious, factor in determining whom you're attracted to."

Nevertheless, psychological factors rather than biochemical ones are usually at work when people in a presumably close relationship feel uncomfortable about oral sex. Dr. Kaplan points out three types of individuals who, for emotional reasons, may not like to participate in either cunnilingus or fellatio. There are, first, those people who don't enjoy it because they cannot help associating the genitals with uncleanliness. This is usually the result of childhood prohibitions about the genitals, although it may be, as an Ohio woman suggested, the result of bombardment by TV:

> Cunnilingus is great, but I don't think all that many women, myself included, feel comfortable about initiating it, the way men feel comfortable about initiating fellatio. So many women feel "dirty" down there. My boyfriend of three years willingly performs cunnilingus, but I have never asked him to, or insisted on it, because I'd feel like I'm making him do something disagreeable, although he protests this. I think my apprehension is partly due to the fact that we women are led to believe we're dirty and smelly. We're bombarded with ads for deodorized tampons, deodorant sprays, "fresh-smelling" douches, and so on. All of that advertising does wonders for making a woman feel dirty, smelly and gross down there. And it's sad, because women really do need clitoral stimulation, not easily achieved with just intercourse. But what really gets me pissed is that those commercials are shown during prime time on the tube. Come on, are we really going to put up with this?

In addition to the people who don't enjoy oral sex because of lingering feelings that it is somehow unclean, there are those who do enjoy it, but find oral sex *so* intensely pleasurable that it frightens them by making them feel emotionally vulnerable. And, finally, there are people who have problems about oral sex because they have emotional problems with their partners. "It's interesting that the semen from the man you really love seems pleasant," writes Dr. Kaplan of fellatio, whereas, "the semen from a man you're angry with or distant from is often repulsive."

Dr. Kaplan advises that if men or women are repelled by a partner's sexual secretions or smells, they should question not just their attitudes toward genitalia but their attitudes toward their partners. It may be that their dislike of oral sex is a cover-up. It may be that the relationship between the couple is an angry or conflicted one. In other words, it is not the absence of oral sex that causes the presence of emotional stress in a relationship, but the presence of emotional stress that causes the absence of oral sex.

Whatever the reasons for discomfort about oral sex, they can be overcome when a partner understands what hinders his or her mate from wanting to participate in the activity. A 37-year-old woman discovered that an aversion to oral sex faded when her lover patiently reassured her that it was "okay" and deeply enjoyable to him:

> I guess I just didn't consider cunnilingus "nice." I enjoyed performing fellatio, but then men are clean, unhairy and dry. I am scrupulously clean, but still cunnilingus worried me. I couldn't believe that anyone in his right mind would want to stimulate a woman that way. My lover had to reassure me each time, and tell me it was okay and that he *enjoyed* it. But he was very convincing, and now I often have earth-shattering orgasms from cunnilingus.

Are there women who feel no initial discomfort about oral sex and enjoy it from the moment they first try it? Yes. An 18-year-old from Michigan writes:

> My girlfriends and I first started hearing about oral sex when we were in high school. Most of them said, "Ugh! You'll never catch me doing anything like that." I never felt that way. My parents have very liberal attitudes. My father said that anything two people want to do in bed is good, or else they wouldn't do it, and my mother said that oral sex was a natural part of making love. So I wasn't afraid to try it, and I did it with my first boyfriend, after we'd dated a few months. I don't need to tell you that when he went down on me it felt terrific. But it also felt terrific when I did it to him. I think that when you care about someone, you just naturally feel great when you see that you're able to make them feel so wonderful. My boyfriend and I talked about it and we both liked making each other feel good as much as we liked feeling good ourselves.

This young Michigan woman succinctly expressed a significant aspect of oral sex: when physiologically pleasurable to the recipient, it provides strong psychological satisfaction to the giver. It may even be that the chief reason for today's widespread practice of oral sex is that increasingly men and women are finding that erotic excitement can be derived from giving pleasure as well as receiving it.

4. Coital Sex: Attitudes

I am so glad you are having this survey. There's something I've wanted to get off my chest for a long time. It's that I really like sexual intercourse. A lot of my girlfriends have been saying there's no point in women having intercourse because intercourse doesn't make us come, and I've been ashamed to admit to them that I really *like* intercourse. It's true it doesn't usually make me come. But I get such a lovely filled feeling when a man enters me. It's an altogether different feeling from the one I get, which is a lonely feeling, when I'm having oral sex. And sometimes, just once in a while, when I'm really turned on through oral sex by the time the man enters, I have an orgasm with him inside and it makes me feel fantastic. I know I'm having it because my clitoris is stimulated. I know it's not because of my vagina. But with a man inside my vagina, I feel like the man and I are one being, like we're some incredible beautiful creature from outer space.

—*a college student from Ohio*

Sexual intercourse has been maligned of late. At a party last year I met an editor from *Playboy* magazine who said to me, "Don't you think that intercourse is simply impossible for women to like? Don't you think that what we men ought to do is give up on having intercourse with them, and just have oral sex instead?"

To give the editor the benefit of the doubt, he may have meant to ingratiate himself by coming on as sympathetic to the great cause of the clitoris. But I found his remarks dismaying. It seemed to me that in newfangled language he was expressing an age-old male copout. "Women don't like intercourse," he seemed to be saying underneath his pose. "What's it got to do with me?"

As the letter that opens this section indicates, there are, in fact, women for whom intercourse is exceedingly pleasurable. It isn't intercourse itself that women dislike. What they dislike is having intercourse without foreplay, or in positions that do not allow them to receive maximum clitoral stimulation during thrusting, or with partners who fail to stimulate them to orgasm through additional clitoral manipulation if intercourse does not make them climax.

Among the *Cosmo* women there were many who were extremely enthusiastic about coital sex:

> I rarely have orgasms during intercourse, but I love it anyway because I love the way men are so intense during it. As long as they've gotten me excited before they start, and as long as they're willing to make me come manually afterwards, then I find it a wonderful close thrilling thing. Nothing beats it for intimacy.
>
> *—a fashion designer from New York*

> I enjoy intercourse, and I especially like the orgasms I sometimes get during it. I get a feeling like I'm climbing a mountain and the air seems to get thinner and thinner and everything seems to be centered on my vagina and then it releases and gives me a warm, delicious feeling all over.
>
> *—the telecommunications analyst from Texas*

> I adore intercourse. It's like being in the middle of an earthquake together.
>
> *—a caterer from California*

True, foreplay and oral sex make a major difference in whether or not a woman will desire coital sex. A 24-year-old woman from New Jersey described in detail a typical progression from arousal to desire for intercourse:

> When my boyfriend is over we usually sit close together on the sofa and he massages my neck and shoulders. Then

he kisses my neck, turns me over, and kisses me hard on the lips while he fondles my breasts. Sometimes I will take my shirt off and let him suck on my breasts for a while, which I enjoy very much. Meanwhile, I will begin stroking his body and then lie on top of him and rub against him and feel him harden. Then after a long time of this, we go into the bedroom. When we go into the bedroom I prefer to have him undress me and in turn I will undress him. Then he will start to fondle my breasts and use his finger in my vagina (this I find most exciting). After he sees that I am aroused, he will lead me over to the bed and while I am standing up he sits on the edge of the bed and eats me. After a few minutes he will lie me on the bed and continue to eat me. By this time I can hardly wait to have him and I will gently raise his head and ask for him to come inside me.

Unlike this woman, many women desire coital sex only *after* they have had an orgasm first, as a result of foreplay or oral sex. Another New Jersey woman of the same age writes,

On a few occasions I've been fortunate enough to have a lover who was sensitive enough to understand that if I achieved an orgasm through clitoral stimulation before we had intercourse, it would be better for both of us. However, I have usually had to explain carefully to my lovers that after they masturbated me to climax, my desire for them would not be less. I have had to explain that, if anything, it would be the extreme opposite. After climaxing that way, my desire for penetration is like 1,000 times greater than before. I *need* intercourse then, when before I just wanted it.

5. Coital Sex: Positions

MAJOR FINDINGS:

Sixty-one percent of the *Cosmo* respondents preferred the "missionary," or man-on-top position during coitus.

Twenty-six percent preferred being on top themselves.

Eight percent favored lateral, or side-by-side, intercourse.

Eight percent favored posterior, or rear-entry, intercourse.

(The figures add up to more than a hundred percent because a few women chose two preferences.)

The familiar story of how the "missionary" position got its name tells something important about intercourse positions. The term first came into use in the 1920s after the great anthropologist Malinowski visited the Trobriand Islands in the South Pacific. Malinowski discovered on his trip that the Trobrianders, who never made love with the man on top, had in the past witnessed British and American missionaries doing so. The Trobrianders had been amused. They had had no word in their own language for what they had seen, since the position was unknown, and so they had dubbed it the "missionary" position, and laughingly caricatured it at their campfires.

It was not just the primitive Trobrianders who didn't make love with the man on top. The highly civilized ancient Egyptians didn't, nor the Hindus, nor the Chinese. In fact, the man-on-top position for intercourse is a rarity in the history of human cultures. Among the thousands of drawings and paintings of coitus that have come down to us through the ages, there is hardly a single representation of the man-on-top position.

Nevertheless, this position became the one favored by western society. One strong impetus for this was that the early Christian Church condemned any other position—for reasons that are obscure—and at one time decreed that making use of any other position had to be confessed. Ultimately the man-on-top position came to seem not a cultural matter to western men and women but a biologically natural one.

It is not, of course, and yet cultural customs linger and change slowly, which helps explain why, although the man-on-top position is probably the coital position least likely to promote orgasm in a woman, the *Cosmo* women still express an overwhelming preference for it. As a result of its sanction by tradition in our culture, it offers important psychological comfort:

Having the man on top makes me feel secure.

—a 24-year-old from Wyoming

He gets on top, you feel all protected, enveloped.

—a 19-year-old from Louisiana

In other positions, I feel exposed and vulnerable.

—a 30-year-old from Illinois

In addition to its psychological benefits, however, some of the women found the man-on-top position physically pleasurable, for reasons such as these:

Sometimes I like to be all laid-back and relaxed during sex. I want to take it all in, not give anything out. Having the man on top is best for times like this.

—a 26-year-old from New Jersey

It's true I can come more easily in other positions, but I like having the man on top because I like the way he can pound into me so hard from that position.

—a 33-year-old from Texas

I like the pressure of a man's body on top of me. It's like having a giant, all-over hug.

—a 27-year-old from Colorado

For purposes of orgasm, however, the woman-on-top position was favored:

I have more control. It's easier to position my clitoris so that it's stimulated during the act.

—a 36-year-old from Maryland

My lover can last longer when I'm on top. It's not as stimulating to him, or at least, when I feel he's getting too excited, I can slow things down myself. So he can wait a long time that way, and the longer he waits, the more likely it is that I'm going to come.

—*a 27-year-old from Michigan*

Being on top means getting my clitoris right wherever I want it. When I'm on the bottom, men are always trying to get deeper inside me. They try to raise my bottom up, or put my legs around them. When they do that, their penises don't get anywhere near my clitoris, so while they're enjoying it more, I'm enjoying it less. Being on top means never having to cope with a man who is trying to get in deeper and deeper while you are struggling to keep sensations on your clitoris and vaginal lips.

—*a 30-year-old from Massachusetts*

Similarly, lateral (side-by-side) and posterior (rear-entry) intercourse were considered desirable positions for orgasm:

It isn't the position itself that's so good, but the fact that my partner can easily stimulate me manually at the same time we're screwing that makes me like doing it side by side.

—*a 32-year-old from Wisconsin*

When my lover enters me from the rear he can thrust into me so hard that it feels as if his penis is even bigger than it is. I like this sensation. But what I really like about the position is that with me on my knees and him behind me, he can stimulate my clitoris the whole time he's thrusting. It never fails but we come together, just like in the song.

—*a 27-year-old from Vermont*

In addition to these positions, 7 percent of the *Cosmo* women reported favoring more unusual positions, among them:

Standing up. It takes a lot of positioning ourselves, and we can't keep it up very long, but it's very exciting.

—*a 25-year-old from Missouri*

Half-sitting half-lying on the edge of the bed, with my lover standing and thrusting into me. That way he can manipulate my clitoris easily, and also thrust very hard. It's very good for both of us.

—*a 28-year-old from Oregon*

Interestingly, there were no significant differences between the positions preferred by older women and those preferred by younger women. So much for those who think tradition exerts more pressure on the old than on the young.

6. Anal Sex

MAJOR FINDINGS:

Thirteen percent of the *Cosmo* women have anal sex regularly.

Anal intercourse was, until not very long ago, so strongly tabooed in our culture that the practice was scarcely mentioned, not just in popular literature but in scientific literature as well. Even the trailblazing Kinsey did not inquire about it among the women he interviewed. But in recent years anal sex has often been written about in both popular and medical journals, and most recent sex surveys have included the subject. In the 1974 Playboy Foundation study, it was found that 6 percent of the female respondents under 35 had anal sex often or sometimes. In the 1974 *Redbook* survey, a survey of women only, it was found that 21 percent of the respondents had had anal sex often or occasionally.

The *Cosmo* women have had somewhat more experience with anal sex than the Playboy Foundation women, and somewhat less experience with anal sex than the *Redbook* women.

Reactions to the sensations of anal sex varied among the Cosmo women:

My boyfriend and I have tried anal sex. But even though he was very slow and gentle, we gave up on the idea. It was just too painful.

—*a 21-year-old from Virginia*

I really like anal intercourse, as long as my husband plays with my clitoris till he's all the way in. That way there's no pain. And once he's all the way in, I can come very easily, without manual clitoral stimulation. It's very exciting. It's as if the penis is somehow pushing against the *inside* of the clitoris, or something like that.

—a 21-year-old from North Carolina

I was brought up very conservatively. My sister and I weren't even allowed outside in the evenings to play hide-and-seek. I'm from a Mexican-American family and sex is a very taboo subject. Who would have thought that today I'd do all the things I do, including anal sex? I'm still shocked that I do it. But I like it, at least with my present lover. He's very considerate. He doesn't hurt me, and he doesn't enter my vagina afterwards without washing up first as it can cause an infection.

—a 28-year-old from Texas

I like anal intercourse but I do not like it when the man comes that way. It feels messy when that happens. So my husband and I do it just for foreplay.

—a 30-year-old from Michigan

Recently my lover and I have been experimenting with anal intercourse. In that area, I was a late bloomer. I wouldn't do it with my husband, although he was always interested in it. I didn't try it until I left him. Now I do it with my lover and ever since we tried it I've been pissed off at myself for not trying it sooner. It is stimulating and feels real good, as long as he is gentle.

—a 30-year-old from Massachusetts

My husband and I have anal sex about once in every two weeks. (We have sex three to five times a week, even though we've been married nine years and have three children.) I enjoy it immensely, and have enormous orgasms that way. I have never had anal sex and not climaxed. In fact, my problem is trying to keep from climaxing too soon, because within a minute after climaxing, anal sex starts hurting, so if my husband doesn't come real soon after I do, he's going to have to pull out.

—a 30-year-old from California

Whether anal sex was enjoyed or disliked, it seemed to be a practice into which the women entered freely, out of a spirit of sexual curiosity. As Morton Hunt stated in the Playboy Foundation report, "Whether one personally finds this practice appealing, neutral or repellent, the increase in its use does not, as some may think, represent the brutalization of wives by sadistic husbands, but generally a more or less free choice by both partners of something they want to do together."

7. Homosexual Sex

What percentage of American women is exclusively homosexual? No one really knows. Due to complex questions of how homosexuality is defined, Kinsey's figures have never been accepted as authoritative, so no solid base line for the past exists, while recent studies have provided only contradictory or inconclusive findings.

Among the *Cosmo* women, 2 percent described themselves as "exclusively" homosexual. Another 3 percent said they had homosexual experiences "regularly." In addition, another 14 percent had had a single, or an occasional, homosexual experience.

Most of these single, or occasional, homosexual experiences had occurred during childhood or early adolescence, and involved petting, mutual masturbation or private masturbation that had been stirred by the thought of another girl. "I went skinny dipping with my best girlfriend one night," a woman of 45 wrote. "She looked so beautiful coming out of the water that that night when I was at home I felt aroused just remembering, and I masturbated. I guess you could call this a homosexual experience."

Often, early homosexual experiences—or arousal through a homosexual attraction, which is really how the experience above should be defined—produced guilt or confusion. "My first 'sexual' experience," one woman wrote, "was of mutual masturbation with a girlfriend at camp. We were 12, and I really didn't understand or think much about the event. But some time afterwards I learned the word 'homosexual' and I got very upset. I felt abnormal. For years afterwards, even when I'd had a dozen male lovers, I was afraid I was secretly a homosexual. It wasn't until I was in my mid-20s that I learned that experiences like mine are very common among young girls, and that being attracted to a girlfriend, or even masturbating with her, was just another part of growing up."

A 30-year-old woman from California described childhood homosexuality, and its confusions, vividly:

> When I was 11 I had a close girlfriend. We were together all the time. She slept over at my house or I slept over at hers. One night we played vampire, and sucked on each other's necks. It was sure fun to me. But my mother saw the hickey marks on my neck and almost beat me to death. I never knew why. When we were 12 my girlfriend's family got a pool. She and I swam naked in it whenever we could, and we would oil each other. I loved it when she would rub my breasts. One night I told her, and she said that felt good to her too. So I sat up and told her to take off her PJ's and we'd take turns rubbing each other. I did her a long time on the back, then she turned over and I did her breasts. I felt the urge to slip my finger down into her vagina. I did it, and she never opened her eyes, so I kept right on until she started moaning and grabbed my hand and said "stop." I felt pleased at what I'd done. I lay down and said "my turn." And she did the same thing to me. We did it as much as we could after that, and then one day she said "no more." She said it was wrong and that maybe we were queer. I didn't know what in hell she was talking about.

Among the women who continued to have occasional homosexual experiences in adulthood, or who first had a homosexual experience in adulthood, there were a number who had done so to satisfy a long-buried sexual curiosity. One such woman was the midwestern lawyer who learned that "taboos aren't set in stone." She wrote, "Probably the one experience that would shock the people who know me would be the times I had with another woman. There was only one woman, however, and I didn't continue the experience after a few days and nights of seeing how it was. I found it highly sensuous, exciting and a little strange, given the forbidden quality of this kind of thing. But I'm glad I did it. I used to have fantasies and daydreams about making love to another woman. Sometimes I had them about my very straight girlfriends. But since having had the experience, I rarely have the fantasies anymore. Apparently what I did was satisfy my curiosity."

Other women who had occasional homosexual experiences in adulthood did so when involved with men who suggested another female be included in their lovemaking. The feelings and experiences of women who had homosexual sex under this circumstance are described in Chapter Nine.

Those women who had exclusively homosexual relationships in adult life seemed reticent about writing to *Cosmopolitan*. Although there were 2 percent of them in the sample, none added details about themselves on their questionnaires or in subsequent letters. Their reticence is not surprising, since *Cosmopolitan* is known as a forum for exploring male-female relationships. Still, it is unfortunate, for it allows us to gain no insight into how the sex practices and feelings of homosexual women have been affected by recent skirmishes in the sexual revolution.

8. Sadomasochistic Sex

MAJOR FINDINGS:

Two percent of the women have regularly experienced flagellation or other sadomasochistic behavior.

While sadomasochistic fantasies were very common among the women (see Chapter Seven), sadomasochistic *experience* was very rare. Only a few women described it in their letters and for the most part their descriptions were of experiences that *bordered* on sadomasochism. A woman studying for a graduate degree at a small Baptist university said, "I'm not into sadomasochistic sex but I really enjoy being strapped to the bedposts and letting my lover do what he wants with me." And a woman from a rural town in Iowa reported that she liked doing the reverse—tying her lover to the bed. She wrote, "Sex in rural areas is a little different from big-city sex. There's lots less orgies and things. Still, we do enjoy sex out here, and I sometimes even get kinky with my boyfriend and tie him up spread-eagle-like and lick him all over. I'm sorry you didn't get more responses from rural areas. We may not be so sophisticated as the city women, but we do have our fun."

Similarly, the dental technician from New Mexico described a fondness for ropes during sex but explained that what she liked about it was hardly the experience of pain:

> I have played at being tied up and roughed up, but what this really means, the form it takes, is gentle handling with a lot of rough, nasty words. I like hearing my men say, "Fuck," "Cock" or "Cunt," while I am at their mercy all tied up, and pretending to want to struggle free.

And a state-government worker from California mentioned enjoying another variation on bondage:

> My husband and I don't allow real pain, just the kind of pleasurable pain that comes from intense sensations. We do such things as having him use the vibrator on my clitoris and inside my vagina, and because I am tied up it means I have to stand these sensations longer than I might if I were free so that I could pull back and avoid them.

One young woman—with an unusually troubled history that had included a teenage pregnancy, an abortion, reform school, a flight to a hippie commune, heavy drug usage and a great deal of prostitution—had slept with some seventy-five men by the time she was 20 but had never had an orgasm. Then she met a man who recognized her desire for being victimized. That was when she climaxed as a result of sadomasochistic sex, and continued to do so whenever sex contained elements of punishment.

She had met the man by accident in the laundry room of her New York City apartment building and, for a moment, as he entered the lonely, dungeon-like room, had entertained the fleeting fantasy that this stranger might rape her. Some days later, having begun to see and chat with him in the building's elevator, and to visit him in his apartment, she mentioned her fantasy to him. He told her that, strangely, although the thought of raping someone had never before entered his mind, it had in fact occurred to him the day he had encountered her in the laundry room.

Perhaps he recognized from the start that the young woman had a penchant for an edge of abuse or violence in sex. Perhaps he sensed how frequently in life she had made herself a victim. In any event, when the two of them struck up a sexual relationship, he used playful humiliations and spankings and pretended rape to please her—and these things did result in her becoming orgasmic:

> When we first had sex I was insane with desire for him, but although I found myself coming right to the edge of orgasm, I just couldn't make it over. He knew immediately I hadn't come. He asked me to masturbate. But I told him I never had and that as a matter of fact, I didn't know how. That evening he called and asked me to come to his apartment. When I got there he said, "I'll show you how." Walking over to me, he put one hand on the back of my head and, by pulling my hair slightly, pulled my face up to his. My heart started pounding, and he kissed me gently but very firmly. Slowly pushing me away, he asked me to take off my clothes. He was fully dressed, but he rolled up his sleeves. I was so excited that I thought I would die. When I was fully naked, he told me to lie on the bed, which I did. At that point, he went into his bathroom and came back with a pair of manicure scissors, a bowl of warm water, some shaving lotion and a razor. He told me he was going to treat me like a little girl, *his* little girl, and I had to look like one.
>
> Holding me down with one hand, he used the other to shave my pubic area. When he finished, he washed me down carefully and rubbed baby oil on my now naked pubic area. How strange it felt. Then he told me he had a gift for me and handed me a vibrator. He told me he would teach me how to masturbate with it. Embarrassed, I told him I didn't want to. He told me I had to, or else he would spank me. I told him to try it. Grabbing me by the arm, he pulled me over his lap and, with one hand masturbating me, spanked me with the other. I came almost immediately. He covered me with kisses, told me how

wonderful I was, and was absolutely ecstatic over my success. So was I.

Our relationship progressed from that point on to one of total submission on my part. I was his slave, he was my master, and I did everything he told me to do. Our sex was magnificent. He was perfect in the role he took. One night he even raped me. In the stairwell of our apartment building, between his floor and mine when he was seeing me home one night, he grabbed me, kissed me, forced me to bend over the banister, and entered me from behind. He held his hand over my mouth the entire time, but it hardly stopped my squeals of pleasure. I was in heaven. He also had me perform for the benefit of our nosy neighbors across the street who liked to watch us with binoculars. He would tie me up (gently) and tease me with his lips and hands until I was about to burst, and then he'd bend me over a chair and take me like that.

The woman who described these events reported that although the relationship broke up shortly afterward, leaving her in emotional turmoil, at the time it was going on she was "obsessively in love with this man and totally happy."

But most of the women who wrote about the subject of sadomasochistic sex, including play-acting at sadomasochism, were ardently opposed to it. "It's dangerous," warned a Connecticut woman. "I have a friend who got seriously hurt because she let a man tie her up." "It's degrading," wrote a California woman. "Why would anyone want to mix shame into something that is beautiful?" And, "When I hear about women who allow themselves to be beaten or tied up by men, I want to cry for my sisters," wrote an Illinois woman. "When, oh when, will they learn that they are beautiful and sex is beautiful and they don't need to suffer or even play at suffering in order to get a man."

There has been a great deal of talk lately about a new fondness for sadomasochistic sexual practices among the American population. Apparently troubled by and disapproving of such practices, *Time* magazine devoted a lengthy article to the subject. Unfortunately, since no statistics existed, the magazine had no recourse but to rely—for at least some support of the hypothesis that sadomasochistic sex was becoming increasingly popular—on the off-the-cuff opinions of a psychologist named Michael Evans. Basing his views, presumably, on his therapeutic caseload at the Berkeley (Calif.) Therapy Institute, Evans estimated in the May 4, 1981, issue of *Time* that a third of all couples have tried spanking at least once and perhaps as many have tied up a sexual partner.

This estimation is hugely contradicted by the *Cosmo* survey. Even were we to assume that the sample of women tapped by *Cosmopolitan* is unusually non-masochistic, or unusually non-experimental sexually or unusually reluctant to admit to out-of-the-ordinary sexual experiences, (assumptions I would not recommend in view of information in further sections of this book), the fact that only a minuscule 2 percent of those women has ever been spanked or tied up suggests that sadomasochistic sex, at least at this time, is not a significant American sexual practice.

Chapter Five
Orgasm with a Partner

1. Doing What Doesn't Come Naturally

I would be more than pleased to help you in your endeavors to write a book based on the recent *Cosmopolitan* sex survey. I had my first sexual experience at 21. The earth did not move for me then, nor did I have orgasms with men with any regularity until around my 25th birthday—only last March. I felt there was something wrong with me, and resigned myself to believing that the closeness between lovers that sex provides would suffice as pleasure enough for me. It didn't, really, and now that I have at last learned to have orgasms, I can truthfully say that while closeness and intimacy are very important to me, I would give them up for orgasms. Fortunately, I have been able to have both, with a wonderful man, who, God bless him, is patient and willing to put out effort to make sex pleasurable to both of us.

But I am writing to tell you not about me but about a friend of mine. Whenever she spent the night with her boyfriend, she would come into work looking noticeably depressed. One day, sheerly on impulse, I said, "You know, it's taken me *years,* but I finally learned how to climax with a man." Not the usual thing one blurts out to a brooding friend, but it worked. She sat up straight and gasped, "You mean you couldn't do it either? It doesn't

121

just happen?" I said that as far as I could tell, you had to teach yourself what felt good and how to do it. My friend burst into tears of what she said were pure relief. Like me, she had thought there was something wrong with her. She had felt inadequate and insecure and cheated. No matter how many books are printed on female sexuality, there is room for one more as long as there are women who feel the way my friend and I did. We must tell each other over and over again that orgasms have to be learned. So all the more power to you. If I can be of help, please telephone me at the number below.

—a 26-year-old woman from Wyoming

I opened the above letter, which was postmarked from Laramie, on a day when I was feeling blue. It was a bright spring day, and I wanted to be out in it instead of working on *The Cosmo Report.* I had just finished the Sexual Practices chapter, and I was thinking to myself, What was the point of going further? Women today are thoroughly informed about sex. The American woman of the 1980s is probably the most sexually sophisticated and experienced woman in western history. Contributing to her sexual knowledge was like bringing coals to Newcastle or lending one's best dress to Nancy Reagan. Didn't we all already know all we needed to know?

The Wyoming woman's letter brought me up short. I had been aware for some months that orgasm evoked more commentary from the *Cosmo* women than any other subject. Virtually every woman who wrote had something to say about it, no matter what the central theme of her letter. Virtually every woman wanted to explain how she achieved her orgasms, or how she struggled to achieve them, or what they felt like, or what it felt like not to have them. But what I hadn't considered until the Wyoming woman's letter was that there might never be enough said about orgasm, no matter how many books, articles and columns of advice appeared. As the Laramie lady said, "as long as there are women who feel the way my friend and I did," information about orgasm would have to be dispensed over and over again. And chances were that there would always be women who felt the way the Laramie lady and her friend did, for what may be most typical about most female orgasm is that it does not come naturally. It takes teaching oneself and one's partner what feels good and what works.

Consider the matter of the duration of time it takes a woman to achieve orgasm. In the foreplay section of Chapter Four it was mentioned that only 10 percent of women reached orgasm with less than five minutes of foreplay, and that most women require ten or twenty minutes of foreplay. Yet during masturbation, women reach orgasm relatively quickly. Kinsey found that most women who masturbated to orgasm did so in less than three minutes of self-stimulation. Clearly, most orgasm with a partner does not come "naturally," or more women would have orgasms after relatively brief foreplay.

But there is more. Sex therapy clinics across America were, at least in their early years, deluged by women who could not reach orgasm even through masturbation. They reported to the clinics and were given courses of instruction in specific techniques to replace the techniques they were using. So orgasm did not come "naturally" to all women, even when alone. And it seems reasonable to conclude that most of the women who do "naturally" masturbate to orgasm actually do so because of techniques they learned not naturally—that is, by instinct—but through trial and error at some long-forgotten point in childhood or earliest adolescence.

Due to basic, immutable facts about female biology, orgasm—at least during partner sex and perhaps even in masturbatory sex—has almost always had to be somehow nurtured—no matter how sexually wise the woman may be or even become.

But why are partner orgasms, specifically, such a problem for women? The first reason is one that most women well understand these days. It is that the clitoris is the woman's chief organ for sexual arousal, as central to orgasmic response as the penis is to a man's. To reach orgasm most women need clitoral stimulation. This is not psychological, but biological.

Which does not mean that there aren't some women who can have orgasms without clitoral stimulation. It has been proven that some women can fantasize to orgasm without any physical stimulation whatsoever. They are, though, the rare—and physiologically mysterious—few. For the rest, clitoral stimulation is a *sine qua non.* Yet while virtually all women recognize this either consciously or subconsciously, many men still do not. Or perhaps will not. And consequently, they concentrate on intercourse.

Now, it is true that intercourse does provide some clitoral stimulation. During thrusting there is some degree of traction on the hood of the clitoris, which stimulates it. And in some intercourse positions there is some stimulating pressure exerted on the clitoral area by the man's pubic bone. But both these kinds of stimulation are limited and discontinuous. From a strictly mechanical point of view, intercourse is an inferior technique for clitoral stimulation. If a couple practices brief intercourse only, or intercourse with only very brief, more direct clitoral stimulation beforehand, a woman may find it very hard to have an orgasm.

So the first reason that many women have difficulties in achieving orgasm is that their partner-sex activities consist primarily of intercourse.

But there is another reason for frequent failure, and it is the more prevalent. Clitoral sensitivity varies widely from woman to woman, and even in the same woman it varies from one lovemaking session to the next. As this chapter will show, while about half of today's women *usually* have orgasms, very few women *always* have them. This is because both men and women tend to assume that whatever time they have spent in clitoral stimulation (whether manual, oral or coital) *should* be enough. After all, thinks the man, it was enough for my last partner. After all, thinks the woman, it was enough for me last time.

But, as mentioned, clitoral sensitivity varies from woman to woman and from lovemaking session to lovemaking session.

So the second reason that many woman have difficulties in achieving orgasms during partner sex is that they are embarrassed by, or ignorant of, their specific, personal, unique and often varying clitoral needs.

It is not surprising, then, that, despite sophisticated sex practices, the central sexual concerns of American women are still: how to have orgasms; how to feel comfortable enough to instruct partners in helping orgasms along; and how to have orgasms not just sometimes or even usually but all the time.

I am grateful to the Laramie woman for getting me back to work that spring day, and for reminding me—and through this work other women—that it is still necessary, and may be necessary for years to come, for women to keep contributing to one another's knowledge about orgasm.

2. What Is an Orgasm, Anyway?

I never used to have orgasms. Then I learned how and now I have them all the time. At least, I think they're orgasms. When I'm making love with a man I really like, at some point I get this wonderful feeling of well-being. I feel happy all over. Please don't tell me this isn't an orgasm, or I will start worrying that I am doing something wrong.

—an 18-year-old college student from North Carolina

It has often been said that if you have to ask what an orgasm is, you haven't had one yet. This is one of those clichés that is, sadly, true. The college student whose letter opens this section probably has not yet had an orgasm. For one thing, despite her saying that she has orgasms "all the time," once she begins to describe them, she sounds quite unsure of herself. For another, she describes a psychological response rather than a physiological one.

Orgasm is not a psychological phenomenon. It is a physiological reflex. So is a sneeze. Has any woman ever had to ask herself, "Did I sneeze just now?" We *know* when that reflex occurs. Our body tells us it has happened. But orgasm has been so dressed up in mythology and misinformation that many believe it is something mysterious and difficult to recognize, something other than the basic response it is.

Essentially an orgasm is an explosive discharge of neuromuscular tensions. The woman about to have an orgasm reaches a peak of sexual activity and suddenly becomes tense. Then, abruptly and instantaneously, the tension ceases. At this point, the woman experiences a series of muscular spasms. The spasms may last for only a few seconds or they may continue for a minute or two. Whichever happens, her mind will be momentarily vacant, as if during orgasm she were temporarily unconscious.

Many women imagine that other responses are involved, that orgasm must be accompanied by the emission of uncontrollable sounds or by the flailing of limbs and torso. Yes, some women moan or even sob during orgasm and, yes, some thrash about in strenuous convulsions that resemble epileptic throes. But there are others who seem virtually paralyzed during orgasm. Their bodies go absolutely still and motionless, and they are mute. Both types of responses are common and normal.

Perhaps the only outward sign of orgasm that can be found in all women (and men too) is a particular facial expression. Oddly, the expression is not what is usually thought of as a happy, pleased one, but a look of seeming agony.

After orgasm, though, most women usually do experience a period of utter happiness, a relaxed quiescence, a feeling of well-being. Indeed, this pleasurable feeling is the most usual aftermath of orgasm. Kinsey pointed out that the famous saying *Triste est omne animal post coitum*—all animals are sad after coitus—is not only inaccurate but a distortion of the original statement, which was made in the second century A.D. by one of the founders of medical science, the great observer Galen. Galen actually wrote, *"Triste est omne animal post coitum, praeter mulierum gallumque"*—every animal *except the human female* and the rooster are sad after coitus.

I've no idea why the rooster is happy, but it is easy to understand why women are, for the experience of orgasm is so intense, and the trance that ends it so restful, that it is as if the body and mind were, however briefly, altogether carefree and at peace.

Such are some of the objective facts about orgasm. What does orgasm *feel like?* Some of the *Cosmo* women were most ingenious at capturing the subjective sensations of orgasm:

> Suddenly all my muscles tense. I stop breathing. And I feel as if I am on the crest of a giant wave.
>
> *—the telecommunications analyst from Texas*

> Sometimes I have two or three little orgasms, but when I have a big one, I feel as though I've passed out. When I come to, my body is all tingly and I'm tired, as if I'd just run twenty miles, and I'm high, as if I'd been smoking joints as I ran.
>
> *—a 26-year-old from New York*

> I feel like small electric shock waves are radiating from my nose to my fingertips to my toes.
>
> *—a 24-year-old from New York*

> It's as if there's an electrical current pulsating from my clitoris and vagina to my extremities, especially my toes and head, and back again.
>
> *—a 30-year-old from Colorado*

I have two kinds of orgasms. One kind consists of body-shuddering spasms. The other of just moaning and wincing. But each is very enjoyable. When the orgasm is the first kind, my legs and thighs shake. I shake like I've got the chills. Then I feel really relaxed and spent for a while.

—a 19-year-old from Illinois

3. How Frequent Are Orgasms?

MAJOR FINDINGS:

During partner sex of any variety—that is, during manual clitoral manipulation, oral sex, or intercourse —only a fifth of the women *always* have orgasms. Half *usually* do. A fifth *sometimes* do. And a tenth *seldom* or *never* do.

It seems clear from these *Cosmo* survey figures that it is the rare woman who can count on having an orgasm every time she has sex with a partner. Still, a sizable number of women *usually* have orgasms. Leaving aside for the moment the types of lovemaking that influence the frequency of orgasm, what other factor is most likely to affect this frequency?

One can examine the question statistically. Age makes some difference. While only 20 percent of *all* the respondents always have orgasms, 26 percent of those over 35 always do. But perhaps the chief factor—once again, aside from lovemaking techniques—that influences a woman's orgastic frequency is having sex with a man she knows well, or, to be more exact, a man she lives with. While only 20 percent of all the *Cosmo* women always have orgasms, 25 percent of those who are married or who live with their lovers do. Among single women who have sex with partners with whom they do not live, orgasmic frequency drops, even when the partners are steady companions. Indeed, only 15 percent of the women who live alone always have orgasms. And if having orgasms always is more common for women who live with or are married to sexual partners, so too is having orgasms usually.

This finding is significant although hardly surprising. Clearly sex—and in particular female orgasm—thrives on both attraction and communication. Attraction may be at its highest level when people first start making love together, but communication is at its highest level after people have become deeply familiar with one another and are able to talk about, or intuit, one another's sexual needs, rhythms and attitudes. In sex, familiarity breeds contentment.

Of course, even when people are deeply familiar with one another, they may not *always* have orgasms. Or they may not even have them *usually*. It is troubling to read letters such as the two that follow, but they describe experiences that all too many women have had:

> I am married, and have two children. I have had only three orgasms in my life. Two of the orgasms were with my second lover, when I was 16, and one of them was with my husband, that I've been married to for the last three years.
>
> *—a 20-year-old woman from Massachusetts*

> Sex is good with my husband, but in our almost five years of being together, I've only had nine orgasms.
>
> *—a 25-year-old from California*

In cases such as these the woman may have a high orgasmic threshold, which means that for emotional or physical reasons she is less easily aroused than other women. (There is a wide range of individual differences when it comes to orgasmic thresholds, with some women having so low a threshold that they can fantasize to orgasm.) Or it may mean that she and her lover are practicing poor lovemaking techniques. Or it may mean that despite living together, the two of them do not communicate about sex.

The last seems the worst deterrent. As most of the letters throughout this chapter indicate, the obstacles to orgasm due to high orgasmic thresholds and poor lovemaking techniques *can* be overcome, provided there is concerned and supportive communication about sex between the partners.

4. How Are Your Orgasms Usually Achieved?

Major Findings:

It is twice as common for *Cosmo* respondents to achieve their orgasms from manual or oral clitoral stimulation than from intercourse. The exact figures were: 34 percent usually have orgasms from intercourse; 71 percent usually have orgasms from manual or oral clitoral stimulation. In addition 9 percent have orgasms from stimulations other than clitoral or vaginal—among them fantasy. (The figures add up to more than a hundred percent because some of the women had regular orgasms from two or more techniques.)

The Hite Report found that only some 30 percent of its 3,000-woman sample had regular orgasms as a result of intercourse. Among the 106,000 *Cosmo* women, similarly, only 34 percent have regular orgasms as a result of intercourse. Does this mean that in the American population as a whole only about a third of the women do and *can* have orgasms as a result of intercourse?

I suggest not. For one thing, as we have seen, orgasm is less reliable among samples made up of younger women, and of women not living with sexual partners. So a study devoted to older or more partner-affiliated women would probably show a higher percentage of women with regular orgasms during intercourse than either the Hite or *Cosmo* studies (*Redbook*'s 1977 study of *married* women found that two-thirds of the sample had regular orgasms during intercourse). Further, the ability to have an orgasm during intercourse can, to some extent, be learned. There are positions, techniques, as well as psychological devices to encourage it. So were intercourse usually conducted in ways that encourage orgasm, it seems reasonable to conclude that more women might have more orgasms as a result.

What positions, techniques and psychological devices did the *Cosmo* women who were orgasmic during intercourse make use of?

I can have orgasms during intercourse provided I'm on top.

—*a 28-year-old from Colorado*

I need to be on top, so I can move to my best advantage, and I need to have good foreplay beforehand. Cunnilingus works best.

—a 30-year-old living in Japan

I love clitoral manipulation to orgasm, but I love orgasm from vaginal entry more. The way it feels is so pleasing to me. To get an orgasm from vaginal entry, I don't let my lovers start intercourse until I signal them that I'm very aroused. All you need is that little word "now!" When I say "now," it means that I'm close enough to orgasm from having had my clitoral area rubbed that once my lover enters me, just a little bit more stimulation from thrusting will make me come. It doesn't matter whether I'm on top or on bottom so long as I'm very close before we start intercourse.

—a 30-year-old from New York

It is easiest for me to come during intercourse if I am on top or if my boyfriend enters me from the rear. Both ways I seem to be able to get that added bit of pressure on my clitoral area, either from pressing down against him or from having my clitoris rub against the mattress.

—a 24-year-old from Washington, D.C.

When I want to have an orgasm during intercourse, and I'm just not close enough, I fantasize. I imagine one of my secret sex plots and it works like a charm and I can come pretty much whenever my lover is ready.

—a 28-year-old from California

Foreplay is the whole secret to orgasms during intercourse. Well, not just having it, but having it in just the right amount. I like to have foreplay until I'm really excited. The amount of time varies. Sometimes it takes a half-hour. Other times just a few minutes. Then, when he knows I'm ready, my boyfriend will enter me. And then we will have intercourse for a while, and I can come any time I want.

—a 23-year-old from Virginia

> The best way to make me come during intercourse is if a man pulls away a little and touches my clitoris for a while. This works best if he's entered me from the rear. It's easiest for the man to reach the clitoris then. But it works in all the other positions, too.
>
> —a 25-year-old from Arkansas

Some women who had regular orgasms during intercourse found that the best "insurance" was to have a *first* orgasm during foreplay:

> If I have an orgasm before intercourse, I often can easily have another, right afterwards, during intercourse itself.
>
> —a 23-year-old from Wisconsin

> Provided I've had an orgasm during foreplay, I can go on having them during intercourse. Sometimes I have so many I lose count. I don't pay attention to how many. Just to how wonderful it is.
>
> —a 25-year-old from Texas

Still, for the majority of the *Cosmo* women, orgasm was obtained not during intercourse, but prior or subsequent to it.

> I like intercourse. It feels real good. But I have my orgasms from having my lover touch my clitoris with his fingers.
>
> —a 29-year-old from North Dakota

> Having my clitoris stroked makes me [reach] orgasm. Some men know just how to do it. Others I have to instruct. I have to tell them how fast to do it, and how hard, but if they're willing to learn, I'll have an orgasm every time.
>
> —a 24-year-old from Delaware

> I always have an orgasm as long as my boyfriend treats me to cunnilingus, at which he is *very* good!
>
> —an 18-year-old from the State of Washington

An orgasm is practically guaranteed by cunnilingus.

—a 38-year-old from Tennessee

I've never climaxed during [intercourse]. It's only happened to me after everything's over. Either my boyfriend
masturbates me, or I masturbate myself and he watches.

—a 26-year-old from California

I like to come by having a man rub my clitoris. I can come
by just having him do that, but it is so much more intense
if his fingers are in me.

—a 29-year-old from Oregon

My fiancé uses a clitoral stimulator ring around his penis
for when we are making love. It was his idea to buy the
ring, which I think was very thoughtful. But it's even
more exciting to me to be manually or orally stimulated,
and when he does this—which sadly he doesn't do all the
time—I have orgasms.

—a 21-year-old from Illinois

While having orgasms as a result of clitoral stimulation before
or after intercourse was twice as common as having them during
intercourse, many women were worried or confused about not having coital orgasms:

I am capable of multiple orgasms and have had up to
thirteen in one session. But I cannot come with vaginal
penetration. It has to be with cunnilingus or masturbation, which is very embarrassing to me, and sometimes
terribly disappointing to my partners, and this keeps
me from trying with many men. I wonder if I have
a very short clitoris, and if so if I should seek surgical
help.

—a 45-year-old woman from Maryland

I can only come if my boyfriend masturbates me. I wish
I could change. We have tried all the other methods for

coming, but it's all been to no avail. I even consulted my
physician, who was of no help.

—a 25-year-old from Colorado

I'm a nurse and you'd think I'd have known better, but
until recently I'd been feeling very inadequate about myself because I almost never had an orgasm from sexual
intercourse. I derive most of my orgasms from having
cunnilingus before sexual intercourse. They didn't teach
us in nursing school that this was normal. I've just begun
to hear about it now. And until now I've been feeling very
bad.

—a 21-year-old from New Jersey

Because worrying about not having orgasms during intercourse
is endemic, it is important to stress how uncommon having orgasms
during intercourse is. The vast majority of the *Cosmo* women do *not*
have orgasms during intercourse. So worrying excessively about the
matter—feeling inadequate, thinking about surgery, consulting
physicians or just plain feeling inferior to other women—would
seem to be unrealistic.

It seems especially unrealistic considering that while sex therapists have had some successes in teaching women to have orgasms
during intercourse (by making use of some of the kinds of techniques outlined in this chapter), they have also had so many failures
that some of them are beginning to conclude that there may be some
percentage of women who simply *cannot* have orgasms during intercourse. Indeed, at some sex-therapy treatment centers, New York
Hospital-Cornell Medical Center's distinguished clinic among
them, it is no longer customary to refer to the woman who has
orgasms during partner sex but not during intercourse as "dysfunc-
tional." She is, in effect, considered par for the course, eminently
functional, altogether normal. She may eventually learn to have
orgasms during intercourse, but until she does, or even if she never
does, she is told to view herself as typical of vast numbers of other
women.

5. The Factors That Affect Orgasm

I have been living more or less on my own since I was 17. The first time for me was when I was 13, and since the first time I have had almost forty lovers. You could say that I believe that variety is the spice of life. But contrary to how it may sound, I do not always enjoy sex. I do not always have orgasms. It all depends on the man, the feelings between us, and the mood I'm in.

—*a 21-year-old from Iowa*

As seen earlier, clitoral stimulation is usually necessary for female orgasm. I say *usually* because there are women who can climax without it. Fantasy, a voice, even an expectation, can make a woman with a low orgasmic threshold climax almost instantaneously. But for most women, it is clitoral stimulation that does it.

There are, however, other factors that contribute to female orgasm—and they may, in their fashion, be even more basic than clitoral stimulation. I am referring to emotional factors. These may exist *within* a woman: for example, she may be so shy about sex that she fears telling any man the kinds of stimulation that would satisfy her. She keeps her desires to herself and hopes a man will sense them. The two letters below are from women whose shyness about sex was all-pervasive. It made no difference who they were with:

I'm a runaway, though that isn't really relevant, except that ever since leaving home a year ago my views of and experiences with sex have undergone drastic changes. I've been able to take a good close look at my sexual attitudes instead of always worrying about my parents' attitudes. I've had three different lovers this year and I enjoy an active sex life. But none of my lovers has (yet?) helped me achieve orgasm. I guess it's partly my fault. I'm still somewhat shy about letting a lover know what really pleases me. After sex, when they've gone, I frequently have to just go off and masturbate.

—*a 17-year-old writing from North Carolina*

Although I have been sexually active since 16, and have been told more than once that I'm very good in bed, I rarely have orgasms with men. I've had to rely on my own "handiwork," and accept my abilities to bring about my own orgasm as the best there is. This is partly due to the fact that I am shy in bed. At work, my personality is 360 degrees away from shy. I've been in sales for two years and I'm outgoing, gregarious and talkative. But in bed I get shy, and can't speak up.

—a 24-year-old from Illinois

The emotional factors that affect orgasm may also exist *between* a woman and a man—one of the most curious aspects of female orgasm is that there are women who are orgasmic with one partner and nonorgasmic with another.

Is the reason simply male technique? Is it because the first man knows more about clitoral stimulation than the second? Perhaps. But it may also be because the woman feels comfortable enough with the first man, but not the second, to guide him in stimulating her. Or because she is so attracted to, or admiring of, the first man, but not the second, that she goes to bed already somewhat aroused, and so in less need of stimulation.

Women's orgasms depend a great deal on trust and exchange between partners. The *Cosmo* women were quick to point this out. For all their concern with mechanical aspects of stimulation, they were insistent about explaining that it was only with certain men, or certain kinds of men, that they felt relaxed enough to ask for, suggest, or even accept the stimulation that best brought them to orgasm.

Typical was this letter from a physiologically well-informed Florida woman:

I am 24 years old and have had thirteen lovers. Five of them were one-night stands. I always need some type of direct clitoral stimulation before or during intercourse in order to have an orgasm. For example, if I'm on top during intercourse I can move in such a way that there's friction between my clitoris and my lover's pubic area. If I'm on the bottom, I can put both my hands on the small of my lover's back, thus guiding his thrusts in such a way that there is sufficient friction or contact with my clitoris and some part of his anatomy to result in orgasm. I rarely have an orgasm with someone the first time we make love. As a matter of fact, that's happened only once. But in a relationship where I can tell a man what I like, feel at ease with him and trust that he really likes and is aroused by me (in other words, know he's not fantasizing that I'm someone else), I always come.

Like the Florida woman, many others needed, in order to have orgasms, to feel that the men they were with truly *cared* about satisfying them. Knowing clitoral techniques was not always a mark of such care:

> I am a college student and I have had twelve lovers. Most of them, except for the first one, have been what you'd have to call very good in bed. I don't have to tell them what to do. They just do it. But with some men you get the feeling they want you to come because unless you do, they think they're not good lovers. They don't care about *you*. So no matter how long or how hard they stroke your clitoris, or even if they have oral sex with you, you can't come. This happens to me a lot. I can only come when a guy is doing it for me, and not for his own self-image.
>
> —*a 22-year-old from Kansas*

> I've had exactly seventeen lovers. The times I've been with people I've really cared about, or who cared about me, I've enjoyed very good orgasms. However, when I've felt like I was pressured into sex, orgasm was out of the question.
>
> —*a 22-year-old from Texas*

What is the quality that makes a man able to assist a woman in the transition from being non-orgasmic to orgasmic? Men have long imagined that sexual stamina—keeping intercourse up for long periods of time—would do the trick. Others, more recently, have assumed it was all a matter of developing clitoral techniques. The *Cosmo* women, interestingly enough, talked instead about such old-fashioned traits as understanding and tenderness. One woman had been afraid to experience orgasms and needed a man who could assure her that an intense sexual response to stimulation was normal and desirable:

I first had sex with a man at 16. No orgasm, of course. In fact, I didn't have orgasms until I was nearly 19. Then, when I first started experiencing those neat feelings, the strangest thing would happen to me. I wouldn't let my boyfriends touch me again until the next session. I don't know why I did this, maybe because I was frightened because my body responded so funny—when actually it was functioning quite normally. Talk about naive! But what was really bad was that when I felt these funny feelings coming on, I could stop them. What a dummy! It was my husband who was the person who finally brought me around to letting these funny feelings happen without stopping them. And I'm not saying this because he's my husband, but because I trusted him completely. He explained things to me. He was patient and understanding. He made me understand my feelings, and enjoy them for what they were.

—A 24-year-old from Iowa

Another woman, a young factory worker, wrote movingly about her May–December romance with a lover old enough to be her father:

I am a 24-year-old factory employee in a small midwest town. I had my first sexual experience at the age of 17 with a boy who happened to be my first boyfriend and who I eventually married. I experienced no joy from sex and no orgasms, although we did everything you're supposed to do. I would have preferred to end any sexual relations for good until four years ago, at the age of 20, when I changed jobs to the one I have now and at the same time met a man whose personality intrigued me. That man was 51 years old. He wasn't even one of those 51-year-olds who look younger than their age or try to. But I felt a strong sexual attraction for him. I was still married and had neither the money nor the independence I needed to leave. But I did it anyway, and started a sexual relationship with the man I mentioned. I could never have guessed or believed that sex could be so good. I came alive and enjoyed every moment. I began to have orgasms. Now this man is my husband and I have never been happier. Many people talk about the exciting places they've made love, but no one could match our list—under a desk, in a sawdust pile, standing up against the edge of a sink in a bathroom, and of course, the bed.

But it's the little things that make each day special. The smiles, the touch of his hand, the extra cup of coffee fixed just for me on a busy morning, or the I Love You's at unexpected times. Many women rave about the many times their men say I love you, but to me that would get old. My husband makes it a point to tell me he loves me only when I need to hear it or when I least expect it. One day I came home from an upsetting funeral of a relative to find a message in the bathroom sink. In red, it said, "I love you." Even better was the morning I woke up a little later than usual to discover a fresh pot of coffee and a note written on a paper towel and hung from the middle of the kitchen ceiling. "Gone to get a haircut. Love you." What a nice way to start a day. What a tender man. He's tender in bed too. That's why I have orgasms now.

6. Sex Without Orgasm

I usually have orgasms but there are times when no matter what my husband and I do, I just can't climax. I'm usually the one who says to him after a while, "Okay, let's stop for tonight." And I really mean that it's okay. It *feels* okay. Maybe what's wrong is that the times I don't have an orgasm are the times I just wasn't too eager for sex in the first place. I don't know. But I'm worried because when I tell my husband it's okay he says I've got the wrong attitude about sex. He says I should expect to have an orgasm each and every time, just the way he does.

—*a 33-year-old woman from Maine*

When a woman has found a partner with whom she is usually orgasmic, she may or may not feel strongly that each and every sexual encounter end with orgasm for her. It is a matter of individual temperament, cultural conditioning, and, perhaps, physiology.

Some of the *Cosmo* women who were usually orgasmic experienced extreme unhappiness or irritability from occasional failure to climax. A 24-year-old from New Jersey who usually has orgasms said, "Sometimes when I don't have an orgasm I just burst into tears. I don't mean to. It's my body's response. I just can't help myself." And an Ohio woman of 36 wrote, "If the kids were smarter, and older, they'd know I didn't come the night before because it's always when I didn't come the night before that I lose my temper with them over little things like not closing the corn-flakes box and spilling milk on the table."

A few women reported demanding of their partners that every sexual encounter culminate in orgasm. A 24-year-old from California wrote:

> I earn close to $40,000 a year, and I own a house, together with a boyfriend. Believe it or not, I never had an orgasm until the age of 20, even though I had sex the first time at 14. Now I have orgasms almost always. And when I don't have them, I get pissed off and frustrated. I tell my men this, and I won't see a man again if he's the type who leaves me hanging there after he has come.

And another 24-year-old, also from California, felt that sex without orgasm should never be accepted by a woman because it could injure her health:

> I am 24 and have had only one lover, a Latino, who always made me have orgasms. The myth about Latinos in bed is no myth. Since we broke up, I have had a lot of fumbly, unerotic men and I rarely have orgasms. I believe that in the U.S. there is a lot of misconception about the grandioseness of sex. Men don't know how to make a woman have an orgasm. They don't think it's important. They don't realize that frustration can lead to emotional problems, even physiological ones, like neurological ones. I believe that orgasm is necessary after the onset of any sexual stimulation.

But for a majority of women who had found partners with whom they reached orgasm regularly, an occasional failure to climax was discounted or minimized:

I usually have orgasms but I don't go to bed expecting to come all the time. There are times when it just doesn't come off. But that has never kept me from enjoying sex. If I haven't had an orgasm, I'm not afraid to admit it. I tell my partner that even if I didn't come, it didn't ruin it for me, so it shouldn't for him either.

—a 22-year-old from Wisconsin

I have orgasms most of the time my boyfriend and I make love. When I don't I just chalk it up to bad luck, and figure I'll have one next time. I don't like to make a fuss. It's all right with me that my boyfriend pleases me most of the time. So even though I get a kind of sad, letdown feeling for a few moments, it's okay. The feeling passes quickly, and I think about how last time I had an orgasm, and the time before, and how I will again the next time we make love.

—a 28-year-old from California

I don't feel an overwhelming need to reach an orgasm each and every time I make love with someone. Most of the time is good enough.

—a 24-year-old from North Carolina

When my man and I make love, I usually [have an] orgasm. Sometimes before intercourse, sometimes during, sometimes after. But once in a while I don't. Do I get mad at him? Not on your life. Why should I? I know I'll come the next time.

—a 26-year-old from Connecticut

The question of whether women should begin demanding orgasm as a result of every sexual encounter is one that was much debated in the seventies, with feminists often making the point that even the occasional absence of orgasm could be emotionally or physically deleterious to women. It was argued that men didn't tolerate the occasional absence of orgasm, and that therefore women shouldn't. But there is some evidence that in fact some men do tolerate—and even enjoy—the occasional absence of orgasm. A 30-year-old woman from Massachusetts writes:

My lover and I have gotten into the habit of having sex sessions that do not end in orgasm for either of us. We agree that on such and so an evening we'll just stroke each other for hours, always stopping short of a climax, and we won't end the sex—that is, have an orgasm—until the next morning, or maybe even when we get together after the next day's work. It is the most delicious turn-on for both of us and when we finally get around to coming, believe you me it's out of this world. He's an older man. Maybe that's why he can hold out. But I've had other older men who couldn't, so I don't know. All I know is sex without orgasm can be wonderful for both sexes, as long as eventually there is orgasm.

And a 26-year-old from Colorado:

My boyfriend likes to postpone our climaxes for a long time. We have intercourse for a little while, then stop, then start again, then stop. When we stop I'm always worried that it must be frustrating to him, but he says it makes it feel even better when we start up again.

In essence, what both these women were describing was sexual play similar to that often advised by Masters and Johnson to teach couples that sexual pleasure—and not just orgasm—can be an end in itself, at least on some occasions. And they further indicate that not just women, but men too, can accommodate to sustaining some episodes of sexual excitement without orgasm, provided, of course, orgasm results from some of their other episodes.

7. The Pressure to Have Orgasms

I'm 17 and I have a gorgeous 6'1" blue-eyed blond boy-friend who really turns me on. He is my first boyfriend and we've been having sex two or three times a week for the past two months. Unfortunately, in these last two months, I've never achieved an orgasm. What can I do? It's starting to bum-out my boyfriend.

—a 17-year-old from California

Time was when women's major complaint concerning orgasm was that men didn't care whether they had one or not. There's a different problem today. Men care. Sometimes, perhaps, they seem to care too much:

> I've been seeing this 30-year-old man. We have great sex. He enjoys it thoroughly. I enjoy it too. Yet I've never had an orgasm. My main concern about this is that my boy-friend may get angry. I think he feels he cannot satisfy me sexually. He's always asking me why I don't achieve orgasm. All his other girlfriends have. I feel so bad. I love sex with this man. God forbid I don't achieve an orgasm!
>
> —*an 18-year-old from California*

Some women, particularly younger ones or those who have not yet had the kinds of relationships that might permit them to de-velop their orgasmic potential, feel that contemporary men's atti-tudes about orgasm get in the way of their sexual pleasure and response:

> It took me nearly three years to discover what brings me to orgasm. I started having sex at 21 and didn't have an orgasm till 24. When I finally did learn, it was incredible! Yet only recently, orgasm has become a barrier to plea-sure again: I've run into two men in a row who feel some-thing isn't "right" unless I come. Under such pressure I find orgasm harder and harder to achieve, and less pleasurable.
>
> —*a 30-year-old from Ohio*

> I like the closeness that kissing and cuddling and hugging bring. I do not think orgasms are always so important. But men think that if you do not have one, they are not the great lovers they think they are. Men see sex as some kind of athletic competition. They really want to perform so as not to dissatisfy women. So they shortchange us on cud-dling and hugging and go just for the clitoris, and it turns me off, not on.
>
> —*a 22-year-old from Indiana*

Clearly, when men feel that a partner's orgasm is their due, or when they chide or judge a woman for being non-orgasmic, they are hindering, not helping, her to respond. On the other hand, without male pressure many women who are today orgasmic might not be. Dr. John O'Connor, one of the founders of the sexual-therapy clinic at Columbia Presbyterian Hospital in New York, advises women who are dismayed by male pressure concerning orgasm to try to understand why their partners are orgasm-directed. "They want to be appreciated," Dr. O'Connor says, "and they view the woman's orgasm as a physical 'I love you.'" That may be an error, but it is hardly a crime.

8. Faking Orgasms

The *Cosmo* survey did not ask women whether they practiced what Masters and Johnson have called "the female's age-old foible of sexual pretense"—faking orgasm. But from the letters received, it would appear that many women still pretend to orgasms they don't have. Typical were these two letters:

> I have had seventeen lovers. Orgasms? Ah, the magic word, and the one thing I am not getting from men. I have hardly ever had an orgasm with any lover. On the very rare occasions I have had one, it's been from manual or oral stimulation. Do I tell my lovers this? No! And am I going to tell my present lover this? No! He thinks I always have them, and so he has no complaints. Please spare me the lectures!
>
> —*a 32-year-old woman from Ohio*

> I don't come all that often—though I generally do when I'm not tired, when I'm not drunk, and when I'm very comfortable with the man I'm with. When I don't come I've found it's usually easier on the male ego to fake than to explain. They always take it so personally, and can't

seem to understand how sex can be at all enjoyable without an orgasm.

—a 23-year-old college student from New York

And even women who were usually orgasmic reported pretending to have orgasms:

> I usually have an orgasm when my husband and I make love. But there are times I'm just not in the mood for one, or just not excited enough. He wants to keep on trying, but I get tired after a while. I know it's going to take a long time, if at all, so just so I can get to sleep for the night, I'll pretend I've come. I don't see any harm in this, really. It's not as if I felt frustrated. (I never fake an orgasm when I'm really excited. Those times I want him to keep stimulating me.)

—a 31-year-old from Iowa

It is not possible to say what percentage of the sample fakes orgasms, or does so from time to time, but it is clear that the practice is still occurring.

On the other hand, a number of women reported having abandoned the practice, and one very young woman happened on a bit of sexual wisdom every bit as "age-old" as faking orgasm. She learned—as many women have—that asking a partner to stimulate her manually to orgasm after intercourse was, if a blow to his ego, also a source of keen sexual excitement to his body:

> My current lover is wonderful about satisfying me sexually. I do not have to masturbate myself to orgasm. He is the one to do it. With other men—there have been a few —I haven't had to do it either. I have just simply had to say, "You'd better finish what you started." They laugh and automatically understand what I'm talking about, and that is that. Nothing else is ever said. I once asked one of my lovers after everything was over if he disliked having to masturbate me when I didn't have an orgasm. He was cool about it and just said that if that's what it took, it was okay with him. But I noticed that it sort of excited him while he was doing it!

—a 20-year-old from Texas

9. Do Orgasms Vary in Intensity?

MAJOR FINDINGS:

Orgasm varies in intensity for most women. Only 3 percent of the *Cosmo* women felt that their orgasms were always of the same intensity.

While virtually all the women agreed that some orgasms were more intense than others, there was considerable disagreement about which kinds of orgasms were more intense—those produced by clitoral stimulation alone, or those produced during intercourse.

A 47-year-old married woman from California who decided seven years ago that she and her husband ought to have an open marriage, and who has had numerous lovers since that time, says, "My experience is that really intense orgasms result from clitoral manipulation, and that orgasms experienced during penetration produce feelings that are diffuse rather than intense."

A 34-year-old woman from Montana disagrees: "I experience ecstasy only with orgasms during penetration. I can have orgasms without penetration, but they are not nearly as intense." And a 26-year-old fashion designer from New York City writes, "Orgasms from clitoral manipulation are localized, but the ones from vaginal entry are more intense because they're felt all over the body."

Perhaps the problem is with the word "intense," which means different things to different people. To some women an intense orgasm is one in which the spasms are of long duration. To others an intense orgasm is one in which the emotional after-effects of tranquility are most pronounced.

Masters and Johnson in studying female orgasm found that it did seem to be true that manual clitoral stimulation produced orgasmic spasms of greater vividness than the spasms produced during coital orgasms. But they also found that their study subjects reported coital orgasms as being more "satisfying."

Love resides in the eye of the beholder. Orgasmic intensity may reside in the psyche, as well as the body, of the participant.

10. Multiple Orgasms

MAJOR FINDINGS:

Sixty-seven percent of the respondents have had multiple orgasms on occasion. Ten percent always have them. Twenty-three percent never have them.

Most women are physiologically capable of being multi-orgasmic. There are four stages of orgasm: initial excitement, a plateau of excitement, the orgasmic—or spasmodic—phase itself, and resolution. During the excitement and plateau stages there is a build-up of sexual tension as a result of stimulation. During the orgasmic phase, there is a release of sexual tension. During the resolution stage, the body gradually returns to its pre-excitement condition. The key word here is "gradually." In most women the clitoris remains tumescent—engorged or swollen—for five to ten minutes after the orgasmic spasms. During that period it is possible for these women to have additional orgasms with relatively little additional stimulation.

How many additional orgasms? Among the *Cosmo* women, 66 percent of those who had had multiple orgasms had recorded up to five in a single sexual episode. A smaller group—13 percent—had had between six and ten. And a very small group—6 percent—had had eleven or more.

Some women, though, find stimulation after orgasm painful, and so don't try for additional orgasms. A 21-year-old married woman from New York: "Most of the time I have one big orgasm and become so sensitive I can't be touched." A 28-year-old woman from New Mexico: "I can't imagine why anyone would want to have more than one orgasm. The experience is so satisfying that I'm content, and besides, if a man tries to touch my clitoris after I've come, it's agony."

Such women—or their partners—may have misunderstood the mechanics of female orgasm. They should not, for example, be attempting to reach a subsequent orgasm through the same kind of stimulation they required for initial orgasm—that is, through direct clitoral stimulation. And indeed, they need not attempt such stimulation. Broad generalized stimulation—that is, stimulation accomplished through manipulation of the entire pubic area (but not the clitoris itself) by manual means or by the thrusting of intercourse

—can suffice. And such stimulation is, in fact, found preferable by many women once they have had an initial orgasm, even though for that initial orgasm they emphatically preferred direct clitoral stimulation.

Physiologically, the preference makes great sense. The clitoris is so sensitive an organ that it seems unable to tolerate direct stimulation beyond a certain degree. So before orgasm, when a woman reaches a high level of sexual tension—that is, once she is very excited—the shaft of the tumescent clitoris invariably retracts under the clitoral hood, pulling away from contact in order to avoid pain. It cannot now be easily touched (if it is touched, acute discomfort results) and orgasm, when it finally occurs, takes place while the clitoris is retracted.

After orgasm, the clitoris reemerges. Yet it is still anatomically close to its immediately pre-orgasmic state. Therefore, just as immediately before orgasm, a direct touch upon the clitoris can be agonizing. But an indirect touch like the generalized stimulation of intercourse can, as just before orgasm, cause the clitoris to go once again into orgasmic spasms. And again. And again. This is why it is common for a woman who has climaxed *before* intercourse to do so during intercourse as well, even though she may ordinarily have considerable trouble having a *first* orgasm from intercourse.

Many people—women as well as men—are ignorant of these anatomical facts, and partly as a result many women do not try to have multiple orgasms. They experience pain when the clitoris is directly stimulated after an initial orgasm, and give up on multiple orgasms. It's worth remembering—and indeed it may be relaxing to remember—this essential: the capacity for multiple orgasms can be the capacity to climax while the clitoris is, so to speak, off the scene.

11. Learning to Have Orgasms

Dear Surveyer:
Read your survey. Here's mine. Seventy-two years. Best of health. Husband, 74. Also best of health. Married fifty years. Several children. All married. Very good sex life. At least five times a week until past 60. Now twice a week. Always enjoyed sex but had first real orgasm at 69. A big

thrill. As husband has slowed down some, he spends more time stimulating me. Orgasm now is like priming a pump, and then a great shock and release and satisfaction.

—a woman from Minnesota

Of all the letters received for *The Cosmo Report,* this one—which was written on lime-green stationery in a spidery, old-fashioned hand-writing—was my favorite. I was touched by the simplicity with which the Minnesota woman made perhaps the most important statement that can be made about orgasm: that it can be learned. And while it was sad to imagine her having sex for forty-five years without experiencing the resolution and joy of orgasm, it was delightful to know that eventually she had done it.

Most of the women wrote vividly about the transition from being non-orgasmic to becoming reliably orgasmic. And, happily, most accomplished the transition at much younger ages than the Minnesota woman:

> I was active in sex since 15 but didn't truly climax until I was 26. I was making love to my boyfriend, and this one night I asked him to pull away a bit. I put my hand between us and with one finger put pressure on my clitoris. Then he took over. From his movements on my hand, and my fingers' pressure on my clitoris, skyrockets went off. I couldn't believe the feeling. Wow! Even he was shocked.
>
> *—a 32-year-old living in Canada*

Among the factors that women identified as contributing to their eventual learning to be orgasmic were the development of personal self-esteem, the acquisition of adequate sexual knowledge, and the establishment of relationships with caring partners.

> I am employed as a senior staff accountant in a worldwide C.P.A. firm. I was 15 when I started having sexual encounters. After the first couple of times, I felt I was frigid, so I didn't even try to bring myself to orgasm via masturbation. But when I was 23 I finally learned to have orgasms. Two things helped me to do so. One was that I started psychotherapy, which made me feel better about myself.

The other was that a few months after I started I found a wonderful 40-year-old lover. The two things combined to enable me to see my body as a thing of beauty although granted it's not perfect. I gradually became able to relax and finally to achieve orgasm. Now I achieve them almost always. I feel that it's just a question of practice (something I enjoyed doing!) and self-confidence.

—a 24-year-old woman from Colorado

I've had between nine and fourteen lovers. I really didn't keep track. Sexually I don't remember being very fulfilled by any of them. I don't think I even knew what an orgasm was at that time. I was in college. Anyway, I was having the affairs more for self-assurance (I felt very unattractive) than for sexual fulfillment. But now I have a boyfriend who I plan to marry the end of this year and sex with him is great. We like many different positions and use them all about equally. We have even invented some great new ones. I always have orgasms. Sometimes it takes me only ten minutes, sometimes up to forty. It always just depends, but my boyfriend always ensures that I do. Having a steady partner is, I've found, infinitely more conducive to having orgasms than having a number of partners.

—a 22-year-old from Oregon

I remember my first orgasm. I was 16 and it was done by manual stimulation. Oh joy! But after that they were few and far between. It was a case of my not knowing what was good for me or what I really wanted. Once I discovered the whats, and wheres, it got better. Now, as a rule, I show my lovers what I want. And if they're at all imaginative or creative, they take it from there.

—a 25-year-old from California

Believe it or not I never had an orgasm until the age of 20. Now mind you, I had sex for the first time at age 14, and from age 16 to 19 I had a steady boyfriend and we had sex regularly. Now again, believe it or not, when I was 20 I read an article about orgasm. If you'd never had one, the article said, you should follow their step-by-step instructions while masturbating. Well, I took the magazine and followed the step-by-step instructions, and that was the first step in the direction of a fulfilled sex life. Now when I have sex, I have an orgasm almost always.

—a 24-year-old from California

Learning to have orgasms during partner sex requires, for any woman who finds orgasm difficult, all three of the factors the *Cosmo* women mention:

Adequate sexual knowledge (without this, stimulation will be inadequate)

Self-esteem (without this, the woman will not feel herself entitled to an orgasm)

A caring partner (without this, the first two become useless)

In addition, it may require the woman's acceptance of the fact that she is just like vast numbers of other women. Only 10 percent of the *Cosmo* women were orgasmic the first time they had partner sex. Yet eventually 70 percent were always or usually orgasmic. No one can say whether another person's life will eventually come to contain sexual knowledge, self-esteem, and a concerned partner. But these days, if statistics are any guide, the outlook is reasonably bright.

PART TWO
Private Sexuality

Chapter Six
Masturbation

1. The Changing View of Masturbation

Another dramatic effect of the sexual revolution has been that masturbation, erotic self-stimulation, has gone from being a subject whispered about, if mentioned at all, to one that is widely discussed and even openly advocated.

In Kinsey's time, when 62 percent of his sample of some 6,000 women said they masturbated, Americans no longer believed—as their forebears had done—that masturbation could produce insanity or dire physical illness. But they did worry about its emotional dangers. They believed that it could inhibit the development of satisfactory interpersonal sexuality. Indeed, there were many psychiatrists and psychologists in the 1950s who argued that female masturbation, in particular, was problematic, since masturbation could cause a woman to become dependent on self-stimulation or at least to fail to appreciate partner-stimulation.

Freudians such as Helene Deutsch, Otto Fenichel and W.S. Kroger believed that in order to stop being sexually "infantile" and to become sexually "mature," a woman had to learn to subordinate clitoral pleasure to vaginal pleasure. Masturbation, by standing in the way of this subordination, could hinder interpersonal sex.

By the mid-1970s mental-health experts were saying masturbation could *help* interpersonal sex. Women who were accustomed to masturbating were not only less repressed about sex but also

153

better equipped to indicate to their partners the kinds of touches that stimulated them, and so were more rather than less likely to be satisfied in partner sex.

If I may be permitted a personal note, I think I can recall when this new view first began reaching a wide public, and what is astonishing to me is how recent it was. I put it in 1975, a mere handful of years ago. In February of that year I had been asked by *New York* magazine to write something about the state of relations between men and women for their annual Valentine's Day issue. As their behavior writer, sex was my beat. I was casting about for a specific topic when someone called to my attention a new book that was to be published on Valentine's Day. Its title was *For Yourself,* by Lonnie Garfield Barbach, a California psychotherapist, and it was the first nationally distributed guide to women's sexual fulfillment that was devoted primarily to self-stimulation. I decided to write about the book, and entitled my article, "Funny Valentine."

I remember that my editor at that time was annoyed when I turned in the article. "I asked her to write about *sex,"* he scolded aloud to a group of our colleagues, "and she wrote about *masturbation!"*

I doubt that editor would make the same remark today. In the intervening years at least relatively enlightened and unbiased people have come to accept masturbation as a part of sex. Books such as The Boston Women's Health Book Collective's *Our Bodies, Ourselves,* Nancy Friday's sexual fantasy volumes, *The Hite Report* and, of course, Barbach's step-by-step guide, *For Yourself,* have helped to popularize this fact of sexual life and have also encouraged women to be more open and truthful about masturbating.

One result has been that today women are increasingly willing to acknowledge that they masturbate. Among the *Cosmo* women, in fact, there was only a small number—11 percent of the 106,000— who said they had never masturbated. The figure is particularly impressive in view of the fact that only four years earlier, when *The Hite Report* was published, 18 percent of that book's sample of 3,000 women had said they had never masturbated. In four years' time admitting to self-stimulation had, it would seem, become more acceptable.

Feelings about masturbation have been slower to change. While acknowledging the practice, many of the *Cosmo* women also said they felt guilty and uneasy about it. Typical were these letters:

I like to consider myself "liberated," but masturbation still makes me uncomfortable. Of course, I do it. I do it manually. And I believe that before a woman can be satisfied by someone else, she has to learn what satisfaction is. But masturbation is a subject I just don't feel altogether relaxed about discussing.

—*a 15-year-old from Louisiana*

From the first time I masturbated until now, I have always felt guilty about doing it. I have read up on the subject and all the articles and books I have read say that it is healthy, that it can teach you more about your body, and that it can help you to enjoy sex with your partner more by making it possible for you to show him what to do to arouse you. But somehow I can't get over my guilty feelings. This doesn't mean that I don't do it, or that I plan to stop doing it. I enjoy it very much. But I wish you could explain why, if I feel so guilty, I continue to masturbate. Perhaps in the future I will be able to stop.

—*a 24-year-old woman from New Jersey*

I have been masturbating since I was 18 years old, but it's something I've never admitted to anyone except my present lover.

—*a 39-year-old divorced woman who has had 25 lovers*

I mostly masturbate when I don't want my husband to have to take the extra time to bring me to orgasm. I'm still a little uncomfortable with it and with him.

—*a 27-year-old married woman from Georgia*

I have done this a few times, but to tell you the truth, no one, not even my boyfriend, knows. To tell you the truth, I think I'd rather die than have anyone find out. I feel so guilty after I do it. And now that I have a steady boyfriend, I am really hoping I'll be able to stop. I just don't think it's fair to my boyfriend. In fact, I kind of consider masturbation "playing with yourself," and that's sickening. I don't even like to talk or think about it.

—*a 23-year-old woman from California*

As the letters show, the story of masturbation is one of cultural lag, of a disparity between a society's practices and its feelings about its practices.

In part this may have to do with how swiftly our society has been changing. And in part it may also have to do with the fact that some of the proponents of masturbation have been talking above—or to the side of—the heads of most women. There was considerable nonsense associated with masturbation in the seventies. There were some masturbation propagandists who, in their efforts to praise self-stimulation and rescue it from ignominy, went to fanciful extremes to get their message across. "Socially institutionalized dependent sex is depersonalizing," wrote the artist and feminist Betty Dodson, and "masturbation can help return sex to its proper place, to the *individual.*" Linda Bisgaard, a poet, wrote a lyrical poem to her vibrator, speaking of it in the sort of romantic language which in the past poetry had used for animate lovers. Often the proponents of masturbation seemed to sound as if masturbation could take the *place* of partner sex.

This was certainly not the view of the *Cosmo* women, not even of those who, like the writers below, had no guilt or embarrassment about masturbating:

> I mostly masturbate when I'm super-horny and my boyfriend just isn't up to sex. But I also do it just for the gratification and release of tension. It does help relieve some of the pressures of life.
>
> *—a 28-year-old corporate executive from Illinois*

> I wish I had masturbated before the age of 24, which is when I started. I had several lovers before that, and I never had orgasms. But masturbating helped me to know my body, and now I often have orgasms—both alone and with lovers. I wish I'd started earlier because maybe sex would have been better for me in those early years.
>
> *—a 25-year-old saleswoman from Massachusetts*

> I didn't masturbate until I was a grown woman and then, strangely enough, it was my mother who first put the idea in my mind. I was complaining about my husband, and she said that her answer to an impatient husband was her

finger. So we discussed masturbation. She said she'd been reading that women need sex biologically, just like men do, and that if you couldn't get it in a love relationship, at least you could—and should—satisfy yourself. I tried it. I liked it. You're never too old to change. Who said life begins at 40?

—*a 35-year-old secretary from Wisconsin*

For these women, and indeed for all the *Cosmo* women who were enthusiastic about self-stimulation, it would be inconceivable to imagine masturbation as a *replacement* for partner sex, or as an activity as gratifying as partner sex. It was a substitute for times when a partner wasn't available to them, or a comfort for times when a partner had not satisfied them, or even a gift to be offered to partners who were aroused by seeing the women arouse themselves. Not a single letter or comment was received from a woman who viewed masturbation as sexually *fulfilling*. Sexual fulfillment was clearly associated with romantic, psychological, and interpersonal fulfillment.

One woman, a 45-year-old separated mother of four from Oregon, vividly stated the difference between the boons of masturbation and those of partner sex:

> I have orgasms with certain partners—not all—and with my vibrator. I only bought the vibrator when I was 40. I love it. But I feel I need a man's need of my body, and the feel of his hands, for my self-image. I can't get that from a vibrator. I can give myself orgasms, but I can't give myself a good self-image.

Some people often confuse masturbation with having a partner stimulate their genitals. At least they do so verbally . . . "I masturbated her until she came" . . . "I wanted him to masturbate me." Even a knowledgeable writer like Gay Talese speaks of being "masturbated" when he describes having a woman massage his penis.

This, it seems to me, is unfortunate. The two activities are very different in their psychological and emotional resonance. How different they were to the *Cosmo* women can be seen in this important fact: Having a partner stimulate their genitals was a subject the women praised and wrote about at length when discussing love-making practices; stimulating their own genitals—masturbating—

was a subject that evoked relatively few letters and comments.

It is obviously because the emotional interchange that human beings experience during partner sex is uniquely satisfying and that masturbation, for all its close physiological resemblances to partner sex, has never been woman's—or for that matter, man's—primary sexual goal.

2. How Widespread Is Masturbation?

MAJOR FINDINGS:

Eighty-nine percent of the survey's women have masturbated.

When Alfred Kinsey studied sex habits in the early 1950s, 62 percent of his sample of about 6,000 women said they masturbated. When Shere Hite studied sex habits in the early 1970s, 82 percent of her sample of 3,000 women said they did. The *Cosmo* survey, done at the very end of the most sexually unrestrictive era in recent western history, revealed a nearly universal experience of masturbation. Eighty-nine percent of the 106,000 women said they masturbated. It is possible that self-stimulation became more widespread during this time, but it is also possible—and I tend to this belief—that it simply became more admissible.

But what of the 11 percent who have never masturbated? Were they mostly women who had been born well before the explosion of sexual permissiveness? After all, Kinsey had found that among the women he studied, those born prior to 1900 were somewhat less likely to have masturbated than were those who were born in less distant decades. Did the decade of a woman's birth still matter when it came to whether or not she was likely to masturbate? Could one actually chart the progress of the sexual revolution by looking at the frequency of masturbation among women born, say, before or after 1950?

The answer is no. Among the *Cosmo* women there was the same small, fairly stable percentage of non-masturbators no matter which decade was studied.

What, then, do those who have never masturbated have in

common? They tend to be women from strongly religious back-grounds. Kinsey had also found such upbringing inhibited mastur-bation. Which is not to say that religious women do not masturbate. Only that the very devout or those raised in structured, religious circumstances are less likely to do so. Several letters came from readers who, while sexually experienced in every other way, had never masturbated because the activity seemed unusually sinful to them. One woman wrote:

> I am proud to say that I have never masturbated. I have done just about every other sex thing in the books. I even once made love with two men at the same time. But God condemned masturbation in the Bible. He said it was a sin. He went out of His way to say so. So I will never do it.

It would seem that those women who, today, do not mastur-bate, are related less by the decades of their birth than by their religious scruples and conditioning.

3. How Old Were You When You First Masturbated?

Major Findings:

Fifty-four percent of the women had started to mas-turbate by the age of 15. Of this group the greatest number—32 percent—began between the ages of 10 and 15; the next greatest number—17 percent—be-tween the ages of 5 and 9, and a small number—5 percent—when they were under 5.

Some began masturbating later in life—of these, 21 percent between 16 and 20, and 14 percent past 20.

Not so long ago most people believed that boys and girls were not sexual at all until the age of puberty. Or they believed that there was a brief period of sexuality in early childhood followed by a long period during which sex went underground, to reemerge at puberty.

Today it is widely understood that even infants are capable of receiving sexual pleasure from touching their genitals, that even 3-year-old girls can achieve orgasms through self-stimulation, and that masturbation can occur *throughout* childhood.

The great explorer of the subject was, as he so often turns out to be, Kinsey. Interestingly, despite all the books that have been written on masturbation in recent years, none has told us as much about it as Kinsey did, nor examined it in all the aspects he did.

He was intrigued, for example, by the question of when self-stimulation first occurs in girls, and wrote about having personally observed six infants under 1 year of age stimulating themselves, and of having read records of 23 3-year-old girls who actually masturbated to orgasm. "It requires some . . . development of muscular coordinations," he observed rather admiringly, pointing out that small boys usually couldn't manage it.

He was also interested in what triggered early masturbation, and wondered why some females attempted it but others did not. To learn more about this, he asked the women he interviewed to try to recall their earliest memories of self-stimulation. But of course many of the women couldn't, or wouldn't, recall masturbation during earliest childhood. Such things are usually buried in the mists of memory. Nevertheless, occasionally a woman does remember early masturbatory experiences. The *Cosmo* survey resulted in a few letters from women who did, and I suspect Kinsey would have been fascinated by them. Like most pioneers, he was born before his time.

> I have been masturbating since I was about 5 or 6 years old. I remember having a favorite blanket. When no one was around I'd roll one end of it up and into a small ball and put it beneath me as I lay on my stomach. I just used to think about school, or anything. Nothing in particular. And after a little while I'd have this strong feeling. I guess it was orgasm, even back then. What I find interesting is that whoever I was thinking about at that moment, I'd just love afterwards. Like if it was some teacher at school, I'd just want to be around that person—male or female—afterwards.

> I first started masturbating at the age of nine. I walked in on my parents—and saw my dad on top of my mom, with

her nightgown pulled down below her breasts. I ran out of the room, and then something made me sink to the stairs where I started touching and playing with myself. I haven't stopped since.

I first masturbated and experienced orgasm at about 11 years of age. I'd had some type of itch, and while I was scratching I noticed a pleasant sensation, so I just kept it up until I had a fleeting orgasm.

I first discovered masturbation at the young age of 6, during my mundane, boring naptime. I was alone in my room, resting but not tired. I was lying on my stomach, and my hands took it upon themselves to drift down to my pubic area. I began feeling rhythmic sensations. I experienced an orgasm, and have masturbated ever since that wonderful day. I even did so again that very night on the couch while my mother was setting the table. She yelled at me to stop and never do it again, but what happened was that I suspected even at that young age that what was really meant was that I was only to conduct the act by myself and not with other people around. I don't believe it scarred me for life having my mother yell at me. Sorry, mom, I had to disobey, but I did learn to control myself in public and save the satisfying event for the privacy of my own bedroom.

As the letters indicate, masturbation usually arises simply from self-discovery. No one instructs little girls or boys to touch their genitals; they do so simply because the human being is a tactile, touch-oriented creature that from the day it is born, explores its world through its fingers. And, sooner or later, children usually stumble on genital pleasure. Kinsey believed that some 70 percent of pre-adolescent girls who masturbated did so simply as a result of spontaneous self-exploration.

Later in life, however, there are other major ways of discovering masturbation. If a girl hasn't masturbated by the time she is adolescent she may begin to do so as a result of hearing about the experience, reading about it, observing it in others (usually boys) or being genitally aroused by a partner. Of these various stimuli, verbal and printed sources are the most predominant. In today's culture there are many books and references to masturbation which encourage and explain it. In Kinsey's time there were virtually none. Nevertheless boys and girls began masturbating even then as a result of hearing and reading about it, never mind that much of what they heard and read were religious discussions urging them *never* to do it.

4. Frequency of Masturbation

MAJOR FINDINGS:

The largest percentage of the women—37 percent—masturbate several times a month. The next largest —25 percent—masturbate several times a week. Thirty-five percent masturbate rarely and 3 percent masturbate daily.

How often a woman masturbates depends on several factors, among them her age, her access to partner sex, and the degree to which she is satisfied by partner sex.

Daily masturbation is most common among women under 18. Eight percent of the under-18s reported masturbating daily. It was extremely rare among respondents over 35—only 1.6 percent of the women of this age reported it.

Frequent masturbation—that is, masturbation several times a week—is, not surprisingly, more common among women who report that their partner-sex lives are not satisfactory or that they make love less than once a month than it is among women satisfied by partner sex and making love frequently.

It is also more common among separated, divorced or widowed women, and among single women who live alone, than it is among married women or women who live with their lovers.

But occasional masturbation—several times a month—is as common for married women as it is for separated, divorced and widowed women, and as common for single women who live with their lovers as it is for single women who live alone.

One can conclude that while older women and women who have steady and satisfactory sex partners masturbate less often than other women, occasional masturbation remains part of women's sexual repertoire, whatever their age and marital status.

5. Techniques of Masturbation

While various researchers have attempted to define the varities of techniques by which women masturbate, their efforts have for the most part tended to be over-detailed, overlapping and therefore unnecessarily confusing. Kinsey, for example, differentiated between women who masturbated by touching the *labia minora*—the inner lips of the vagina—and those who masturbated by touching the *labia majora*—the outer lips. Shere Hite avoided the use of this particular bit of cumbersome categorization and wrote simply of "vulval" stimulation to cover both sets of labia, but she differentiated between, for example, women who masturbated while lying on their back and those who did so by lying on their stomach. Such over-specificity has, it seems to me, tended to obscure somewhat the essential facts about female masturbation. Basically there are only two principal types of masturbation:

I. Indirect stimulation of the clitoral/vulval area

II. Direct stimulation of the clitoral/vulval area

Women who masturbate the first way do so by rubbing their thighs together, or pressing the clitoral/vulval area against some soft object, such as a pillow, or some firm object, such as a mattress.

Women who masturbate in the second way do so by touching the clitoral/vulval area with their hands, or with water spray, vibrators or other objects (see pages 165–169).

There is a third masturbatory technique, one called vaginal penetration or insertion, but it cannot be considered a principal type of masturbation. It is extremely rare, at least when used in and of itself. This is not surprising, since the walls of the vagina have no nerve endings and the only part of the vagina that is susceptible to arousal is its entrance. Still, a few women do masturbate in this way. Here is a letter from one of them:

Usually when I masturbate I use my fingers in my vagina. Occasionally I use a narrow-necked bottle or the end of a hairbrush, but I seem to enjoy using my fingers most. I get the urge to masturbate when I read sexy men's magazines. I try to imagine myself in the magazine articles or pictures, try to feel the way the person portrayed is feeling, and then I become aroused very quickly. By the time I have finished the articles, I feel intense sexual tension, and I masturbate and climax.

This woman was in a distinct minority. As Kinsey said, way back when, women who masturbate by vaginal insertion alone usually do so because the technique has been "recommended by a male friend" or because they haven't yet "acquired an understanding" of their "own anatomy and sexual capacities."

Such women were so rare, even in Kinsey's day, that he listed no percentage for them. However, he did note that some 20 percent of his women used vaginal penetration *along with* one of the other masturbatory techniques. He felt they did this largely in an effort to recapture some of the psychological pleasures of intercourse.

An example of this is in the following letter:

> Sometimes when I masturbate I get myself all aroused by rubbing my clitoris and then I put my fingers up inside my vagina as far as I can. Then I slide them in and out till I'm all wet outside. I could come any time now just by pressing hard against my clitoris, but I hold off on doing that, pretending I'm with a man. Putting my fingers inside delays my orgasm, but it's nice, because it reminds me of making love.

Technique I: Indirect Clitoral/Vulval Stimulation

This is the less common of the two principal masturbatory techniques. It occurred most among younger *Cosmo* women:

I like to masturbate every night that I am not sleeping with a partner. I usually lie on my stomach and use my nightie to form something firm to rub against. I don't touch myself with my hand unless very aroused, as this does not particularly turn me on.

I've been masturbating since I was a small child, although I didn't understand then what I was doing. I just rub against the seam in my jeans or a pillow.

When I masturbate I squeeze my legs together hard and concentrate on sexy things, like fantasies or dirty magazines.

My method is to read a book and then use the pressure of the book in a rocking motion to stimulate my clitoris.

I have a beautiful way of masturbating. By rubbing my legs together. *No one* can tell. I used to do it all the time in grade school—at my desk—especially when I was under pressure taking a test. (Now you know where I got my 3.5 to 4.0 average in college.)

Technique II: Direct Clitoral/Vulval Stimulation

By far the greater number of women masturbate by direct clitoral/-vulval stimulation. They outnumber those who use indirect stimulation by four to one. They may, of course, add indirect clitoral/vulval stimulation, or direct vaginal, anal or breast stimulation, but they concentrate on direct clitoral/vulval contact:

When I masturbate it's usually right before I go to sleep at night. I turn off the light, visualize one of my favorite fantasies, and in a minute or two I have an orgasm. I always masturbate manually, using two fingers. I rub my clitoris up and down or around, and sometimes I pinch or rub my nipples with my left hand. My orgasms from masturbation are terribly intense. The orgasm comes from my clitoris, but there is also a feeling of intense desire (not quite the right word, but I can't think of a better one) in my vagina.

There is only one position that is effective for me—lying on my stomach. I use my fingers, but by lying this way my clitoris receives the maximum stimulation. My orgasms vary from small crackling ones to long and toe-tingling ones.

I masturbate in lots of different positions, but mostly on my back. Or on my knees—that's my favorite. In that position I can really stimulate my clitoris. I can rub it all I want, and I can reach down and rub against the entrance to my vagina and then touch my rectum too. Sometimes I use hairbrush handles or candles, both vaginally and anally, just going inside a tiny bit, as this does add to my excitement. But when I'm ready to come, I just use my fingers on my clitoris.

I like to experiment with different textures. I've rubbed myself wearing gloves, and with bits of soft underwear, and with a feather.

I touch my clitoris with the lightest kind of brushing stroke. Too much pressure irritates it.

I use two hands, holding the lips of my clitoris with one, and rubbing hard and directly on the clitoris itself with the other.

While there are only two principal techniques by which most women stimulate themselves, within those techniques there is an enormous range of individuality and idosyncrasy. Some women prefer faint pressure on their genitals, some prefer strong pressure. Some prefer lying on their back, some on their stomach. Some prefer to use their hands, some prefer to use mechanical devices. Some prefer to reach orgasm quickly, some to extend the excitation period for a long time. One woman's treat may be another's boredom. *Vive la différence.*

6. Vibrators

MAJOR FINDINGS:

Twenty-six-and-a-half percent of the women use vibrators during masturbation.

One of the more surprising findings of the *Cosmo* survey was how widespread the use of the vibrator for masturbation had become. Vibrators were being used for masturbation even in Kinsey's time, but only rarely. He said he had found them in an unappreciable number of cases. Today vibrators are much in vogue. They were employed during masturbation not just by 26.5 percent of *all* the respondents, but by 37 percent of the women over 30.

Such prevalence of vibrators is something of which many people are unaware. A young speech pathologist from the midwest wrote:

> I wish I had the guts to buy a vibrator. I know this sounds corny, but I leaned over a running vacuum one time and really got excited. But I just don't think I have the nerve to look a sales clerk in the eye while purchasing a vibrator. And I don't think my friends use vibrators, even though I'm sure that, like me, they'd like to.

Most of the women who used vibrators swore by them, sometimes becoming so attached to them that they gave them names, as in the letter below:

> My husband travels. He is gone all week, and comes home just on weekends. I don't mind. My life is great. I work in the daytime, take college classes in the evenings, and go to bed at night with Victor—my vibrator.

Why have vibrators become so popular? For one thing they are what might be called fail-safe. It seems almost impossible for a woman not to have an orgasm if she uses a vibrator. Here is one survey-taker's experience:

When I was young I hardly ever masturbated. I'd tried it a couple of times but nothing ever happened. So I gave up in frustration and looked for the "perfect penis," assuming that would be the answer to my problems. It wasn't. I had dozens of lovers, and I married one of them, and eventually—after thirteen years—the marriage broke up. I still had never had an orgasm. After the divorce I had dozens more lovers. I was unutterably lonely and would take almost anyone to bed, not for sex, but to have a warm body next to mine. Sex wasn't very satisfying. I still didn't have orgasms. Then one day a man whom I'd known for many years and was having an affair with wanted me to try the two vibrators he had brought over for me. I was mortified, shocked, embarrassed. And intrigued. I refused to try to use them in his presence, but I asked him to let me keep them and, the next day, experimented. At first, there was no sensation, I guess because mentally I couldn't condone masturbation. But after a few tries, a few days later, I had my first orgasm. I was 38 years old! Now at last I knew what everyone had been talking about all those years. Orgasm really wasn't a figment of people's overactive imaginations, as I had thought. What a relief! Six months later, I was lucky and met the man with whom I'm now living. With him I have two types of orgasms, one when he touches me and either inserts his finger into my vagina and/or just applies pressure to the area after stimulating my clitoris, and the other, more earth-shattering, through oral sex. And of course, when I'm not with him, I have orgasms with the vibrator.

Because they are apparently so effective in producing orgasm, vibrators have become important in certain aspects of sex therapy. When sex therapists work with women who have never been able to have orgasms, they often begin treatment by advising their patients to masturbate with vibrators. The concept is that the patients will then learn what an orgasm feels like, and afterward be able to use this sense-knowledge to repeat the orgasmic experience during manual masturbation, or—as the woman in the above letter did—during a partner's touching of the genitals.

Some sex therapists, though, have lately been advising against the use of vibrators. Among them is one of the field's leading practitioners, Dr. Helen S. Kaplan. Dr. Kaplan believes that vibrator stimulation is so intense that a woman can become dependent on its sensations for orgasm. When this happens, a woman "may find herself unable to experience orgasms from the less intense stimulation offered by manual masturbation or a partner's touches," says Dr. Kaplan.

A number of *Cosmo* women reported having experienced this phenomenon:

> I knew nothing about the possibilities of masturbation until, some years ago, I stumbled across a vibrator in my parents' bathroom. I simply played with it and found it made me go into spasms of throbbing. I was young then and thought I must be sick, but I later found out my reactions were natural. Afterward I used the vibrator frequently. But then I found that, using it so frequently, I couldn't have an enjoyable time with men. They did not do exactly what I wanted, or stimulate me with the intensity that the vibrator did. I have not masturbated with the vibrator in years because once I stopped using it, I had a better sex life.

> I use a vibrator if I've made love with a man and I haven't climaxed. Most men feel threatened by this at first, but they get over it. But I'm afraid the vibrator has spoiled me a little. It's now harder to climax with a man. Also, it's even harder to climax while masturbating manually. I used to do this all the time, before one long-term boyfriend gave me my first vibrator. Once I began using it, I lost my desire to masturbate manually because it is harder and takes longer to climax. I'd like to give up my vibrator but am afraid I won't be able to do it until I'm married and in a very sexually satisfying relationship with my partner. On the other hand I'm not sure how I'm going to accomplish this, unless I give it up.

7. Do You Continue to Masturbate When You Have a Steady Sex Partner?

MAJOR FINDINGS:

Of the 89 percent of women who masturbate, 54 percent continue to engage in the activity when they have steady sex partners.

A majority of women masturbated even after establishing steady sexual relationships, although they tended to masturbate less frequently in this circumstance (see page 162). Some felt comfortable about the matter, others not. One wrote:

> I masturbate both when I have a steady boyfriend and when I don't. Masturbation gives me unlimited satisfaction and I see no reason to give it up. I have orgasms both with my partner and as a result of masturbation.

Another said:

> I almost always have orgasms with my husband, and yet sometimes I masturbate. I do this when he's at work, and feel very ashamed about it afterwards. Why do I? Am I the only one? Please don't tell anyone my name.

The two women were so different in their attitudes toward what they were doing that is is almost difficult to believe they were practicing the same activity. Yet of course they were, and it is an activity which is not only common to 54 percent of the total sample of *Cosmo* women who masturbate, but to 58 percent of the women over 30 who masturbate.

8. Masturbation in View of a Sex Partner

The *Cosmo* survey did not attempt to discover how many women engaged in masturbation in front of their sex partners, but quite a few of the letters that were received commented on or described the practice:

> A couple of guys have requested my solitary performance, to be shown to their uninformed minds. I must admit it's a turn-on for me to be showing the sacred ritual to a man.

> I usually only masturbate in the shower. That stream of water is something else! But sometimes when my man is not in the mood for sex, he's just lying there tired, I say okay, no problem, and start masturbating. Well, the sound of my moans and moving of the bed excites him no end, and before I know it we're in each other's arms . . .

> I have found that most men I've been with like me to demonstrate masturbation to them. I not only use my fingers but a vibrator. The men always get turned on. But it is quite a turn-on for me also to watch their expressions as they see me getting myself turned on.

Most of the women who described the activity were, like the writers above, stimulated by exhibiting their masturbatory techniques. But some women did not enjoy the practice yet did it anyway. They were offering their masturbation to their partners as a kind of gift:

> I've done it a few times, but I didn't get aroused. My partners did, though. They liked it an awful lot.

> I have been with a few men who enjoy watching me masturbate in front of them but I feel that this is a very private thing to do and so, when I do it, I cannot get into it as much as I do when I masturbate by myself.

These women were offering their masturbation willingly. Others, like the woman below, felt pressured into masturbating in front of a partner:

> My husband has on several occasions asked me to masturbate to orgasm in front of him. I've done it, but it makes me feel very funny. It makes me feel as if in some way he's saying, "Satisfy yourself, baby. If you can do it to your-

self, why should I take the trouble?" We've talked about it. He says, "No, it's not that I don't care about satisfying you. It's just that watching you is such a turn-on. I get excited for days afterward just thinking about it." I should explain that after I make myself come, he usually masturbates too and makes himself come. What upsets me is that it's as if we aren't together, aren't lovers. It's like we're just objects to each other. I'd rather not come at all than have to come all on my own, right there in front of his eyes. But I'm afraid to say I won't do it anymore. I'm afraid he'll find another girl who won't refuse.

Finally a few women reported masturbating *only* in the presence of a sex partner:

I have never especially liked masturbating. I much prefer having a man. I almost never masturbate, except when I'm with a man who asks me to. I have indulged in masturbation on occasion, but usually in the presence of a man and because it turns him on. I really don't masturbate to satisfy myself. I find I can go for long periods of time without sex. I simply put it out of my mind.

There is something very touching about many of these masturbation-in-front-of-partner letters, with their suggestion that some of the women who wrote them do not actually crave sexual stimulation but enjoy only its fruits—the pleasing of a man. The letters are also, it seems to me, ironic. They say that in spite of all the masturbation-advocacy of recent years there are still some women for whom self-stimulation is so guilt-producing that it can only be considered acceptable when it is performed in front of a man, and that some women . . . to please . . . will do what men ask them to do even when they feel greatly conflicted about doing what is asked.

The existence of women like these, among a sample of women sexually liberated enough to take part in a sex survey, suggests that in the rest of the population there is even greater confusion over masturbation. It also makes one wonder if all that glitters, so to speak, is really gold. Surely, saying, "Yes, I masturbate in front of my partner," *seems* uninhibited. But is it? To know, one also needs to know *why* it is done. And if a woman does it without experiencing pleasure, or only because a man asks her to do it, can she really be said to be uninhibited?

In later sections of this book, where women's attitudes toward their lovers are explored, questions such as these loom large. But the fact that they must be asked even when one looks at that bastion of private sex, masturbation, surely seems to suggest that America's sexual revolution isn't all that it appears to be.

Chapter Seven
Sexual Fantasies and Dreams

1. The Mystery of Sexual Reverie

I'm a librarian, a married librarian with three kids. But in my fantasies I'm always a prostitute, and I have a pimp who says that if I don't make love with one customer after another he'll beat me black and blue.

—a 34-year-old woman from Virginia

There are many kinds of sexual fantasies and dreams. "Sexual fantasy" need not refer to a detailed masturbatory reverie featuring forbidden acts and a cast of hundreds of partners. It can also mean the reliving, in the mind's eye, of an encounter with a particularly satisfying old lover, or the anticipation of sexual experience to come. "Sexual dream" does not refer only to a dream that induces orgasm complete with sex flush and orgasmic spasms, but also to vague dreams from which the sleeper awakens feeling stimulated or merely sensual.

Mysteries abound about these various kinds of sexual fantasies and dreams, but one of the most puzzling is that there seems to be no direct or predictable relationship between the propriety of the dreamer's life and the lasciviousness of her sexual imaginings. Like the librarian whose letter opens this chapter, women who are outwardly conventional and restrained in the extreme may, when they are alone, experience—and enjoy—hours of day- or night-dreaming

174

about sexual situations that are unconventional and bold in the extreme.

Consider this letter from a 33-year-old hospital administrator:

> My current fantasy is of having an affair with my boss. In this fantasy my boss is alone in his private office working on a project. I enter to get a book from the bookshelf behind him. As I walk past he hardly looks up until I brush against him in a very suggestive way. He stops what he's doing and caresses my buttocks, then slowly moves down my leg caressing me lightly. I bend over to kiss him and his hand finds its way under my skirt and up my leg, slowly and gently. He soon discovers that I'm wearing nothing under my skirt and I can see his penis bulge against his pants. He begins manually stimulating my clitoris, then he slowly lifts my skirt and lightly traces the outlines of my vaginal lips with his tongue. This drives me wild and as I moan, he licks and sucks and caresses my clitoris until I come so close to a climax I can hardly hold it back. He senses this moment and quickly unzips his pants exposing his engorged penis. In one quick movement he grabs my hips and lowers me down on his throbbing penis while we move and thrust in the chair, but finding that too restricting, he lifts me to the top of his desk with my buttocks against the edge of the desk and he resumes thrusting in and out of me as I moan for him until he calls out my name in a husky cry and I feel his penis throbbing with the ejaculation while I climax and the juices flow on his papers. We both kiss deeply and we laugh at the mess we made of his desk. Then we adjust our clothes and he sends me back to work with a pat on my rear.

The woman who wrote this letter never exchanged intimate conversation with her boss, let alone spent an intimate evening with him. The letter writer says she isn't particularly interested in her boss, except in her fantasy. What really interests her, she explained elsewhere in her letter, is her 6-year-old daughter and getting pregnant again—the experience of motherhood has been "the most beautiful and cherished experience of my life."

Amateur analysts, not to mention professional, might find

ready, even pat answers, to such apparent contradictions between fantasy and real life. The lady is classically repressed, she wants her boss but is afraid of her desire . . . It's not really her boss she wants but her father or another man, for either of whom the boss is a relatively less threatening stand-in . . . She's really miserable in her marriage and motherhood, protests too much about the joys of motherhood and the desire for a reprise. . . . All plausible, perhaps, but really with no discernible basis in the facts of the woman's life, at least as communicated by her rather lengthy letter. Is it not leaping to perhaps too easy a conclusion (and making the leap merely from the need for reassuring closure) to assume such facile solutions to a genuine mystery? Fantasy and dreams aren't *necessarily* reflections of neurotic yearnings or worse. This is not to discredit or argue with the genius of Freud or other experts in the field. Of course dreams and fantasies have proved useful in the analysis of troubled people. But not all women who have fantasies—albeit in apparent contradiction to, at variance with, the feelings and desires that occupy their apparently fulfilled lives—are subjects for the couch. And fantasies themselves are—to the bane of amateur or professional analysts—the stuff of wondrous mystery that still defies scientific explanation.

Small wonder then that they are devastating. For example if the sexual daydream of this ardently maternal hospital administrator is less than easily explicable, consider this reverie sent in by a 31-year-old Texas housewife who lives with her husband and his 16-year-old son by a previous marriage:

> My favorite erotic fantasy involves something I'm sure I would never dream of doing in real life, but nonetheless it is my most prevalent and sexually stimulating fantasy. In this fantasy I am sexually dominating my 16-year-old stepson. I assume the role of a castrating stepmother and verbally and physically abuse him, as well as force him to satisfy my insatiable sexual needs. When he does something which fails to please me, I force him to strip nude in my presence. He must wear a harness which binds his arms. It consists of several leather straps which go over his shoulders and attach to a wide leather belt in back. A small metal ring at the end of another short strap hangs down from his waist. When he has the harness on, his penis and testicles are drawn through the small metal ring

and form a tight grip on his genitals. By pulling upward on the leather belt around his waist, his balls are tugged upward causing him pain. I use a long black whip on his bare buttocks. I enjoy seeing him squirm and hearing him scream out in pain, and this spurs me on to flog him even more. I do not stop until his buttocks are scarlet red and until he begs for mercy. He is required to perform cunnilingus on me for hours at a time, bringing me to orgasm after orgasm. Finally, he is required to service me sexually, making sure that I enjoy intense and pleasurable orgasms. His penis is enormous, at least ten inches long and very thick. (In real life I have seen my stepson naked several times, and he does have an extraordinarily large penis, in fact much larger than his father's.) He is forbidden from ejaculating, so his penis remains constantly erect and ready for me any time I want it. He is *required* to maintain an erection at all times, and learns that if he doesn't he will be whipped over and over again, until his penis stands upward again and he can resume his duties. He also serves as my houseboy. He performs all household chores nude, with his beautiful prick in full erection. He bathes me, massages me, and accepts his role as a totally helpless slave boy. I dominate him completely and his existence soon becomes one of total submissiveness with sexual servitude and adoration for me.

This erotic fantasy with added variances reoccurs over and over again. I've never understood why it had to be about my stepson.

The woman who wrote this letter was puzzled not only by the main character in her fantasy but by the elaborate sexual imagery in it. There was nothing in her prosaic daily life to account for her imagination's delighted dwelling on leather harnesses, whips and bleeding male buttocks.

But that is characteristic of sexual fantasies and dreams. They are no respecters of respectability. They can make "monsters" of us all. "Everyone has felt (at least in fantasy)," writes the essayist Susan Sontag in "The Pornographic Imagination," "the erotic glamour of physical cruelty and an erotic lure in things which are vile and repulsive." Sontag sees in this a reminder that "tamed as it may be, sexuality remains one of the demonic forces in human consciousness."

Perhaps. At times. But many sexual fantasies are also romantic. A 20-year-old from the Canal Zone wrote: "I masturbate to the fantasy of a handsome man who comes to town in a custom-made van. He takes me away with him, and we travel and travel, and screw and screw in the back of the van." Many sexual fantasies are also voyeuristic or exhibitionistic. But whatever they are, there is no way of knowing which woman will have which sort of fantasy. Certainly, as already noted, real-life experiences provide few if any clues. The most proper, the most sexually reserved woman may have wildly quirky fantasies about gang rapes and intercourse atop the Eiffel Tower. And the most bawdy, most risqué woman may have idyllic dreams of a lover who never touches her body. Which doesn't mean that people's fantasies necessarily tend to be the opposite of their experiences. All it surely means is that to know the outer woman is to know little or nothing at all about her sexual fantasies.

This should be reassuring to the many women who worry about the content of their fantasies.

A New Jersey schoolteacher apologized at length before describing her fantasies: "I am so embarrassed by my fantasies that I have never before now been able to describe them to anyone, not even to the man with whom I've been living the past five years. Let me explain why I am so embarrassed. I am by conviction a pacifist, and actual violence upsets me very much. Yet when I masturbate or have sex, I fantasize about being killed. I have done so ever since I first began to masturbate at age 13. I have amassed a number of favorite fantasies, all of them about all sorts of horrible painful deaths. Some of them even involve cannibalism and all involve sex before, during and even after my killing."

A young nurse from the southwest wrote, "I really hate to admit this. I consider it truly perverted. But I love to masturbate to fantasies of bestiality. I imagine a dog licking me. I would *never* want to have such an experience, and I would never stand back and watch it happen to an unwilling woman, but I do get awfully aroused thinking about it."

And a 24-year-old law student from California: "I often fantasize about being humiliated in front of a group of men. They tweak my nipples and force me to go down on them, and all the while they just joke and chat with one another. Sometimes one or another of them throws me on my back and fucks me, or two of them hold me down so that a third can enter me from the rear. Always they ignore my protests, or laugh at me. I get very excited during these fantasies, and always have orgasms; but afterwards I am troubled. I don't know why I have such fantasies, and why they turn me on. And I'd die if I ever had to confess them to a partner, or if one of my boyfriends ever figured out that that's the kind of thing that turns me on."

Worrying about the content of sexual fantasy is endemic, and for every letter *Cosmopolitan* received containing a sexual fantasy, there was another letter asking *"Why* am I turned on by such a thing?"

The question began to haunt me, particularly after I read this letter from a 22-year-old Long Island woman who works in a real-estate office. Her sexual initiation had occurred in early adolescence, the result of a rape by a man more than twice her age:

> My first time was painful and scary. I was raped by a 37-year-old neighbor. It made me think all sex would be bad and for years afterward I was afraid to get sexually involved. I waited until 18, and when I first started having sex I didn't enjoy it at all. But I do now, and am living with a lover. We have a marvelous sex life. I almost always have orgasms, either as a result of oral sex or when I am on top during intercourse. What puzzles me is my fantasies. I always fantasize during masturbation, and sometimes during intercourse. When I fantasize, it's about my lover, and I always have him forcing me to have sex with him. I am a virgin and he is beating me. Or I accidentally meet him on a street or on a bus, he invites me to his place for a drink, and then suddenly he hits me, ties me up, and beats me. Once he even held a gun on me. These fantasies really turn me on, but I honestly can't say why, especially since when I was really raped, it was terrible.

I could empathize with the deep bewilderment of this woman. The experience of rape had turned her away from sex for years, and now, at last, she has a satisfying sex life with a man who not only doesn't impose himself on her but makes love to her in her favorite ways and positions. Yet now she augments her pleasure, both with him and away from him, by imagining scenes of rape. Is it because she actually, despite her protestations, enjoyed being raped? I doubt it. Something else is going on. But what is it?

So far, *no one* has been able to explain adequately the prevalence in sexual fantasies of activities disapproved of and even despised or viewed with terror by the fantasizer.

The most common explanation is, of course, a developmental one. Basing their interpretations on Freudian psychoanalytic concepts, as already suggested, some psychologists and psychiatrists explain fantasies as a result of childhood learning. If a child was punished for masturbating, such mental health practitioners say, or even if a child simply absorbed a sexually punitive parental *attitude,* he or she might associate sexual pleasure with punishment and might then have sadomasochistic fantasies. Similarly, if a female child absorbed a parental attitude that held that sexuality was wicked, she might need, in order to enjoy sex, to fantasize herself in situations in which sex is imposed on her and she has no choice but to submit to it.

These are the traditional interpretations for the prevalence of sadomasochistic and forced sex fantasies among women. But over the years they have been questioned by various serious scholars and sexologists—Kinsey for one. He wrote: "It has long been recognized that there is a relationship between . . . sadomasochistic interests and sex, but the relationship is probably not as direct and invariable as current psychologic and psychiatric theory would have it." And indeed, it does seem as if the old theories are somewhat inadequate. For one thing, today there are clearly more and more women who have been raised in homes that are not sexually punitive, and clearly more and more women who do not seem to require that sex be imposed upon them. Yet sadomasochistic and forced-sex fantasies persist. It seems likely, then, that such fantasies may have their origins in something other than development.

Perhaps the answers will come from biochemistry. Many contemporary scientists are today working toward decoding the biochemical changes that occur when an animal experiences fear, stress or general arousal. They believe that there are specific hormones released in the brain under such conditions. It is not implausible that the hormone that is released during the expectation of pain produces a similar effect to that of the hormone released during the anticipation of pleasure, and thus in the imagination the two cognitive sensations become fused, producing pleasure-pain fantasies.

Unfortunately, brain hormones are still not understood. Until they are, what is important to know about sexual reveries is that they are virtually universal and that there is nothing wrong in having them. They are pleasurable, they harm no one, they increase arousal and allow for release of sexual tension, and unless they are shared, they cannot be divined by another human being. It is virtually impossible to anticipate, whether from looking at a woman or even from knowing her intimately, what her fantasies will be like, or whether, for example, she will be titillated by imagining gentle sex with Prince Charming or forced sex with a brutal stranger. Or a group of such strangers.

Should a woman share her fantasies? There has been a growing body of sex literature urging the exchange of fantasies among sex partners, and even the acting out of fantasies. But there may be psychological dangers in fantasy-sharing. A woman who tells a man with whom she is having sex that she is imagining him as Robert Redford, or Johnny-from-around-the-corner, risks injuring her partner's ego and thereby their sexual rapport. A woman who tells her partner that she fantasizes having him beat or rape her, risks having him reject her as bizarre or, potentially worse, having him attempt to make their sex relations brutal. (And, as we have seen in Chapter Three, few women actually *desire* brutal sex, although many fantasize about it.) But worst of all—and here is one last mystery about sexual reverie—sharing a fantasy usually destroys its potency. For some inexplicable reason, once told, a fantasy generally loses its efficacy as a stimulant.

2. The Prevalence of Sexual Fantasies and Dreams

MAJOR FINDINGS:

Virtually all the *Cosmo* respondents had sexual fantasies and/or sexual dreams. Only 2.5 percent said they had not.

As mentioned, Kinsey anticipated much of what has been learned in the past twenty-five years about masturbation among women, coming to conclusions that still hold up.

This is not true of Kinsey's conclusions on the subject of women's sexual fantasies. Because he found that some 85 percent of the men he had studied had sexual fantasies, while only some 66 percent of the women did, he concluded that women did not have the same neurological capacities for erotic reverie that men did. Interestingly, he did not hedge his bets, as was his habit when he found differences between the sexes. He did not consider that perhaps the women he had interviewed had been a little less than forthright with him because of social taboos; he did not suggest that, in another climate of opinion, sexual fantasy among women might become more common. He presumably felt that his women, who after all had been exceptionally honest with him on many stressful and taboo subjects, were being equally straightforward with him about their fantasies. When they said they didn't fantasize, he believed them, and did not speculate that perhaps sexual fantasy was an *exceptionally* distressing subject for women.

It is. Many of the images that erotically arouse women cause them embarrassment and concern even today, as seen in the first section of this chapter, so it is easy to imagine that women in a more repressed time would simply have denied that they fantasized.

Whatever their reasons, many of Kinsey's women did not admit to fantasy and Kinsey built a castle of speculation on—as it turned out—the unsteady ground of his findings. He postulated that psychological stimulation was significant to men but not to women, and that women—unlike men, who could be aroused by memories, anticipation and the contemplation of new sexual situations—were dependent on physiological sources of arousal as opposed to psychological ones. He suggested the difference might be neurological, speculating that the disparity between the two sexes' abilities to fantasize, or needs to fantasize, might account for the frequent failures in adjustment that occur between so many men and women. The ability to fantasize might account for "the male's desire for frequent sexual contact," he wrote in *Sexual Behavior in the Human Female,* and for "his difficulty in getting along without regular sexual contact, and his disturbance when he fails to secure the contact which he has sought." And the female's inability to fantasize might account for her failure to understand "why her husband finds it difficult to get along with less frequent sexual contacts," or to know why he won't "abandon his plans for coitus when household duties or social activities interfere."

Kinsey's description of the differences between the male's attitude toward sex and the female's attitude still rings true today. The discrepancies he cites still exist. But they can't be related to the proclivity for fantasy, for we now know that most women do fantasize.

What we did not know, until the *Cosmo* survey, was how big a group that "most" could be. Many sexologists have, since Kinsey's time, argued that "most" women fantasize. But their arguments were based on impressionistic data only. Now, with the *Cosmo* survey, we at last have a sound statistic. *Among the Cosmo women, 97.5 percent have sexual fantasies and dreams.*

3. When Do You Have Sexual Fantasies?

Although I don't fantasize while having sex, sexual fantasies occupy my mind throughout the day. They can be triggered by a song I hear, a face I see, a memory. Sometimes they get very intense, and I feel as though I could climax right where I am, wherever I am.

—*a 20-year-old from Alaska*

The *Cosmo* women reported fantasizing about sex in their dreams and in their waking hours. Among those who had waking-hour sex fantasies, not all the fantasies occurred during times when the women were being sexually active. Sometimes such fantasies occurred when the women were, like the woman above, just driving to work, standing in a supermarket line, writing up a report, talking to a client or customer; at times like these, their minds would drift and, unaccountably, turn to sex with a compelling intensity. They would remember a man with whom they had once made love, or someone with whom they hoped to make love, or the fragment of a sexy song, and they would feel instantly stimulated.

Sixty-one percent of the women reported this kind of idle-hour sexual fantasizing.

Nearly as common was masturbating to a sexual fantasy, with 58 percent of the women reporting that they did this.

In addition, 61 percent of the women reported that during sleep they frequently had dreams that had sexual content.

Interestingly, according to the letters, there were some who fantasized about sex only when they were asleep. The phenomenon probably has to do with inhibition. One woman, a model, reported that she thought until a year ago that masturbation "was terrible" but that now she has "no guilt about it at all." Nevertheless she still doesn't have conscious sexual fantasies. She writes, "I have experienced some incredible sexual fantasies in my dreams. I can't remember exactly what I fantasized about, but I do remember having a great orgasm." If one cannot recall one's sexual fantasies, one need not feel guilty about them.

Guilt is, in fact, a common problem among women who fantasize during partner sex. Fantasizing during sleep, during masturbation and during sexually inactive waking hours seems to have become relatively acceptable among women since Kinsey's time, but fantasizing during intercourse still causes intense anxiety among women. "I don't like to admit even to myself that I do this," wrote one woman. "It makes me nervous to realize that when I'm imagining my lover is Bill Walton, he's probably imagining he's in bed with Cheryl Tiegs. Or Bo Derek." Another wrote:

> I have always been very free about having sexual fantasies during masturbation, and when I was young, or even nowadays when my lover is away on a business trip, I can have a fine old time inventing stories and making myself come. But I don't feel good about having fantasies during sex with my lover, and the few times I've had them I've felt uncomfortable afterwards. I summoned them up because I was having trouble coming. He'd be inside me and I'd be hanging on the edge, all ready to come but unable to do so, and so I'd tell myself one of my favorite masturbation fantasies. I'd imagine he was someone else. Or two people. I'd pretend that while he was inside me, his alter ego was entering me from the rear. Or stroking my clitoris. The fantasies made me come instantly. But afterwards I felt I'd betrayed him.

These and other women may be relieved to know that 36 percent of the *Cosmo* women have on occasion fantasized during partner sex. And in other groups of women the rate may be even higher. In a 1974 study of women's fantasies during sexual intercourse, psychologists E.B. Hariton and J.L. Singer found that 37 percent of the older married women in their sample "very often" fantasized during partner sex. And in a study of the erotic fantasies of college students during coitus, conducted by David Sue and published in *The Journal of Sex Research* in 1979, it was found that 6 percent of the female students questioned almost *always* fantasizied suring partner sex, while 53 percent of them did so at least sometimes.

4. Who Do You Fantasize About?

MAJOR FINDINGS:

> In most cases, the subject of a woman's sexual fantasies is a person she knows well.

It has often been speculated that nameless, faceless strangers are the partners most often featured in female sexual fantasies, but the *Cosmo* women's answers did not bear this out. A large majority of the women—71 percent—reported fantasizing about sexual partners with whom they were already involved. A slightly smaller group—68 percent—reported fantasizing about people they merely knew. What kinds of people? One woman detailed "old boyfriends, my friends' husbands, my husband's friends, even the paperboy are the subjects of my sexual fantasies."

Those women who did fantasize about strangers were only 38 percent of the sample. This is a bit surprising. But the *Cosmo* survey grouped both masturbatory and sexually inactive fantasies together in the question "Who do you fantasize about?" It may be that strangers are featured in masturbatory fantasies, and that familiar figures are featured in erotic reveries that are not masturbatory (i.e., the daydreams of sex that fill the women's time at work, at child-care, and so on). There is evidence for this belief in the letters evoked by the survey: "My fantasies are usually about my husband. I think about what we did last night, or what we're going to do tonight, and I get all turned on, no matter where I am. But if he's ever away for a few days, and I'm turned on and want to mastur-bate, then when I'm lying alone in bed I have to have a different sort of fantasy, one about a stranger or a strange situation, not just our usual lovemaking, in order to bring myself off." Another woman, a 16-year-old high-school student, wrote, "I usually start off a fantasy by thinking of either my boyfriend, or one of my girl-friends, masturbating. This is a great turn-on for me. I envision how my boyfriend does it. Or I pretend I'm doing it the way my girlfriend told me she does it. But when I'm ready to come, the person in my fantasy isn't the person it started out to be. It's someone unidentifiable. It changes, the way people do in your dreams. You know how in a dream you start out with something like you're talking with your Aunt Mary and then somehow Aunt Mary turns into your third-grade teacher Miss Edwards and then Miss Edwards turns into the boy at the checkout counter and you're running away from him and you say, 'Hey, but it *was* Aunt Mary!' "

Another surprise was how few women fantasized about celebrities, fan magazines to the contrary. Only 17 percent had sexual fantasies involving famous people. One woman who does have such fantasies describes how they started—and where they have taken her:

> My first orgasm, which occurred during my first act of masturbation at the age of 6, was prompted by the thoughts aroused in me by a character in a television show. The name of the program was *McKeever and the Colonel.* It has long since been buried, and perhaps even cremated, in the archives of television storerooms. But I still remember it fondly. Little McKeever somehow turned me on. I doubt that the producers of Little McKeever were aware they were starting a future masturbator on her way, but that's the way it happened. Then, as time progressed, my fantasies grew, and while they continued to feature various television personalities, I also imagined sex with certain movie stars and character actors. To this day, especially during masturbation, I think about some TV show or movie I've seen recently, pick a prime subject from my memories of it, and dwell upon his body, what he'd be doing with me if I knew him, and the things he'd tell me about how much he adores me and can't live without me. I fantasize mostly about seeing the men masturbate, and this builds me to such a passion I can hardly contain myself.
>
> This past January I had a marvelous experience. I was fortunate enough to have the opportunity of enjoying a one-night stand with a handsome local newscaster. Making love to someone who was formerly a sex fantasy was certainly an event I'd repeat time after time, if given the chance. [An interesting coming together of fantasy and fact.]

Among those who fantasized about strangers, what kinds of strangers did they envision?

Some of the women's fantasy lovers were immensely sympathetic. They were rescuers or saviors: "In my favorite fantasy," writes a 26-year-old divorced woman from upstate New York, "the man of my dream saves me from someone who is threatening to harm me and we end up making love in his cabin in front of a fireplace."

Some were callous: "I am in a bar and the guy on the stool slides his hand up my skirt. I ask him to stop and he won't. He keeps fingering me, his hand going inside my panties. There's nothing I can do to stop him because if I scream everyone will know," writes a Florida woman.

And some were quite brutal, as in the case of this 23-year-old from Iowa: "I like to fantasize about a man who wants me so much he rapes me in the woods." . . . "I fantasize about a powerful man who is standing over me, a huge hard penis in his hand," writes a Colorado riding instructor. "He insists I look at it, and take off my clothes, and lie down, and then he pisses on my clitoris with it."

But whatever their nature, the strangers tended to clone themselves, to come in multiples:

> I am having some sort of foreplay with a group of men whose faces are hidden from me. They don't have intercourse with me. They just use their hands all over my body.

> I am taken hostage by a cruel dark man. After he has had his way with me, he brings his friends into the room where I am confined. He urges each of them to do what they will with me.

> I am watching a man masturbating. He is joined by another man. After a while I join them too and they are no longer interested in one another, only in me. I masturbate them.

> My husband shares me with two of his best friends. While my husband is caressing me, the others have intercourse with me, one in my vagina, the other from the rear. Then they switch places.

The partners were not always males:

> A group of women in harem outfits decide to initiate me
> into their rites. They take turns petting my body and
> licking me.

Only rarely were they animals. Although dogs and horses and other animals are frequently presented in porno magazines as being favorite sexual fantasy companions of women, they turned out to be decidedly unpopular, at least in the *Cosmo* survey. Only 5 percent of the women reported sexual fantasies involving animals as partners.

5. What Do You Fantasize About?

Despite differences in their specific details, sexual fantasies tend to be alike. There are only a limited number of fantasy themes and they occur with surprising regularity.

Typically, people fantasize not only about particular types of partners (numerous partners, strangers, same-sex partners), and particular types of activities (sadomasochistic activities, oral-genital contact, anal intercourse and intercourse itself), but also about being with their fantasy partners and performing their fantasized acts under certain particular kinds of circumstances. These circumstances consist of such situations as being observed, observing others, being forced, forcing others.

The *Cosmo* survey did not poll women concerning their most frequent fantasy circumstances. But many women volunteered this information. The fantasy circumstances most commonly reported involved: being observed prior to or during sex, and being forced to have sex. (These two types of fantasies were, incidentally, also the most frequent fantasy circumstances reported in the David Sue study of college women: of those college women who fantasized during sex, over half fantasized about forced sex, and a third fantasized about being observed.)

Among the *Cosmo* women, observation fantasies were sometimes blunt, as in the three fantasies that follow:

I fantasize while I am masturbating or having sex with my husband that someone else is present. Someone is watching me from the shadows, or through the keyhole, or from outside the window.

—*a 25-year-old Virginia woman*

My lover is going down on me in front of a circle of men who are all watching. I don't know any of them, although my lover does. Each of the men has an erection and my lover asks me to perform fellatio on them, one by one, and then, in the end, on him.

—*a 29-year-old nurse from Maine*

I love to fantasize that I am doing a strip on a table in a nightclub. The men in the audience go wild. They press around the table where I'm standing and want to have wild sex with me.

—*a 27-year old California woman*

But some observation fantasies were elaborate, with settings and story lines resembling those in romantic gothic novels or old-time costume movies:

I have a repetitive fantasy about a burly, muscular man who is somehow very important. A king or a nobleman. What happens is that for some reason he picks me for his lover. He has many servants, mostly women, and he orders them to prepare me to have sex with him. I am bathed, massaged, powdered and perfumed, all of the servants commenting on me as they prepare me. Then I am dressed in a thin satin slip and placed on satin sheets, awaiting the man's arrival. At last he comes. The servants drift into the corners. I am aware that they are still there, observing me, and am a little uneasy about their presence, but when the man touches me, I melt under his strong hands, and we drift off into heaven.

—*a 23-year-old graduate student from Chicago*

I live back in the time of Scarlett O'Hara and Rhett Butler. My father is very rich. We live on a horse farm, and there are plenty of handsome young ranch hands. It's like a tradition there. There is always an auction to decide who gets the girl. I am auctioned off to a ranch hand who offers a whole month's pay. When the day comes, he takes me into one of the barns and leads me up to the hayloft. All the other ranch hands, the ones who lost out to him, come too. But just to watch. The man who has won me then proceeds to undo my dress and take off one of my many petticoats. Then the next. And the next. And so on, until I am naked. Then he undresses himself. He makes love to me there, in the hay, with everyone watching. I protest, but he goes ahead anyway.

—a 24-year-old from Maryland

No matter how such fantasies are expressed, their essence is the same: The fantasizer's sexuality is being appraised by others.

Why are they so prevalent? In observation fantasies the dreamer assures herself about her sexuality. In her fantasy she may long for sex, or be reluctant about it, but no matter how *she* feels, those who observe her are ineluctably drawn to her. They look at her or stare at her. She is the center of their gaze and attention. Her sexuality is inviting, a calling card. It is, in a way, irresistible.

Irresistibility is also a dominant element in the second most frequently reported group of fantasies—those involving forced sex. In forced-sex fantasies, the dreamer is usually reluctant or fearful, and must be tied down, restrained, provoked, tricked or teased into sex. (Some forced-sex fantasies also contain observation elements, but some do not.)

Among the *Cosmo* women, being tied down was the most common forced-sex situation: A 16-year-old high-school student wrote, "My fantasies are all about being tied up." A 21-year-old bank teller: "My favorite fantasies are of being overpowered, tied up, and teased until I'm begging a man to enter me. At which point, he does. There's no pain, but I am not able to resist what he is doing to me." A 19-year-old factory worker: "I fantasize being tied to the bed posts and teased to death! I fantasize spankings until I agree to masturbate in front of a man or men." A 26-year-old who works for Western Electric in Louisiana: "My main fantasy deals with being tied down while a man makes love to me. I am protesting. But the man's friends are there and they keep urging him on." And a social worker from Colorado:

I live with a man who makes me go about naked and wait on him, hand and foot. He never has intercourse with me, but what he likes is to have me kneel on all fours and have fellatio with him while he reads his newspaper or eats. If I don't do it properly, he gets angry. He has these pole lamps in his living room, and when he's angry with me, he ties me to one of them and leaves me hanging there for hours. Of course, I'm naked. Every once in a while he passes by and he strokes and teases my clitoris. He gets me very excited, but he says things like, "If you come, if you dare to come, I'll leave you tied here forever. I'll let you starve to death." Then he strokes and teases me some more. I want to come. I want to come so badly. And I can't help myself, I am going to do it. But suddenly he stops touching me and goes away. He leaves the house. He slams the door. I hurt. My arms hurt. And I'm so excited. I am going to faint. He comes back and starts all over again with me.

Forced sex can also occur under other circumstances:

My favorite fantasy is that I spot a very attractive man at some crowded public place. It could be anywhere. A sporting event, a club, even at the store. He throws me to the ground and we engage in very rough sex in front of other people, mostly men, but sometimes women too. Afterwards each person there does something to me. The men fiercely screw me, almost raping me, and the women finger or lick me. And sometimes, believe it or not, the women have penises, and they screw me too. Or they have dildoes, and they screw me with these.

—*a 19-year-old supermarket clerk from Missouri*

My sexual fantasies are about being a call girl. Men rough me up, but I go along with whatever they want or do, because I figure "it's all in a day's work." And in the end, I am very sought after. I'm treated like a queen.

—*a 40-year-old postal clerk*

I am sitting on a dais at a business luncheon. I am making polite conversation with the women on either side of me.

Then I feel something under the table. Someone is slipping off my panties. Someone is fingering my clitoris. I want to stop this person, but I am embarrassed. Now he is licking me down there. I want to tell him to stop. But then again I don't. I slide down in my chair a little and let him go on and on, and all the while I smile and talk with the ladies on either side of me.

—a 35-year-old insurance saleswoman

And sometimes—although only rarely—a forced-sex fantasy involves the imposing of sexual bonds, teasing or demands not on the fantasizer herself, but on a partner. A 19-year-old Nevada woman reported such a fantasy:

I am tying a man down onto the bed and licking him all over, and teasing him, and he can't touch me at all. I keep him that way for a long time. I suck his penis and just when he thinks I'm going to suck him off, I stop. He begs and begs me to continue. I give in after a while. I start in again. But sure enough I stop just on the verge. I drive him wild. I sit on his penis and then get right off. At last he breaks through the bonds and fucks me fiercely.

At first the similarity between observation fantasies and forced-sex fantasies may not be obvious. Certainly the partners in forced-sex fantasies are nearly always callous, or even cruel, while in observation fantasies, although they *may* have these personality traits, they can also be adoring and tender. Nevertheless, even if at first glance it appears that in a forced-sex fantasy the fantasizer is imagining herself as being unable to resist her partner, if one looks closer one sees that what is happening is that her partner cannot resist her. In forced-sex fantasies, even those involving sadism, the partners of the fantasizer can never be dissuaded from giving up their preoccupation with imposing themselves on her because the fantasizer's sexuality is once again, just as in observation fantasies, *irresistible.*

Understanding this is essential to an understanding of female sexual fantasy. It also lends a poignancy to what superficially seems cruel and cold. At least in her mind every woman can be a *femme fatale.* And so sexual fantasy, aside from serving the important physiological function of increasing arousal, also can serve an essential psychological function—making it possible to feel incredibly desired, and regardless of any reality to the contrary.

One can see this at work in the fantasies of the *Cosmo* women. In their erotic reveries they may be call girls or plantation heiresses, striptease dancers or slave girls, and they may be peered at or pummeled, but the one constant is that attention is lavished on them. This attention may be adoring, as in the auction fantasy of the woman from Maryland, or it may be brutal, as in the rape fantasy of the supermarket clerk, or it may even be humiliating, as in the urination fantasy of the Colorado riding instructor. But whatever it is, it is *intense* attention, giving a sense of the woman's singular importance to all the fantasy partners encountered.

In fantasy can be found a sexual reassurance that goes beyond —and may exist in spite of—prosaic reality.

PART THREE
The Human Arithmetic of Sex

Chapter Eight
Lovers

1. The Pleasures and Perils of Change

Few things define the sexual revolution of the past decades as clearly as the fact that today's women tend to have sexual experience with numerous men. Indeed, the old custom of sex with one man throughout one's lifetime—a custom practiced universally by our grandmothers, and quite widely by our mothers—seems on the verge of disappearing into the mists of memory. It is not inconceivable that one day soon it will smack of the barbarous, like the Hindu custom of immolating widows on their husbands' funeral pyres, or of the outlandish, like the Moslem custom of garbing women in long black veils.

How many lovers is a woman today likely to have? The women who participated in the *Cosmo* survey tended to have had, on the average, nine each. But some had had many many more.

The situation has its pleasures and its perils. Clearly there are joys to be had from having numerous lovers. There is the sheer joy of sexual variety—a near-universal fantasy throughout history. There is the joy of emotional variety as well, the opportunity to know and understand a medley of men and thus, ideally, to grow deep and wide oneself. And, above all, there is the hope common to most women, that by virtue of sexual exploration they will be

197

able, if they want, to settle down into a more rewarding, more *desired* relationship than would have been possible with little or no previous sexual experience.

But there are also dangers, pitfalls. There is the increasing complaint among women that sex has become trivialized, that it is now mere sport, where once it was a deep emotional experience. There is the fact that, much as we try to close our eyes to the knowledge, venereal diseases have been spreading at an increasing rate throughout the United States. And, above all, there is the nagging suspicion that being able to pick and choose among lovers may not, after all, enable us to establish ideal relationships once we settle down with one particular lover. If anything, it often appears that despite the new sexual freedom (or perhaps because of it), the relationships of Americans are in at least one respect less ideal than they used to be: They are less enduring. According to the latest census figures, almost one out of every two marriages today ends in divorce. Living-together arrangements break up even more frequently.

And so while many women are immensely pleased by being able to have numerous lovers, they are also uneasy about the advantages. Ambivalence rules the day.

So does uncertainty about sexual etiquette. One-man-in-a-lifetime has changed in only a few short decades to I'll-take-as-many-as-I-please. The situation is too new for sexual mores to have become clear. Women with as few as two or three lovers worry that they are promiscuous, while women who have had dozens fear they have been too selective. Women who have had one marriage and one extramarital affair fear they are degenerate, while women who have taken on a rock band or a mini-platoon of Hell's Angels (see p. 202) say they have "old-fashioned values."

It is all very confusing, for we are in a time of transition. Should one go to bed on a first date? Should one carry one's diaphragm with one at all times? A condom, to reduce the dangers of herpes or VD? How many lovers is too many? How many too few? Is it okay to have sex with one man one night, another the next? Or, for that matter, to let a stranger sleep over? And is he a stranger if he has made love to you?

Questions like these plague women today and make the sexual going less smooth than one might presume from the advertised fruits of the new freedom.

In time society will no doubt thrust up new rules for sexual relationships, rules that will be as firm and clear as those that once applied when such relationships had to be approached slowly and with formality. But at present, the rituals are not clear, and relationships with lovers seem a bumpy and uncharted territory, even to today's most uninhibited explorers.

2. How Many Lovers Have You Had?

MAJOR FINDINGS:

The majority of the women have had numerous lovers. The median was nine lovers per woman, with 10 percent of the women having had only one, and 15 percent having had more than 25. The exact breakdown was:

One lover: 10 percent
Two to five lovers: 28 percent
Eleven to twenty-five lovers: 25 percent
Twenty-five or more lovers: 15 percent

No other figures yielded by The *Cosmo* Sex Survey seem as much a revelation as these. Indeed, in an important sense, the sexual revolution can be characterized as today's widespread practice of picking and choosing among lovers. And the number of partners a woman of today is likely to pick and choose is, frankly, stunning.

How many partners? Among the *Cosmo* women, while two to five lovers was the most typical amount, a sizable 15 percent of the respondents had had more than twenty-five lovers. And the letters revealed that there were some women who had had thirty lovers by the time they were out of their teens, and some who had had well over a hundred by the time they were thirty-four.

The woman who wrote the following letter lives alone on an island off the coast of Mexico. She is an artist who has recently been successful enough to support herself entirely through her painting:

> I'm 34. I've worked in factories. I've trained horses. I've painted ten large murals and sold them. I've had over a hundred lovers, have never married, and am absolutely content.

This woman was something of a free spirit, independent in many ways. But here is a 23-year-old who describes herself as having been brought up in a very strict home:

> I married four years ago, at 19. My upbringing was so straitlaced that my husband-to-be and I didn't even have sex until the wedding date was set. But the marriage didn't work out. It broke up a year ago. And in that year, I've been to bed with twenty-six men.

Another woman, similarly brought up and currently again living at home after the failure of her nine-year marriage, writes:

> I really don't know how many men I've made love with in the three years I've been separated. It's somewhere between fifty and one hundred.

And a 20-year-old college student says:

> How many lovers have I had? Goodness . . . at least thirty.

She sounded a bit startled by her own behavior, but she was way behind some of her peers. Another 20-year-old, also a college student, claimed:

> At this point in time, I have had 134 lovers. I am proud to say that I remember the names of all but three of them.

There is no doubt that women today are engaging in sex with numerous partners, and that some women are having sex with extraordinary numbers of lovers.

How women *feel* about their options to have numerous lovers is explored in the next section.

3. What Is It Like to Feel Free to Have as Many Lovers as One Pleases?

I am 31 and I feel free to have as many lovers as I please. But there are times I envy my mom. She's 50 and she's still with my dad; he was her first lover, and although they have their fights I think they'll be together always. Whereas me, I had a number of affairs before I got married at age 23, I got divorced at 29, and since then I've had at least a dozen short-term affairs and two long-term ones.

Mind you, I'm not saying I get walked out on. It's almost always been me who's broken up the relationships (and it was me who broke up the marriage). I'd get to feeling, at some point in my relationships, No, this isn't what I want for the rest of my life. But here I am 31 and still trying to decide what man, if any, I'll share the rest of my life with. So sometimes I think, Why didn't I just stay with any one of those guys and just make a go of it? Like mom did with dad. But that's only sometimes.

The rest of the time I think how lucky I am. Each of my serious affairs—and, of course, my marriage—has added to my depth as a human being. I've learned a lot from the men I've loved. I don't mean just sexual things but emotional things, intellectual things, different ways of looking at the world. My mother may be a more protected woman than me, but I'm a more sophisticated woman, and who's to say which is better. I guess my mother played the love game according to the rules of her time, and I play it according to the rules of mine.

—a woman from Illinois

The rules of the game of love today stress choice. Increasingly men and women alike have the option to have as many partners as they please.

This is not to say that the goal of the game is altogether different from what it was yesterday. Most men and women still seek emotional bonding—long-term commitments—with one another. But the bonds are often weaker and the terms are often shorter than they were a few decades ago. Living-together arrangements substitute for marriage, or precede marriage. They are rarely permanent. And marriage itself is not permanent. It has not gone out of fashion but it has given way to serial marriage. Thirty-eight percent of *first* marriages today end in divorce; among women whose first marriages have ended in divorce, twenty-nine of every hundred will remarry. Thirteen of those twenty-nine will get divorced again. And some of those thirteen will remarry yet again. And will divorce. So, although people do tend still to seek long-term emotional commitments, they tend to seek them repeatedly and at various times in their lives. And while they are seeking, they often take up with an extraordinary number of lovers.

Most of the *Cosmo* women were greatly interested in long-term emotional bonding. They had *various* lovers in order to settle down, for a time at least, with *one.* They had various lovers in order to choose the *right* lover with whom to settle down. Here is how a 24-year-old assistant buyer for a Chicago department store who has had twenty-three lovers described the situation:

> I prefer long-term monogamous relationships. I've had three of these, one which lasted two years, two which lasted a year apiece. But in between them, I do tend to try out what sometimes seems like battalions of lovers. It's not always a happy experience, but how else am I to get into a relationship with a man with whom I can be monogamous?

A similar note is struck by this woman from an entirely different background who lives in the west and has had the kinds of experiences of which movies are made:

> I'm an average type of woman, age 27. I've had a lot of affairs, some of them with men I wish I'd never had anything to do with. One was a drug dealer, some were ex-cons, two were drug freaks, a whole lot were Hell's Angels. Also there were the more usual types— high-school jocks, a few nice, decent businessmen. There have been maybe twenty altogether. The drug dealer had long blond hair and a beautiful body and I became pregnant with his child and had an abortion— something else I thought I'd never do. Right now I've got two lovers, one a kid of 19, the other a man 15 years older than myself. In a nutshell, I am somewhat promiscuous. But I retain small-town values of love

and marriage. Living together is fine, but unsatisfying. Marriage, to me, is a promise to try—no matter how difficult things get. I want to get married. And when I find the right man I will.

Of course, not all the women were having sex with numerous partners just to find one to settle down with.

"I have lovers because sex feels good," wrote a minister's daughter from Texas.

"I have lovers because lovers are food for the mind," wrote a wine taster from California. *In vino veritas?*

"I have lovers because what else is there in life that's so much fun as turning on a new man, interesting him, conquering him," wrote a French-restaurant waitress from Washington, D.C.

"I have lovers because each one teaches me something new both about sex and about humanity," wrote a midwestern telephone operator.

"I had sex with every man I dated to prove to myself that I could please a man and be pleased in return," wrote a woman whose husband had returned from Vietnam shattered and depressed. This is what she had to say about being able to have as many lovers as she pleased:

> I am 39 and have been divorced for seven years. I got married in 1966 to my childhood sweetheart. Sex between us was explosive and ecstatic. But then he went off to Vietnam, and when he came home he was altogether different. He almost never wanted to make love. He'd try to get in the mood by watching stag movies or asking me to perform fellatio on him. But something inside him had shattered. He never really got excited. Then he got mean. Blamed me for the way he was. Told me sometimes I was an insatiable pig because I wanted sex, and sometimes that I was cold and sexless because he didn't want me. Eventually I left him. And guess what happened? I was like a wild woman, an animal unleashed. After not being fulfilled by my husband, my sexual appetite was insatiable. I had sex with every man I dated. Since then I have taken a look at myself and realized that what I was doing was trying to prove to myself that I could please a man and be pleased in return. I've stopped going to bed with everyone I go out

with. But I don't regret that I used to do it. I had to learn
that I was a satisfying and satisfiable woman, and I'm glad
I did.

Clearly, people exercise their option to have many lovers for
different reasons. But whether they want to find a steady partner,
to experience bodily pleasure, to develop a better self-image, to
make friends, or what-have-you, how they feel about the option
depends on whether they get what they want.

The 27-year-old union organizer whose letter follows got what
she wanted:

> I was married at 18 to the second man I had sexual rela-
> tions with. We divorced when I was 24. And now at 27
> I am living with a lover. Between the divorce and this
> current relationship I had two wildly exciting years. My
> sex life with my husband had been one of those every-
> Saturday-night-at-nine kind of things. I walked out on
> him. I moved into an apartment, then bought a condo-
> minium and with the money I made in my high-paying
> union position was able to party three or four nights a
> week. I love to dance; disco was just becoming popular;
> I had a ball. I had a score of lovers in those two years. I
> very rarely went home with any man I met while danc-
> ing. We usually exchanged phone numbers and only
> after he had called me would I go out with him. I always
> strived to be very up-front. If I found a man attractive,
> I would tell him I wanted to go to bed with him in a
> very straightforward manner—usually verbally, but
> sometimes through body language. I tried not to lead
> any man on to the point where he expected me to go to
> bed with him unless I really meant to do it. I never felt
> that I was being taken advantage of in sex, and have a
> hard time relating to what women mean when they say
> men "use" them as sexual objects. I usually went to bed
> with men with the idea not only of satisfying them but
> of getting plenty of satisfaction for myself. I don't place
> sex on a pedestal. It's something you can do to have fun,
> and sometimes out of that fun you'll find yourself build-
> ing an ongoing relationship with one of your partners, as
> I did.

The union organizer got a husband by the process of having many lovers. Here is a letter from a woman who got not just a husband but a whole entourage of friends and caretakers:

> I am 24 years old and have just gotten married to a wonderful man with whom I lived, before our marriage, for almost a year. Before that, from February 1978 until March 1979, I had over twenty lovers. I never saw just one person at a time—usually I'd see three or four different men during a week. Most of my relationships lasted a few months. But when we broke up we'd stay friends. I had a sexual relationship with my dentist, and he's still my dentist, even now that I'm married. Same for my doctor, and my stockbroker.

Both of these women were very high on their options to have as many lovers as they chose. But if a woman's goal in having many lovers is to find a husband or live-in lover, and she fails to do so, her view of the game of love today can be bitter indeed. Here is what a 24-year-old from Ohio said:

> These last three years have been filled with so many short-term dead-end relationships that I'm beginning to wish there was a law against sex. Most of the men I go to bed with never call again, or when they do it's just for sex again. Never for seeing friends, going places together. I used to love sex. But now it all seems absolutely pointless to me. It doesn't get you a man. At least not one you can count on to stick around.

And even if a woman is exercising her option to have as many lovers as she pleases, not to find a steady partner but just because she enjoys physical pleasures, she may sometimes grow disillusioned with the option. Again, it depends on whether she got what she wanted: Writes a 27-year-old from Mississippi:

> I used to find sex fun, and had loads of lovers just for the fun of it. But I found out the hard way that sex with strangers tended to make *them* make me feel cheap and sluttish, even though I had considered our sex a precious thing to share.

Her despair was as nothing compared to that of this office worker from New Jersey:

> I am 32 years old and am writing to you about the last man with whom I had intercourse. I was out with some of my co-workers for a much-needed Friday afternoon happy hour. I started talking to the bartender. He was good-looking and funny and I went home with him. He introduced me to my first and only experience with cocaine, and we made love, and a few nights later we made love again. By this time I had become aware that he used drugs extensively, and I decided against seeing him on a permanent basis. Besides, I had a boyfriend. This new guy wasn't worth endangering my previous relationship for. I quit seeing him, chalking it all up to a fling. Then a few months later I was having my gynecological checkup and the doctor noticed vaginal warts which could only have been contracted from the bartender. After two visits with my doctor the warts disappeared and I thought that was the end of the trouble. Unfortunately, I later developed cancer of the cervix. The specialist who is treating me says that it stems from the same herpes virus that caused the venereal warts. I have since had my cervix removed in two operations and may have to have a hysterectomy later this year. My thoughts about being able to have lovers whenever and wherever I please have changed drastically as a result. Women should take care to know and [be able to] trust their partners and not treat sex as casually as I did.

Playing the game of numerous sex partners is like playing any numbers game. You win some, you lose some—usually more than you win.

All the women quoted so far had had fewer than twenty-five lovers. But what of those who had more? They were 15 percent of the sample. Were they different from the rest? True, there was a letter from a 40-year-old who declared:

> I've had upwards of a hundred lovers, have never married or lived with one, and don't expect I ever will. Why should I? Why should I put up with the inconvenience of

men, their sloppy habits, their snoring, their stinginess, when I can have the best thing of all: sex whenever I want it, and no strings attached.

And yes, there was a 20-year-old cocktail waitress who had had forty-two lovers:

> I love to bed down with a new guy. With me, the time leading up to the first time you sleep together is incredibly enjoyable. Probably it's my ego. Whatever it is, I wouldn't want to give it up and stick with any one guy. I'm sure it would be boring.

But mostly the women who had had more than twenty-five lovers were little different from those who had had fewer. Most of them, just like the others, said they were looking for intimacy, for a man with whom to settle down, at least for a while. They had just had worse luck at finding such a man. Or better luck, and more opportunities, for finding sufficient men with whom to pursue the search for the special man. In any event, they reported the same joys and the same miseries as the women with fewer lovers. They did, though, have an added complaint: that having so many lovers eventually robbed sex of dimension. They could not, for example, always remember their partners:

> I have had twenty-eight lovers, one for each of my years. When I started having sex at seventeen I felt daring and it was fun to have a lot of different guys. But lately it seems almost boring. Sex is just something you do after a date—what a kiss goodnight must have been in the past. It's lost its meaning for me. I don't mean that I don't enjoy it. I do. I've had wonderful lovers, for the most part, and I've learned to have orgasms easily. If a guy doesn't know how to make me come, I always tell him. But the thing is, in the beginning I used to remember each of the guys I'd been to bed with. I'd remember the way they looked, the things they said, and what I liked or didn't like about them. But lately I find I can't even remember the names of a lot of them.

> *—a 28-year-old from New York*

And:

> I've never been married and have had dozens of lovers. Last month a weird thing happened to me. I went to a party and I met a guy who was pretty terrific-looking and I started to talk with him and he said, "Don't you remember me?" I didn't, and he said, "It was at Michigan. We spent a weekend together." I nearly died. It all came back to me, and I remembered I'd had a fling with him in my sophomore year. It wasn't all my fault that I didn't remember him, because he'd lost a lot of weight. Still, I felt really terrible. My girlfriends are always saying that the guys they sleep with don't see them as people, and that they're so busy having sex with lots of girls that they can't keep one straight from the next one. But here I was, being just that way. I felt terrible.
>
> *—a 32-year-old from Illinois*

An administrative assistant from a midwestern university had a clerical solution to the problem:

> I have kept a sex journal since 1962, and though eighty sounds like a lot of men to have made love to, I have a written record of their names and the places.

As did an insurance broker from Atlanta:

> I am 28 and keep a list of all men I've had sex with. I include their names, a brief description of their appearances, statistics, on their height and weight and the frequency with which we made love. I also rate their performance and desirability. I use a code: stars from one to five for sexual performance; plus checkmarks from one to five for humor and intelligence.
>
> That way I figure I'll not only remember every man, but know if I ever want to look him up again.

But many women who had had numerous lovers felt uneasy once they listed all their partners: A personnel assistant at a large northeastern city hospital wrote:

I am 27 years old, have a 4-year-old child and have had dozens of lovers. Once, when I was 23 or 24, I sat down and listed all their names. I was shocked and terribly ashamed of myself.

A meaningful repetition in the stories of the women who had an unusually large number of lovers in their early twenties was that by the time they were in their late twenties they ceased being as sexually active as before. 'Slowing down," they called it, or "calming down." So many women described the phenomenon that it appeared to be a distinct pattern:

I am 28 and have had sixty-three lovers. Thirty-eight of them were one-nighters. I had most of them when I was between the ages of 18 and 26. Since turning 26 I seem to have become more reserved, less willing to share myself with a casual stranger. I still enjoy the one-nighters, but not as much as I used to. I seem to want more intimacy these days.

—*a nurse from Massachusetts*

I am in my late twenties. I used to have lots and lots of lovers. One year I had over a dozen. But I've slowed down a lot because I didn't like what I was doing. Now the quantity has decreased, but the quality is definitely on the rise.

—*an airline stewardess from California*

I've had fifty-five lovers that I can remember. That's not counting the ones I don't remember. I am not bragging. You see, I am a mobile woman and I've lived in quite a few different areas. But from my experiences I've found that men really don't care about you if you're only with them for one night. Not to be vulgar, but really, to them it's just another hole unless there are some emotions involved. And out of my fifty-five men that I can remember I can honestly say that only four satisfied me mentally, physically and emotionally. So I don't give myself so freely anymore. I don't look at the past with regret, I just chalk it up to the experience. But the past has influenced my present attitudes, and changed me and slowed me down.

—a saleswoman now living in Missouri

I am 30 years old and have had forty-five lovers. The funny thing is that I had most of them before I was 25. In the past five years I've only had three lovers. It seems that the older I get, the calmer I am.

—an actress from California

Having the option to have as many lovers as they choose seems to be something the women aren't likely ever to want to give up, but one which is nevertheless causing some of us more than a little confusion and conflict.

One woman summed this up with exceeding pungency—the telecommunications analyst, the woman who, in Chapter One, described eagerly shedding her virginity by telling her fellow student at the southwestern engineering college that she was afraid to be alone. After their affair broke up she had thirteen lovers over the next five years. Six were one-night stands; the balance were men with whom she had relationships of two months' to a year's duration. She says:

> Hooray! That's my main feeling about having lovers, but maybe I should change that to a qualified hooray. I love men and I love sex. I know a lot more about men and sex than my mom and my grandma put together. But my mom never has experienced the feeling of self-disgust after a disastrous one-night stand, she's never had sex with a man she didn't love, she's never had a man say "You were great baby" as he's putting on his pants to leave you thirty seconds after he's gotten his rocks off, she's never had to wonder what-in-the-hell-am-I-going-to-do-if-I'm-pregnant, she's never had to consider the possibility of VD and she's never had to hide things from her mother. I, on the other hand, have had all of these problems and more. I can't imagine living without feeling free to have lovers whenever I chose to do so, but life would be an awful lot less complicated.

4. Sexual Etiquette: How Quickly Do You Go to Bed?

MAJOR FINDINGS:

Thirteen percent of the women have often gone to bed with men during a first date.

Fifty-five percent have done so occasionally.

Thirty-two percent have never done so.

To a large extent it is age that determines the practice. The younger women, those aged 18 to 24, were somewhat less likely to go to bed on a first date than were the women over 24.

While there was much more sex in the 1950s, and even in the earlier decades of the twentieth century, than many of us today assume there was, sexual etiquette held that certain things simply weren't done. One such was sex on a first date. When I, for example, went to college in the fifties, although quite a number of my fellow freshmen were sexually experienced, another smaller group of girls was not only still innocent but still mortally wracked by the question: Should you let a boy kiss you goodnight on the first date? This group, for the most part, consisted of girls from small towns and rural areas. They got past the question quickly enough in their first year in college, but they did pause to reflect on it for a tortured (if short) time, and to have forceful attitudes and strong opinions pro and con.

The question had been handed down to them by the 1940s. War years. Years of social upheaval. In the family magazines of the time, there was some recognition of the fact that sexual etiquette might have to be amended to suit the sad realities. I came across an article written in the forties in which a woman reported a debate between her daughter and herself over whether or not a first-date kiss was permissible. The daughter said her friends believed in allowing this as an extra social fillip, provided the boy had been particularly attentive, or particularly polite in requesting it. The mother disagreed. A first-date kiss was never appropriate . . . well, *maybe*, if the boy was a soldier and was soon going overseas.

As for *sex* on the first date, I doubt the matter ever reached print in the forties. Nor did it reach it, except rarely, in the fifties. But had it done so—had for example, the subject been investigated by Kinsey (even he, intrepid as he was, didn't inquire about it)—there would surely have been relatively few voices raised in the wilderness to suggest that it was ever appropriate, under *any* circumstances. (Which, of course, is not to say that behavior did not often go beyond what was acceptable. But that is the point—it was not considered the norm, was not appropriate social behavior.)

Today, of course, we talk about it, and most of us have attitudes about the whens, whys and, above all, the with-whoms that make it appropriate or acceptable. A college-student respondent from the midwest writes:

> I sometimes go to bed with a guy on a first date. Definitely in the first week. I'd say I usually sleep with a guy before I truly get into having oral sex with him.

An ex-groupie:

> I used to have super, exciting sex with bands, like Kiss, Tull, Heart, etc. When I was a groupie I had sex very quickly. Usually the first night. Why? Because you might not have a second chance.

A 28-year-old computer technician:

> I like to get to know a man and find out if I care for him non-sexually before going to bed with him. My attitude has cost me a lot of men, but I don't care. If a man is ready to turn away from me just because I won't sleep with him right out, then that's the kind of thing I need to know about him, in order to decide if I *could* care for him non-sexually.

A divorced TV production assistant:

> I wait before making love with a man until we're comfortable with one another. I feel it makes all the difference. I'm still friends with most of my ex-lovers and I attribute this to not rushing into bed too quickly.

Moreover, not everybody who has sex on the first date feels too sanguine about it. Writes a 24-year-old from Colorado:

I have often had sex on a first date, whether I've wanted to or not. When I've done this on occasions when I really didn't want sex, it's been bad sex, and the man and I have ended up not wanting to see each other again. I suspect that if I'd said, "No, I don't want it tonight. Maybe another time," I might at least have kept a friend.

A 30-year-old from the same state offered:

I've had some terrible experiences with first-date sex. You just don't know what you're getting into. Which of us is such a good judge of character that she can really be sure the man she's been out with for just a few hours isn't cruel, coarse, crazy? I'd rather masturbate than repeat some of the experiences I've had with first-date sex. And I don't like masturbating that much. I love the intimacy of two bodies lying together. But I'll settle for my fingers anytime if I have to choose between them and a stranger.

Men are pressuring women into first-date sex, says this Missouri woman:

How quickly do I go to bed with a man? Immediately! It's a shame. I do it because there's just so much pressure to go to bed. There's a saying that friends become lovers, but lovers don't become friends, and that's been true for me —at least when I've rushed into sex.

And a Massachusetts woman agrees:

About half of the men I have gone to bed with, I have done so with on the first night. I feel the slower you are to get in bed, the better the chances are of having a meaningful relationship. But in today's world it's very hard not to go to bed with a man because they all expect sex. If you say no, they don't respect you. They think you're a prude and they don't want to know you.

But the California legal secretary whose story we have been tracking in previous chapters felt that men *preferred* waiting for sex:

I've had sexual intercourse with seventy-four lovers. Quite a high number for a 26-year-old single woman, but it's true. I've discovered a lot of men can't deal with women who give themselves too quickly, so although I used to go to bed on first and second dates often, I've tried to change my ways somewhat. These days I play coy or shy for about as long as possible to get their juices flowing and their lust going before the actual event takes place. A lot of one-night stands come about when you give in easily on the first date, so it's much better to hold men at bay, and make them await more heated and more anticipated sexual pleasures.

Like the secretary, a woman in the military service believed that making men wait for sex increases their appetite for it:

I am currently stationed on a large ship with approximately 1,100 males and forty-five females. I used to feel there was nothing wrong in two consenting adults making love on their first encounter, but I have changed my mind because it makes sex seem less special and exciting. For the past year I have been holding off on the sexual part of relationships until I have dated the men for some time. That way they look forward to it more.

(It's interesting that in the past it was men who presumed women would be more responsive and ready if they held off. They were the presumed manipulators, planners of the sexual act.)

Most women, however, were not rigid in the matter of first-date sex. The majority favored deciding each case on its merits. Typical of their attitudes were these letters:

If the feelings are right, I'll go to bed on a first night. But I'll never do it if the feelings aren't right.

—*a 21-year-old college student*

On a few occasions I have had sex with a man on the same night I met him, but I prefer to know a man well, as a friend, a companion, a playmate, a person, before having sex with him. I'll consider first-date sex when a man is really special.

—a 25-year-old motel manager

It happens when it happens. If I feel that a man is genuinely interested in more than just getting a little bit of sex, and if I have found something about his personality to make me feel I want to share myself physically with him, then it's fine. But some men take longer than others to reveal desirable personality traits, so I have waited as long as two years. In other cases, I have made love only five hours after meeting a man.

—a 27-year-old disk jockey

5. Sexual Etiquette: Have You Ever Gone to Bed with One Lover, and Then Another, in the Same Twenty-Four-Hour Period?

MAJOR FINDINGS:

Most of the women (53 percent) never do.
Thirty-five percent have done it once or twice.
Thirteen percent have done it occasionally.
One-point-five percent have done it frequently.

The story that follows comes from a New York City woman. She is divorced, 32, the mother of two young children, and works as an assistant producer in television:

I never thought, when I got divorced, that it would be easy to meet appropriate men. You know, men who would care not just for me but for my children too. Men I could consider seriously. I thought they'd be few and far between. To my surprise it wasn't as difficult as I'd thought. I guess it's because of all the divorces. There's a large pool of available men out there. After all, for every divorced woman, there's a divorced man.

Of course, I was looking for someone a little special. Someone with a lot to give, and a family sort of man. After my divorce I had an affair with one such guy, but we broke it off. Then I had a bad period. I withdrew. I was lonely. I was horny, but there was no one to make love with.

Then my friends came through. Someone introduced me to a very nice guy, a physicist. Not much in the conversational department but, you know, steady, kind. I started sleeping with him. I knew he wouldn't be the love of my life; he was too taciturn; we couldn't talk deeply to one another. But I was horny. And lonely. And there was good comfort just in our two bodies making contact. Then, at a Friday-night cocktail party, just before I was to meet the physicist for dinner and a sleep-over date at my house, another friend introduced me to another guy—a talkative, sensitive, attractive lawyer. I felt very turned on by him and I thought he was by me. He promised to call me first thing Saturday morning. What to do? I wondered if I ought to call off my date with T.—the physicist. Would I feel uncomfortable the next morning, getting up out of bed with him to make a bed date with the new guy? Suppose the new guy wanted to see me that very night? Would I feel uncomfortable if we ended up in the same bed T. and I had just lain on? And for sure it would have to be my bed. I don't sleep *out* with guys—because of my kids. Then I decided that even if I would feel uncomfortable, I couldn't chance calling off the night with T. Suppose the new guy *didn't* call? Why should I hurt T.'s feelings for nothing.

So we had our date. We went to bed. It's true my mind wasn't altogether on what we were doing, but that happens in the best of relationships and for all sorts of reasons. It could be work or the kids or anything. Then in the morning, first thing, sure as his word, the new guy called. T. was still in my bed. Worse, the new man wanted me to meet him at one o'clock for a walk in the park, with his kids and mine, and I knew, I just felt, that that night we would be making love.

Did I feel badly? Dirty? No. I just told T. I had to go into work because of a sudden crisis, got him to leave, and changed the sheets. That was my only concession to Emily Post. I knew I couldn't let a potentially ideal relationship slip away just because I had pretty feelings about not going to bed with two different men in one day. So I just compartmentalized. I shut down that part of my brain that said, Hey, you just had sex with T.—what are you *doing?* It wasn't difficult to do this. *After all, having sex isn't all that personal. Having a close relationship is.* (Author's italics.)

Men have always known this. That's why, with plenty of sex available to them, they'll still choose one girl over another, and want to be with her and her only. It isn't the act of love that makes them choose her, but other things. The way she talks, the things she says, her soul. Things like that are personal. I wouldn't want to bare my soul to every guy who comes strutting into my life. But I don't mind baring my body. I'm serious about this. You'll never catch me sharing my life history and my deepest thoughts with one man one night, and then telling these things all over again to another man the next. But sex? Sex is just a path in the road we take so that we can knock on the door of another person's soul and see if there's someone we like in there.

Sex as a path in the road we take to knock on the door of another person's soul. I was moved by the television producer's metaphor. For a long time after I learned her story, I kept thinking of the image she had used. It seemed almost emblematic of the *Cosmo* women. Seventy-four percent of them had said, when asked whether good sex was possible without love, that it was. But alongside the question, thousands of them had gone to the effort of penciling in onto their survey sheets, "Good sex is better with love" and "Sex is sex, love is love." And others had scrawled, "I've had a lot of sex partners, but only a few lovers."

Not only did it seem that a new sexual etiquette was developing, but also that a new vocabulary would soon evolve, and the word "lover" would be reserved for those few men who, in any woman's lifetime, touched her in more than a physical way.

Chapter Nine
Multiple Partners

1. The Spread of Group Sex

It has become largely acceptable throughout American society for a woman to have several—or even numerous—sexual partners over the course of her lifetime. This arithmetic of sex now causes relatively few heads to shake. But there is another component of sexual arithmetic that is startling and disconcerting to most Americans, but which nevertheless seems to be proliferating—the having of several, or numerous, sexual partners at the same time. Group sex. The spread of group sex was one of the more surprising developments on the sexual scene during the 1960s and '70s. Group sex began to flourish in those decades both in settings where it was prearranged (at organized mate-swapping parties and at sex clubs like Plato's Retreat in New York and Sandstone in California) and in accidental circumstances.

True, according to all studies participation in prearranged group sex has involved only a small percentage of the population. Nevertheless it has received a great deal of publicity and attention from the press. Less noted, but to my mind more significant, is the phenomenon of spur-of-the-moment group sex, for it seems to involve a larger number of young American women than many people recognize.

Among the *Cosmo* women only 11 percent of the sample had ever participated in an orgy, or gone to a sex club or partner-swapping party. But nearly 19 percent of the sample had experienced sex with more than one partner at the same time. It was multiple-partner sex that came about as an impulsive arrangement, the unexpected follow-up to a night of marijuana-smoking or cocaine-sniffing or drinking heavily with friends. A couple would pair off; a companion would hang about; soon all three would find themselves in bed.

This form of multiple-partner sex, rather than the ones more often written and talked about, is the more prevalent experience today.

Throughout history sexual utopians have dreamed idealistically about group sex and have invented ideologies to support and spur it. Some of their dreams have materialized in our time. Yet from the descriptions of the *Cosmo* women it would appear that the recent marked spread of group sex has far less to do with sexual ideology than it does with the pronounced spread of drug-taking. Regular marijuana and cocaine usage among college students has nearly doubled in the past decade, according to a 1981 study by a team of Harvard Medical School researchers. There has been an increase, if not necessarily proportional, in the population at large. Realizing such social change is crucial to understanding the group-sex experiences of the *Cosmo* women—experiences that until only yesterday seemed so unlikely that they were never even asked about in any national sex survey.

2. The Frequency of Group Sex

MAJOR FINDINGS:

Nineteen percent of the women had had sex, on at least one occasion, with more than one partner at the same time. Six percent had had such sex occasionally; 13 percent had had it one time only.

A surprisingly high percentage—nearly one-fifth—had experienced sex with more than one partner at the same time. Typically, the experience came about in an unplanned, unexpected way. A 32-year-old woman from California who had had multi-partner sex on five occasions wrote, "Four out of the five times I was high on pot. The fifth time I was high on booze." A college freshman from Ohio said, "I had sex with more than one partner this winter when two fellow students came to my dorm room at four o'clock in the morning. I was under the influence of cocaine." A college junior from California reported, "I had sex with two partners at once. I probably wouldn't have done it if it hadn't been for the cocaine and David Bowie singing 'Ziggy Stardust' on the stereo." And an established, successful businesswoman also attributed her one experience with two-partner sex to cocaine. She is 29 years old, owns her own business—a dance studio, where she instructs children, adults and professional dancers—and is active in her city's politics, sitting on and often chairing civic and cultural committees. Two years ago, when the events she describes took place, she was living with a man she has since married—but had gone on a vacation without him:

> I decided to spend my vacation down at the shore at my grandmother's house. I went alone, but once I was there I realized I didn't want to have to spend all my time just with my relatives. So I did something I've never done before or since. I went to a local disco, mainly to find a good dancer and have a fun night. I did find a nice guy, about my own age, and he turned out to be a pretty good dancer. We danced all night, and he bought me drinks and we talked. He had come with a friend, and when the club closed he and his friend invited me to their summer house for a few joints. Well, having been with grandma dear, and aunts and uncles, and therefore unable to get high, I jumped at the chance. I went with them. The summer house was neat and attractive and the pot was great. They also had loads of cocaine. I had never tried coke before but I was willing, and before I knew it I was having sex with both the men. At once. I kept asking them over and over whether they'd ever done this before, and they kept saying no. We partied until the morning, when I finally left.

Appraisals of this, the most usual kind of group sex, varied. The college junior who had been stimulated to try it by the music of David Bowie, said, "Although I probably would never have planned to have sex with more than one person at once, I'm glad

I did it. The pleasure was incredible—hands all over me, two men meeting my every desire, two men to receive everything I had to offer. I'd do it again if I had the opportunity."

But the California woman who had tried group sex five times said, "I'd always fantasized about sex with multiple partners, but through my experiments I found out 'pretend' was better than 'for real.' " She itemized the experiences and what occurred:

#1—two guys and me. All of us were novices, and the guys got to laughing so hard at feeling each other's hairy legs that we all gave up.

#2—one guy, my girlfriend, and me. He had a problem remembering there were two of us needing stimulation. Failure again. The two of us kicked him out.

#3—this was the booze time. Two guys, my sister, and me. Both the guys had staying-up problems. Frustration again.

#4 and 5—with my lover of the time, a married man, and his wife. I lived with them for a while, and we tried three-way sex twice. The sex was good, but obviously the situation was extremely stressful emotionally.

What kinds of women are likely to have sex with more than one person at the same time? It would seem, at first glance, that they would have to be highly uninhibited, independent women, free spirits who follow their sexual curiosities wherever they take them with not much concern for social convention. But from the survey letters it became apparent that this was not entirely the case. There were also women who were surprisingly timid, inhibited, and otherwise conventional. Indeed, it appeared that there were two distinct personality types among the women who had tried multiple-partner sex, two enormously different groups.

Typical of the first group was the legal secretary from California who gave up her virginity to "Pencil Dick." We have gotten to know her a little in previous chapters, heard about the seventy-four lovers she had had by age 26, listened to her cope lightheartedly with impotence and some male disdain for foreplay, grown familiar with her optimistic humor and devil-may-care bravado. Here she is at her high-spirited best in describing, with some mixed feelings, her mixed group-sex experiences:

I've done it three times. Twice with a once-a-month lover of mine and his male roommate, a cute guy I'd always liked. It happened this way. I went to their apartment. Apparently they'd already discussed the subject, and had some plan in mind before I'd even arrived. We'd smoked some pot and had some wine. I mostly feared for my reputation, and didn't think at first about the possible pleasures of the act. It turned out to be fantastic. I felt like a queen having two lovely men, both passionately out of their minds over me, taking turns on top, with the only pressure on me being that when one of them was not on top, he wanted my hands and lips to be engaged with his lips and body. I did not have an orgasm that night, as I was too self-conscious to relax, and too occupied (my hands were full, to say the least) to care. But even so, I had the time of my life, and when the two of them asked me for a repeat performance a week later, I gladly accepted.

The second time was not as much fun. I believe we were beginning to realize it's difficult enough to handle a one-man, one-woman relationship, let alone a two-man, one-woman relationship. I still keep regular company with my friend, although his roommate and I have just become friendly acquaintances, and it's a pleasant memory between us, but we never tried it again.

My third more-than-one-partner experience occurred while I was dating a musician and it involved his entire band (four members at that time). We went to a party and enjoyed ourselves considerably. The next thing I knew, everyone in the band was in the bedroom, and my boyfriend and I had been invited to participate in whatever was going on in there. I figured it was some unappealing drug I'd have to turn down, but when I looked around the bedroom, I was shocked. The band members were lounging around on the bed, with no clothes on, and watching a bar waitress and one of their ever-present groupies kissing and fondling each other. I'd never seen a lesbian act before, and I must admit I was quite mesmerized at the whole thing. The next thing I remember my boyfriend was starting (although reluctantly) to strip me of my precious clothing, and was doing the same thing to himself. But I could tell his heart wasn't really in it, and so we just kissed and petted each other as the rest of the band began what I can only call an orgy. The next thing that happened was, I sat up, looked my boyfriend in the eye, and asked if he wanted a cigarette. Since we could have had a cigarette right there in the bedroom, we both knew my question meant, Get your clothes on, we're leaving. Which is just what we did. I didn't feel bad the next day. The boys in that band were crazy ones to say the least, and since some of my close girlfriends knew the band, and dated them on and off themselves, I enjoyed telling them the story.

The seemingly unflappable legal secretary from California is a woman who feels "great" about today's sexual atmosphere. "It's given me a chance to taste all the erotic delicacies life has to offer although it has also often given me some nightmarish episodes—the semi-rapes, the unwanted orgy parties, and the rest of the trials and tribulations of the single girl's existence. But that's life, as they say, and what would life be like without sex?"

But the legal secretary represents only one side of the group-sex spectrum—a woman who has sex, even the most exotic far-out forms of sex, with *sangfroid,* pretty well convinced that she does only what she wants to do, and exercises control over her choices.

On the other end of the spectrum is a 22-year-old court reporter from the south. She first had sex when she was 17 with a steady boyfriend. "We went to a party and got—as my friends call it—'commode-huggin' drunk.'" But unlike the legal secretary—who had welcomed first sex even though it had not been physically pleasurable—the court reporter felt "mostly fear and guilt and kept hearing in my mind Peggy Lee singing, "Is That All There Is?"

In the intervening five years, the court reporter has had twenty lovers, and last year she had sex with two partners at the same time:

I went to a college football game with a man I had met only recently. I remember that I was in a daring mood, and when this man said he had an extra ticket for the game, but doubted whether I'd come down and use it, I took him up on it and even arrived the night before the game. We made love several times that night, and I felt good about it. The next day, at the game, I met his friend. I was instantly attracted to him. At the after-game party, the two of them began feeling me out on the subject of group sex. I was a little apprehensive but I was still in a daring mood, and since I felt sexually confident about the first man, and attracted to the other, I finally agreed to try it.

The event itself took place in a nearly pitch-black room, which made me feel more comfortable, even though I generally prefer dim to moderate light. The men did nothing sexual to one another, except watch each other, but they each engaged in prolonged and intense foreplay simultaneously on me. They seemed quite at ease in this situation and I later found out they had engaged in this kind of arrangement several times before. Their practice paid off, because they were able to get me to climax six times that night, two of the times being multiple orgasms —my first. The men themselves climaxed once each in roughly two hours of sex play, during which I orally and manually stimulated them, and then had intercourse with each. They climaxed within minutes of each other. It was a sensually exciting night, but I had difficulty in coping with it emotionally.

Unlike the legal secretary, the court reporter is a woman who feels that the chief reason she has sex—and in particular the chief reason she tried something as socially disapproved of as two-partner sex—is that men expect it of her. "It is hard to say 'no' to men these days," she explained, "and the men I've met know this. So they tend to be very self-centered and demanding. It is sad, but any Joe Blow today can be a stud, and a woman is obligated to give in to him sexually because sex has become mandatory."

When women like the court reporter, who felt extremely uptight about sex, experienced two-partner sex, they did so out of acquiescence rather than out of desire, worrying that unless they agreed they would be considered prudish or uninteresting.

While two-partner sex is still highly untraditional, a considerable amount of it seems to spring from the traditional female fear of not being able to catch a man. As an unmarried colleague put it recently, "Not being able to say 'no' to one is bad enough, but not being able to say 'no' to two is worse."

3. Threesomes: One Woman/Two Men

MAJOR FINDINGS:

Of those women who had experienced sex with
more than one partner at the same time, the majority
—59 percent—had had two male partners.

In fantasies, women will often experience equal enthusiasm for
multiple-female-partner sex as for multiple-male-partner sex. In
reality, there is more enthusiasm for, and more practice of, multiple-
male-partner sex, at least among the *Cosmo* women. It is no wonder,
for the two experiences have entirely different psychological motivations among heterosexual women, and the *Cosmo* women were
markedly heterosexual. Interestingly, these motivations are so particular that they can make multiple-female-partner sex seem degrading or shocking even to women who find nothing at all unac-
ceptable about multiple male partners.

Once again to the legal secretary from California, who illus-
trates this unique double standard: When the lover with whom she
was eventually to have two-partner sex first mentioned group sex
to her, she thought it "disgusting." They were out on a date and "he
told me about a *ménage-à-trois* he'd had with two girls, and how great
it had been. I told him, 'How disgusting. You'd have to tie me down
and force the act.' It wasn't appealing at all. But when it came out
that he was trying to have me have sex with him and
roommate, that put it in a different light."

Many letters from women who had not tried group sex, but
who said they had considered it, indicated similar feelings. Typical
was this comment from a 24-year-old Nevada woman who had
been toying with the idea: "I told my lover maybe. I told him I'd
maybe do it with two men. It might be nice to have all that luscious
attention paid just to me. But I'd never do it with another woman
and a man. I'm much too selfish and insecure to share."

Clearly, sex with a male partner and another female was
viewed as potentially demeaning, an unwanted sharing, while sex
with two male partners was viewed as at least potentially ego-
salving, a special event for the woman . . . the situation promised
to make her feel flattered, the central figure in a bedroom drama, the
magnet of two males' attention and, better, competition. One such
woman is a 34-year-old from Texas who has tried two-partner sex

twice. She says of herself, "I guess that I love being 'the star'—surprising or startling a man, having his undivided attention, and making him remember me as someone special. And being the star for two men is even better."

But while playing a starring role was often the underlying motive for two-male-partner sex, it sometimes turned out that the women felt, in the end, like bit players:

A 38-year-old from Pennsylvania who tried two-male-partner sex on three occasions said:

> I found it boring. The men talked to each other a lot, and not much to me.

A 21-year-old bookkeeper from Wyoming who tried two-male-partner sex once said:

> The men were a friend of mine and his friend. One "rested" and watched while the other entered me. Then they changed positions. It was sexy, but later I felt rotten about it because I was nothing but a hole to fill to those two guys, no matter how I pretended it was flattering that both wanted me so.

A 34-year-old from Alabama said:

> I had sex with two men twice, both times with my husband and another man. I didn't find it especially enjoyable. I found I was too concerned about not making one or the other of them feel left out. I also found that my own enjoyment took a back seat to theirs.

And a 20-year-old from New Jersey who described herself as "a person who wants to try everything at least once" said:

> I had sex with two guys after a party. Everybody got drunk and, mostly, everybody went home. But seeing that I am a liberated woman of the '80s, I stayed out. What a dumb move. The boy who had given the party said, "Okay. Who wants to sleep in my bed?" His girlfriend was still there, passed out in the living room, but I said, "Great idea," and so did a boy I'd met at the party, a friend

of the host. We got undressed. Both the guys touched and teased me. We kissed and caressed. Then the host put his tiny penis in my mouth while the other boy started to go down on me. I was bored to death! I did not have an orgasm and I hated myself for letting these men see my body. It was great fun for them. Not for me.

In general, reactions to sex with two men were more negative than positive. While some of the women said they had found it extremely exciting on a physical level, nearly all commented that this was largely offset by disappointment on the emotional level.

Which is why, one suspects, that while 19 percent of the *Cosmo* respondents had tried two-partner sex, only 6 percent had tried it more than once.

4. Threesomes: Two Women/One Man

MAJOR FINDINGS:

Of those women who had experienced sex with more than one partner at the same time, 42 percent had had both a male and a female partner.

As in the previous combination of group sex, one male and two female partners can and do get together in bed without planning. A 24-year-old from Georgia describes how she came to it:

I did it because a) the man was the sexiest thing I had ever seen; b) I had been inundated with pro-*ménage à trois* material at the time so it didn't seem so weird; c) I knew the other girl quite well; d) we were all high on champagne and my first cocaine.

And a 21-year-old from Connecticut says:

I recently had my first experience of sex with two people —another woman and a man. The woman and I were very

close friends. Mostly, she and I got it off sexually while
the man watched.

I might do it again, if the situation ever presented
itself again, but I would have to be in the right frame of
mind. We were very drunk, coked up, etc.

But more often than in two-male-partner sex, two-female-
partner sex was arranged in advance, usually by the male in the
triangle. A 22-year-old from Georgia had been working as a waitress in a nightclub featuring nude dancers, and she had become
involved with a married customer who, she said, "can only be
described by the word 'lusty.' He kept the dancers too busy to
dance, as they were practically standing in line to go out with him
after work." She was very proud when this man left his wife and
moved in with her, but she knew that "he was the type who would
never pass up anything that was offered to him" and consequently:

> I made up my mind I would just have to work at keeping
> him happy. So when he suggested we try adding another
> girl to our love fests, I went along with it. It was erotic to
> plan it as well as to do it. We planned it for months ahead.
> It isn't something you could just try on the spur of the
> moment with just anyone. There are a lot of feelings in-
> volved, and compatibility is important. He found the
> other girl, and we did it, and it turned out better than I'd
> expected. In the morning, waking up sober, I didn't have
> the guilt feelings I'd expected to have, and after she left,
> my guy and I talked the events over and over, and he got
> excited again and we started planning for another time.

Similarly, a 47-year-old from Oklahoma had, when she was 37, a
fairly lengthy affair with a man she met in a bar shortly after
separating from a long marriage. In her marriage she had not been
orgasmic. "I had never been turned on by sex," she said. Nor had
she even thought nudity agreeable. "I had always been ashamed to
show my body." But the new man changed all that:

> We went around his house in the nude, and had sex any-
> where the mood struck us, and it was a whole new world
> for me, so when he suggested we bring another woman
> into our sex play, I was all for it. I let him pay a prostitute

> to come to our home and perform cunnilingus on me. I loved it. But the greatest turn-on was afterwards when he had sex with her. I watched them and I couldn't help masturbating the whole time.

In both these cases the third woman was a paid participant and the women themselves had met their male partners in somewhat shady bars. But the same pattern of having the "other" woman selected by the male emerged in circles in which nude dancers and prostitution played no part. Men would obtain a second female partner for the triad by calling upon an old girlfriend.

The situation was sometimes agreeable:

> I had sex with two people, one male, the other female. I met the man at a fashionable disco and was very attracted to him. We started off talking and soon, during the next few weeks, were occasionally having sex together. We discussed our fantasies with one another and I mentioned the fantasy of having sex in a threesome. One day soon after, I received a call from another girlfriend of this man, a woman I had never met. She told me she was interested in getting together with me and that like me she had fantasized about making love with a female. Well, one day, she, me, and the guy got together at his place. Everything just clicked. We liked each other a lot, both mentally and physically. Of course, we were all nervous. But it happened fairly easily. The other woman and I made love to each other very tenderly, and the guy joined in. It only occurred twice, as I soon moved away. But we all stayed in touch for a long time.
>
> —a 26-year-old from Virginia

More often it produced feelings of jealousy:

> I was married for ten years until last year and now I am experiencing (without guilt) many fantasies I harbored for years. A short while ago I met the "other girlfriend" of a man I've cared deeply about ever since meeting him in Bermuda a few months ago. This man and I see each other about once a week, always ending up in bed, and he dates this other woman too, and I also date other men. Anyway,

the three of us had dinner out, and talked and got acquainted. Then we went back to this man's apartment. After much drinking and drugs, we made love together. First the other woman and I shared our boyfriend, then we explored and made love to each other. It was delightful, really. I enjoyed pleasing both of them, but I was very jealous when watching them make love.

—a 31-year-old from Massachusetts

Some of the women felt they were being asked to share not just the male partner's sexual favors, but his affection as well. When this was their feeling, they usually decided the excitement derived from the experience was not worth it:

I've had sex with one of my lovers and another woman, a friend of his. I found it quite nice. At first I felt guilty, but then I asked myself, Why? I realized there was no reason. Nobody gets hurt. So why not. All three of us had a good time pleasing each other. But I don't think I would do it again because I don't like sharing. All the times I did do it I was not straight. I was tipsy a few times, and high on pot and cocaine the others.

—a 24-year-old from Florida

I'm upper-middle-class and recently married for the second time. I'm extremely happy in all respects. I had two-partner sex in my previous marriage. It was all right. It was with my ex and a good girlfriend of mine. We (the girlfriend and I) didn't really have sex, we just performed sex on my ex-husband. It was all right, and maybe I'd enjoy it again, but I don't want to share *this* husband.

—a 24-year-old from Colorado

And one woman, who had tried it several times and decided not to repeat it, wrote:

I can't think of anyone who is ready emotionally for the experience of seeing a man she imagined she was giving the thrills of his life to suddenly turn from her and moan and groan as he comes because of another woman. I don't care how excited she gets from having that other woman fondle and caress her, or from doing it to the other woman, or having the man in the middle with one hand on each of you. There always comes that moment of truth when he gets it off, and he's panting just as loud from being in her, as being in you, or from touching her, as touching you, or from her lips on him as from yours. It makes you feel so trivial, so unimportant that the turn-on isn't worth it.

—a 28-year-old from California

Even those women who had liked two-female-partner sex more than this California woman tended to evaluate the experience in unusually bland language. There was the woman who said, "I found it quite nice." The one who said, "It was all right." The one who termed it "delightful, really." This was a far cry from the unreserved language the same women used in their letters when describing other sorts of sexual experiences. In fact, when evaluating two-female-partner sex, the *Cosmo* women sounded just a bit stuffy or polite, as if they were describing a luncheon, or endorsing a new product for a television ad. As if, in short, they were unwilling, being presumably "cool" women, to acknowledge the depth and intensity of their negative feeling.

5. Sex Clubs, Orgies and Partner-Swapping Parties

MAJOR FINDINGS:

Seventeen percent of the respondents had attended sex clubs, orgies, or partner-swapping parties. Eleven percent had attended such events only once; 4 percent had attended occasionally; 1 percent had attended often. Of those who had attended, only 11 percent had participated in the sexual activities; the others had been observers.

Based on the above figures it would appear that quite a number of women today have been curious enough about sex clubs, orgies and partner-swapping parties to attend them, and to a considerably lesser extent even to participate in them. Few, however, relished the experience enough to become habitués of these activities. This is not to say that there weren't some *Cosmo* women who spoke enthusiastically of these kinds of group sex, but they were fewer than promoters of group sex might have expected.

In the matter of sex clubs, only one woman, a 34-year-old from a suburb near New York City and a devotee of Plato's Retreat, was enthusiastic. And the subject of orgies evoked unanimous complaint. The *Cosmo* women had been to all manner of orgies: the organized kind to which male participants must bring a female partner and pay an admission fee; the unplanned, noncommercial kind that happens among friends, usually in connection with getting "stoned"; and even religious-cult-group orgies. A 26-year-old from Mississippi who was a frequent participant at commercial orgies said:

> Sometimes it was good. Mostly it was a total burn-out. At these orgies, I sometimes had sex with as many as three men at once. I prefer one at a time. Three men at once are very hard to please. They think you're a machine. Or that you're made of rubber. One wants this while the other wants that. It's tiring.

A 23-year-old from upstate New York who had been part of a spontaneous orgy told a particularly sad story:

> I was part of an orgy when I was 18. It was after a party. I had sex with five of the guys there. I'd never do it again. I became pregnant afterwards, even though I was using an IUD, and I didn't know whose child it was.

And a former member of a religious cult, a 29-year-old from California, wrote:

> I joined a religious cult on my 18th birthday. After I'd spent two months with them I had a husband "chosen" for me. Unfortunately he was someone I loathed. But fortunately he did not like sex, so we only "knew" each other four or five times—and only because there was group pressure to produce children. (I have two as a re-

sult.) I remained in the cult for five years, gaining power and leadership. The cult's views on sex kept changing, and one day the top dog said that God had told him that He wanted us to share all things, bodies included. So now I entered into orgies—called "sharing experiences"—with the other leaders. A number of the male leaders outranked me in power, and so I was used at their whim. The sex was all right, but the experience sure taught me the value of having sex with someone you care about, and having it with that someone *alone.*

Partner-sharing had more support than sex clubs or orgies did. A 35-year-old woman from Virginia praised both its sexual and affectional role in her life:

> I'm just your average, medium-sized-town housewife who is into mate swapping about once a month. No kidding. We are doing it even in Virginia! Actually it's not quite as sordid as it sounds. My husband and I became intimate with our best friends about three years ago and have been carrying on ever since. It began very innocently and worked its way to swapping, and now has turned into a lasting beautiful thing for all four of us. The emphasis is now more on friendships, shared growth, mutual likes and dislikes, and meaningful time spent together, than it is on sex, though for myself I'll add that sex from someone new, with a different perspective, adds quite a bit to a ten-year-old marriage.

Often the women would find themselves more attracted to or more satisfied by the new man. Then they secretly would move from sharing themselves with the new man in front of their husband's eyes to having sex with this man in private. A 32-year-old Pennsylvania woman, who meets the "other" man for secret sex, described the situation and its emotional complexities:

> My husband and I have been married for ten and a half years. Our marriage was very good on all counts except in bed. Sex never seemed quite as exciting or important to me as it did in the days when we were dating back in college. We had numerous discussions and occasional fights about this. My husband accused me of not loving

him because I didn't care much about having sex with him and I kept insisting that I *did* love him, and I'd say, "I guess my sex drive is just not as strong as yours." The fact was that I was only trying to smooth his ruffled feathers. I really didn't care and it bothered me, but I didn't know what to do about it. I had orgasms whenever we tried hard enough, but most of the time I didn't even really want to make the effort.

One thing we fought about was that he wanted us to have sex occasionally with other people. We even tried it several times with one or two others, male and female, and he loved it. I *didn't*. This finally seemed to become the focal point of all his frustrations. When one day last spring I finally put my foot down and refused to ever do it again, he hit the ceiling. His feeling was that I thought sex was dirty. And if I thought that, I must also think *he* was bad for enjoying it. Maybe he was right, I don't know what was behind my attitude.

Anyway at this point he'd had it with our marriage. Because of our two children he didn't walk out but he announced to me that he intended to find women who *would* respond to him, and for several days that were hell to me I think he did just that. Finally in desperation I approached his best friend, who is the husband of my best friend. I'd been physically attracted to this man—I'll call him Rob—for years. What I wanted was for the three of us to try it in bed. I figured that since I liked Rob, maybe I could fake liking group sex and convince my husband that I was at least willing to try to change for him.

Rob said sure, he'd try it, and my husband reluctantly said okay, not believing for a minute that I could change. But that afternoon I surprised him. And myself even more —I *loved* it. I had I don't know how many orgasms and, after several hours, both the men were worn out but I wasn't. My husband was convinced that I had gotten over my sexual problems, and over the next few months sex between us was great.

Rob, who still joins us in bed occasionally, never really got used to the idea of making love to someone else's wife while that someone was there watching. He was always slightly uncomfortable when we were to-gether. He made it clear to me that although he enjoyed it with the three of us, what he really wanted was to be with me alone. Neither of us had ever had an affair [a nice distinction] before, but we finally got up enough nerve and began meeting alone.

That is still going on and sex between Rob and me is also sensational, sometimes even more so than between my husband and me. My husband doesn't know that we meet in private. Sometimes I think he may suspect it but that in a funny way he doesn't mind. After all, he was the one who wanted me to be a truly sexual person. Rob's wife doesn't know a thing. Sometimes when the four of us are together we seem to be heading for some kind of four-way sex play, but that hasn't happened yet. I feel lucky. I have a lover who is also a dear friend, and a husband who will allow me to express my sexuality in all kinds of new ways. But there have been times I was worried that Rob and I might fall in love with each other and ruin two marriages. We don't want this to happen. Our respective marriages mean more to us than the affair, and that's the way we want it.

A 26-year-old New York woman who *has* fallen in love with the "other" man in a partner-sharing arrangement wonders where the situation will end:

> I met the man I'm living with nearly two years ago. At the beginning of our relationship we made love in every position imaginable, in every corner of his apartment. All my sexual fantasies were fulfilled, and because I could be myself with this man (I enjoyed him physically as well as mentally) I moved in with him.
>
> We never discussed partner-sharing. I'd fantasized about it, but the thought of really making it with another man and my lover in the same room made me feel guilty, and the thought of making it with another woman embarrassed me. It didn't occur to me that my lover wanted to try things like this until after we'd been together for some time. Then it came up. We talked about sharing. We both said we had fantasized about it and wouldn't mind trying it, provided it could be done in a situation where neither of us would get hurt feelings.
>
> One day soon after, my lover's best friend, I'll call

him Tommy, was alone with me in the apartment. (I should add that Tommy had a very attractive girlfriend.) Tommy asked me what I thought of him as a person. We ended up talking for hours. We came to realize how much we had in common, and he finally told me that he wanted to make love to me. I told him that I'd like the same thing but, not wanting to mislead him, I added that it would have to be with his girl and my lover. After the initial shock, he was thrilled.

The four of us sat down and talked openly about everything, got drunk and ended up having a wild time. Since then (about six months ago), we've been meeting regularly every two or three weeks.

I don't always reach orgasm when we have our intimate meetings, but the physical and mental pleasure is so great that I truly feel satisfied the next morning.

Sometimes we all wake up and just start all over again, while other times we just get up and begin a new day. It's really an odd and exciting feeling walking down the street with three close friends and knowing that what we experience together is something rare and magnificent.

Tommy's girlfriend has become the best friend (as far as a girl is concerned) I've ever had. We share secrets, good times (in and out of bed) and lovers.

As for Tommy, however, here's where the sad truth comes. You see, Tommy and I have discovered that we love the same, feel the same about everything. We've discovered what love between two people really means. It's not just a physical attraction or an understanding of personal needs. Tommy and I love each other, but we also love the two other people involved. We don't want to hurt them. I'm sure you're wondering where this kind of relationship can eventually lead. I don't know the answer myself.

This New York woman seems to have understood, if on a subsconscious level, that she could avoid her feelings of jealousy and competition in a four-way-sex situation if she was the one who chose the partners for that situation. By making the extra male a man who had already revealed a strong interest in her, she gave herself the emotional upper hand over both her lover and Tommy's girlfriend. For her and Tommy, the four-way-sex situation appears to have been a success; for her lover and Tommy's girlfriend, it is most likely another story. They are not really equal sexual sharers, more outsiders.

This is a familiar pattern in open marriage and partner-sharing arrangements. It is rare that the situation gives equal satisfaction to all members of the sexual quadrangle. Usually it is the instigator— the person who first proposes four-way sex or who selects the partners—who benefits the most, while the accommodator—the person who merely goes along with the idea because it sounds erotic —feels he or she is being shortchanged. Usually the instigator has in mind not just extra sex but extra attachment, and has chosen a partner to obtain it from.

But it *can* happen that it is the accommodator who becomes emotionally attached to a new partner. Merely by suggesting the arrangement, the instigator has made the accommodator feel a little less loved than usual, and a hidden urge for a new attachment emerges and develops.

Many, reasoning that sex is merely a physical activity, believe that it cannot threaten their primary relationship. But sex and emotions—especially over a period of time—can rarely be kept separate, never mind the degree of liberation or sophistication. So it is common for people to discover that they or their partners have become emotionally entangled with another member of the sexual quadrangle—and subsequently to find their primary relationship on the rocks.

The emotional complexities of sustained group-sex arrangements have been reported by numerous investigators. Gilbert Bartell, an anthropologist who studied the budding phenomenon back in 1971, reported in his book *Group Sex* that although in its idealized conception group sex was thought to be a system that could flourish without jealousy, in actuality envy and competition frequently marred group arrangements. Morton Hunt, who studied group sex among the Playboy Foundation men and women, also found that it was often accompanied by considerable emotional stress and wrote that while group sex could be "a temporary release from confinement and responsibility, and a brief chance to live out one's wildest fantasies . . . its advantages are heavily outweighed by the manifold conflicts, emotional problems and practical dangers involved." He concluded that because of these conflicts, problems and dangers, ritualized group-sex experiences were not likely ever to appeal to any great group of Americans.

The *Cosmo* research would seem to bear out this opinion. Although some women found their experiences highly erotic, most felt the emotional stresses had outweighed the sexual advantages. But the statistics are even more telling than the letters and opinions. While more than a tenth of the women had attempted through sex clubs, orgies and partner-swapping to live out that most common of female fantasies—sex with multiple partners at the same time— only a minuscule 1 percent had chosen to repeat these experiences "often."

Chapter Ten
Infidelity

1. The Rise in Women's Infidelity

If multiple-partner sex seems a shocking, late-twentieth-century development, there is another matter of sexual arithmetic that is as old as David and Bathsheba—infidelity, the having of more than one sexual partner while committed, either through marriage or a living-together arrangement, to erotic loyalty.

Throughout history men have courted women who were not their wives. And, in fact, there was always more female infidelity than is generally realized. Starting with Bathsheba, and continuing on through Helen of Troy to Phaedra, Augustus' daughter Julia, Isolde, Francesca da Rimini, Queen Caroline of England, Madame Bovary and Anna Karenina, the pages of history and literature bear witness to a parade of adulterous women. But today, women's infidelity has been rising precipitously. While in the past some women were unfaithful, today many are.

A number of factors have contributed to the increase in female infidelity. Contraception is one. But so too are obstetrical advances. In England as late as the 1880s, the average female had a life expectancy of only forty-six years, and it was expected, rather than astonishing, that she might die in childbirth. Women in the past *feared* sex and childbirth. And the very changes that made them cease to fear and begin to enjoy it, are also contributors to the rise in their adultery rates.

239

But while many women today have, on occasion, been adulterous, they do not necessarily *believe* in adultery—that is, admire it and proselytize for it. A large number of the *Cosmo* women have been unfaithful, yet four-fifths of the women disapprove of infidelity and wish that both they and their husbands could be sexually faithful. The urge for sexual loyalty seems to be a powerful and omnipresent female yearning. Why there is sometimes a discrepancy between this yearning and a woman's actions is a major theme explored in this chapter.

Also investigated is a new and confusing matter: the question of fidelity not between husbands and wives but between men and women who live together, trying to carve out new social rules; and an old and confusing one—single women's affairs with married men.

2. Marital Infidelity

MAJOR FINDINGS:

Fifty-four percent of the women who were married had had one or more sexual experiences with partners other than their husbands since marrying.

Not only are affairs outside marriage today far more common among women than they used to be, but wives today also tend to feel as free—or perhaps entitled—to have affairs as husbands used to feel. Kinsey found that about half his men and a *quarter* of his women had had extramarital sex. A quarter century later the *Cosmo* survey has found extramarital sex among about *half* its women. So it would appear that extramarital sex is today twice as common among women as it was twenty-five years ago, and that it is exactly as common as it used to be among men. Apparently, as suggested, women now feel that infidelity, once chiefly a male province, is theirs to explore as well.

But what about men? Are they more or less adulterous today than women are? No definitive study of male infidelity has appeared in recent years, but the 1981 *Hite Report on Male Sexuality* addressed the matter and reported that among the 7,239 men who agreed to write about their sexual experiences for that book, 72 percent of those who were or had been married had been unfaithful. This figure suggests that male infidelity is still outstripping female infidelity, and that it is doing so at about the same rate as it was in Kinsey's time.

Whether or not the Hite or the *Cosmo* findings on adultery will prove, as Kinsey's did, to be representative of Americans as a whole is a matter only time and further sex research will tell. Meanwhile, most observers of the American sexual scene would probably concur that infidelity has risen dramatically, both among men *and* women, since the days of the Kinsey reports. Half of American marriages today end in divorce, and there is a tendency on the part of men and women who are on the verge of divorce to attempt at least one extramarital affair prior to separating.

Nevertheless, and despite the growing prevalence of infidelity, our society's marital goal is still, emphatically, the traditional one of fidelity. Among the *Cosmo* women who had been unfaithful to marital partners, there were many who still believed strongly in fidelity despite having eschewed it. A twice-married 32-year-old woman from Georgia, who was unfaithful in her first marriage but has been completely faithful in the second, stated what was a typical attitude:

> Although I had three affairs during my first marriage, I believe in fidelity. To have an affair breaks a trust and shows a lack of love and respect. I had to break the trust in my first marriage. I was married to a man who showed no sexual interest in me whatsoever. This made it impossible for me to tolerate the marriage. But you don't just wake up one day and realize that what you ought to do is divorce. It doesn't happen that way. First, you think, well, maybe if I had an affair I could keep the marriage going. So you do that. It's only after a while that you realize that if you're willing to jeopardize your marriage this way it probably isn't worth holding on to. It took me five years and three affairs to get up the gumption to let go of my first marriage. Now I've been married for the second time for five years, with no affairs. Why? Because I love my second husband, have a good sex life with him and wouldn't want to jeopardize this marriage. So even though I've sometimes been attracted to other men—one

just is, you know—I'd never ever have an affair. This marriage is just too precious to me.

Like this Georgia woman, most of the *Cosmo* women expressed a strong liking for the concept of fidelity. Eighty percent of the sample affirmed that they wished for fidelity on their partner's part, and the vast majority of the mail was in favor of mutual sexual loyalty. This marital goal was most firmly expressed by young women and by women who had never been married. For them infidelity was unthinkable and even contemptible. They wrote such things as:

> I have recently decided to share the rest of my life with a man. As far as fidelity is concerned, I believe that once two people are ready to make a commitment, fidelity must be part of it. Period. It's easier said than done, but I believe it is absolutely necessary if they are to maintain a bond of trust in their relationship. If you aren't willing to forsake sex with all others except your mate, you aren't ready to form a relationship.
>
> —*a 26-year-old woman from Wyoming who has had six lovers*

> I am not living with a man right now, but who knows, perhaps I soon will be. When I do, I will be faithful. I believe in fidelity. I feel that's the way love should be, one man and one woman together forever sexually. I may sound hysterical to you, considering I've had so many lovers, but in the last year and a half I've changed, and now I want just one man in my life forever.
>
> —*a 23-year-old from Wisconsin who has had thirty lovers*

> I am currently maintaining a separate residence from my man, but entertaining the idea of sharing a home with him. I will not marry him until I am convinced that I will always be able to be in that percentage of people who can stay faithful to their spouses, and that he will be in that percentage too.
>
> —*a 24-year-old from Arizona who has had twenty-five lovers*

> When and if I ever marry, I know that I will be faithful. I think that if a person makes her decision wisely, she

won't have to be unfaithful. I would also hope that my husband will be faithful. I don't know what I would do if I married a man and found out he wasn't faithful. But I imagine I will make a man a good enough wife and lover so that he wouldn't want to stray.

—a 22-year-old from Michigan who has had nine lovers

I am about to get married. I love my fiancé and I know neither he nor I would ever do such a terrible thing to each other as be unfaithful. Doing something like that is totally unforgivable and never justifiable, at least not in this day and age when people can have sex before they get married and so can be sure that the person they are marrying is satisfying to them.

—a 22-year-old from New York who has had eight lovers

Obviously the young and unmarried do not always take into account what can go wrong in marriage, the sexual and emotional provocations that can cause even strong believers in fidelity to stray. Would these younger women, one wonders, feel contempt for the woman whose story follows, a considerate grandmother from Pennsylvania? Or would her words help them to understand the complex wellsprings of—and, yes, even loyalties behind—some adultery?

I am 58 years old. I was married at age 26 to a man seven years older than myself. The double standard was very strong in those days, so although he had had a lot of sexual experience he expected to marry a virgin. And he did. He was my first and only lover until six months ago. We had sex three times a week most of our lives, then for the last ten years about once a week, and I was true to him and he was true to me for thirty-two years. I was true to him even though sex with him was never interesting to me. He never turned me on. Or, who knows, maybe I just didn't give it a one-hundred-percent effort. But I did always try to make it good for him. I never refused him sex. Never, even when I really *did* have a headache.

Still, I don't think it was bad sex that drove me at last, after all those years, to have an affair. It just happened. I think it happened because my husband, as he got older, stopped being interested in anything except his job, his beer, his TV and our home. With all the children—there were four of them—grown and out of the house, I'd be bored to tears. But I could never get him to go out, or even to have friends in. I have lots of interests. I love hiking, dancing, beachcombing, visiting museums, driving. But my husband just likes to stay at home. So eventually I had to start filling my time on my own.

Six months ago I met a man of 65 (the same age as my husband) who likes to do all the things I like to do. He is divorced and has been alone for five years. We've gone driving and hiking and gallery-hopping together, and one weekend we went sightseeing to another city and stayed in a motel. During our two-day stay there, we had sex. We had it twice that weekend. I couldn't believe a 65-year-old man could be so loving and caring and exciting. Although I didn't have an orgasm, as I was very nervous, I believe I could have one with him, and next time we have sex I hope I will. My new friend and I are both so happy we're in heaven. We feel 16 again.

I thought I'd feel guilty but I don't. Since my husband has settled for old age, whereas I'm still full of pep and energy, what's wrong with this? My only trouble is that my friend doesn't like my being married. But what can I do? I could never leave my husband. After all these years of our being together, I think it would kill him. He was never a man who liked change. That's why he just loves to do nothing but go to his same old job and come home and watch TV. He's such a stick-in-the-mud. If I upset the applecart, he'd probably just die.

Of course, the Pennsylvania grandmother is an unusual adulterer. She resisted sexual temptations for years, and only succumbed to them after her husband had clearly withdrawn not just from her but from any sort of active life altogether. But what of this next story, again from a Pennsylvanian, this time a woman in her forties. She lives in a town in the western part of her state, a town that sounds very much like the sort of place depicted in the movie *The Deerhunter.* The letter-writer, like her grandmother and her mother before her, married young after an unwanted pregnancy, and each generation of women handed down to the next a legacy of sexual and emotional despair:

I grew up in a small steel town where almost everyone was Polish and everyone knew everyone else's business. My grandmother and grandfather were immigrants. She became pregnant before they were married, and then they had seven or eight children and they fought a lot and he beat her. My mother got pregnant at eighteen and got married so she could get out of that house, but she only moved next door. My father didn't beat her, but they fought a lot too, with lots of bad language between them. I had very little love and holding and right after high school I made love in a car and got pregnant and got married.

I'm 41 now and I've been married for twenty years. My husband likes cars and machines. I guess he likes sex too, but he is very cold and shows no outward sign of emotion. He doesn't even blink when I touch him. It's always been that way, since I can remember. But now we have had no sex for the past four years, except three times, and those times it was mostly my doing.

All these years my husband had his Friday nights out alone. Then it was stock cars, and so then it was Wednesday and Friday nights out alone. I was always at home with the children. My husband hardly ever took me out or said I looked nice. When we did go out it was dinner (nothing special) and a movie. No visiting, dancing, sightseeing, vacations.

One day I met a telephone service repair man by accident and he started coming over for quickies in the afternoon. He wasn't much warmer than my husband but still, it was quite a change from my drab life. Then some years later I met another man, different from the others. He brought me things, complimented me, wanted to take me places, and in bed he could hold out until I was completely satisfied. But he told his wife about us, and she in turn told my husband, and he threatened to kill us and that was the end of that.

That was a long time ago. Now my husband and I live in a bigger house, about two and a half miles from a small-town shopping center. We have three kids and two big dogs. I never get to go out with friends for an evening, never have sex, have no allowance or even much money to spend on groceries, am beginning to drink, am fifteen pounds overweight and have just about given up on life.

Fidelity is important in marriage. But I sometimes wish people could know what it's like to live all those years with a man who thinks you're fat, or dumb, and how just hearing a man say something halfway nice to you is enough to make you want to sleep with him.

There are, of course, many different types of infidelity, some of which are far less poignant than the kinds we have been reading about. Sometimes an unfaithful partner seems bent on humiliating a mate. Sometimes an unfaithful partner seems to have no cause for his or her actions beyond a shallow urge to add to a hidden sexual scorecard. Infidelity is a complex matter. But one thing is certain. One cannot always predict from people's attitudes and beliefs prior to marriage whether they will be faithful. The nature of the marriage, what it gives to the partners and what it denies them, affects the odds for fidelity more than either partner's philosophy.

3. The Mechanics of Marital Infidelity

I am 26 years old and have been married for six years and having an affair for the last three. He was a co-worker. We used to go to lunch together with other people on the staff. Then we started going to lunch alone. Then we started going to his place for lunch. Then we started having sex. After work he goes out with other women, and I go home to my husband and my 5-year-old son. I never thought when I kept on working after I got married, and then again after the baby, that work was going to bring me such fringe benefits.

—*a market researcher from Connecticut*

In short stories and novels about women's infidelity, it is usually the idle wife who has an affair, the woman tucked away at home in the suburbs, while her husband is off at work and her children at school. The milkman and the mailman and the newspaper delivery boy are the storied beneficiaries of the housewife's alleged lust, and she herself does not have affairs so much as she has plain, unadulterated sex, a quick tumble on the patio, a hasty roll in the rumpus room.

This is myth, and most likely male myth. The picture is somehow reassuring and perhaps enables some men to believe that a woman's extramarital affair is nothing serious, nothing she actively sought out, and thus nothing they need be deeply concerned about. If it is a cuckolded husband, he can more easily rationalize it, avoid feeling too outraged.

The bored-housewife notion has been a long-lived one. Back in the mid-1970s when I had occasion to interview a number of psychiatrists concerning women's adultery in connection with my book *Playing Around,* I heard several of them assure me that once women got back into the workforce there would be less and less infidelity. Ah, the power of wishful thinking! For, of course, it has been just the opposite. More often than not, working has given the potentially wandering woman precisely the opportunity she requires to find a suitable partner, and to be with him at times when she is *supposed* to be elsewhere.

One *Cosmo* woman, an economist from the midwest, has been having an affair for five years with a man she met through her job. Here she explains how it came about, how she manages her meetings with her lover, and what the affair is like:

> I've only had two lovers in my life—my husband, whom I married when I was 20, and for the past five years my "friend," a man I met while I was at work. My sex life with my husband wasn't bad. In fact, we still make love often and I always have orgasms. But I think that what happened to me is that I became more interested in sex— or maybe I should say I became sexually mature—after my child was born. And that happened at a point that my husband was slowing down. It wasn't a matter of age—my husband is only a year older than I am—but of responsibility. We had our first home—four bedrooms, three baths. My husband worried about finances and seemed less free and interested in fun than before, and I was the same, or more interested. Anyway, my friend and coworker provided me with an awful lot of emotional support during this period. We weren't having sex. We were just friends and colleagues. And then he was transferred to another city. His new job entailed his giving profes-

sional seminars all over the country, but whenever he was back in the home office we'd have lunch or dinner. He never pressured me to have sex with him. But I'm sure he must have had a lot of frustrating plane rides home. Then, after six months of daily long-distance phone conversations in the office, and as many dinners as we could manage, I finally called him and made a request for sex. A girlfriend of mine was visiting, so I asked her to babysit while I went on a "job interview" after work. (To this day, over five years later, she doesn't know what kind of "job" I was interviewing for and how interesting the interview/ interviewer/interviewee was!) My friend flew in that morning. We spent the afternoon and early evening together. And he took a dinner flight home. I went home too, and since I didn't have time to cook I ordered a pizza —a dinner which has since become routine around our house—my friend is just as much a part of my life now as he was five years ago.

Sex with him is wonderful. When we don't see each other for several months I plan what I want us to do when we do meet. I am very creative and sometimes I come up with ideas to top *The Sensuous Woman* and to rival *Penthouse* 's Forum. The last time he was coming in I bought some oil on my way to the airport to meet him, planning to tell him my fantasies of our massaging one another. I never had to mention my fantasies. He fulfilled every one and then some. We didn't get to the massage, though we did use the oil, according to his excellent prescription and to unbelievable pleasures. These are my concrete experiences with fidelity. As to fidelity in the abstract, I don't know what I think—at least about whether it's ever possible.

Another woman, a medical receptionist from Minnesota, had an affair with the doctor who employed her:

This is a perfect opportunity for me finally to reveal my wonderful love affair. I am 34 years old now, and the affair happened when I was 22 and lasted four years. I'd been married four years when it started. I went to work for a doctor as his receptionist, and for some reason this man made me feel funny. I had difficulty looking directly at him, and I would drop things whenever he was around.

He always teased me about what was the matter. I never knew. Then one night after all the patients left he called to me and took me in his arms and held me. Every night for two weeks I would sit on his lap and he would hold me. He always wanted to kiss me and I always said no. Finally I gave in and it was the most exciting kiss I ever experienced. I was also feeling a stirring of sexual excitement and desire I'd never felt before. My husband had been my first and only lover and I thought I was sexually happy with him, but this was different. But although the new stirrings I felt were fantastic, my relationship with the doctor was just one of kissing and hugging for almost a year until one day, close to Christmas, he took me in his arms and picked me up and carried me to the examining table and made precious love to me. It was the most beautiful experience of my lifetime.

After our first taste of sex, we couldn't make love enough. Each experience was more wonderful than the last. We made love on lunch hours, after-hours, in the office, in his car, in his boat, and in many hotels. My lover was able to climax two times in every lovemaking session and I learned how to be multi-orgasmic. He introduced me to oral sex and the sensations were great. Our sexual relationship lasted four years. But once we nearly got caught. After sex my chest would always break out in a red flush. One time my lover's wife came to the office and we were all standing around talking when she noticed that my neck and chest were red. She said, "What's wrong? Do you have a rash?" I just said, "Oh, nothing. It will go away." Eventually I left my husband, but not to marry my lover . . . he wanted to stay married to his wife. He and I continued working together, and having stolen kisses and sex, but we tried to cool down emotionally. Then he decided to leave town. We were getting too involved. But we still keep in touch platonically. We still care for each other deeply, and we always will. I've married again, but even my present husband doesn't compare to my old lover.

Like the doctor's receptionist, a 32-year-old woman from the midwest had an affair with a man with whom her work brought her into frequent contact. She was a social worker, he a minister:

I have been married ten years, have two kids, and last year
I had my first—and I hope only—affair. I had good sex
with my husband, and a nice enough life, and I can't
explain why I had the affair, just that this minister and I
used to see each other at work sometimes, and it happened. My husband found out, but he forgave me, and
things are all right between us now. Maybe if I'd stayed
at home, instead of working, it wouldn't have happened.

And a 27-year-old secretary from Texas who went back to
work after staying home three years with a child felt that infidelity
was "the inevitable" once she resumed her career:

I had been programmed, in my typical middle-class Cath-
olic upbringing, to believe that the ultimate life goals were
being a faithful wife and a devoted mother, and having a
beautiful suburban home. No divorce. No working mothers. No mess or untidyness. But having achieved the goals
and at such a young age (I've always been an over-
achiever, I guess), I one day discovered that they weren't
enough for me. I was miserable. What could I do about it?
Since I had six years of solid secretarial experience behind
me, work seemed the most logical place to start the ball
rolling. I made a few phone calls to former associates and
within a few days I was back in the workforce, freelancing
with two clients. I was out there in the "real world" for
about six months, my business doing well, me feeling
happier (yet still somewhat confused), when the inevitable finally happened. I went to call on a prospective client,
one thing led to another, and suddenly this nice 27-year-
old wife and mother found herself in bed with someone
else's nice husband.

Of course it is not work itself that brings about infidelity. The
Texas secretary went on to explain:

Six months later I left my husband and moved in with my
lover. I am still with him now. In the beginning I thought
I was having the affair just to get it out of my system. I
thought I'd soon get back to the business of living the
"good" life again. But then a very strange (and not so
funny) thing happened. I began to realize that I loved my

lover and not my husband. It was when I had sex with my husband that I felt unfaithful! That was why I left my husband. Adultery is a very complex and multi-faceted subject. Is it possible that many marriages have never really been marriages at all, because the partners have never been in touch with each other? Is it possible that adultery exists because there has never been a true commitment? That is what I think mine was all about. I was married, but I did not love and respect my husband. I do love and respect my lover very deeply. Our need for each other has continued to grow in spite of ourselves and all the other forces in our lives.

As this woman's letter suggests, most women who have affairs while married do so because they do not *feel* married. They cannot commit themselves entirely to their spouse. They *feel* single, alone. And sometimes they actually are alone. A 26-year-old factory worker from Massachusetts told a fairly typical story:

I have been married for four years. When I got married, my views were very conservative. I believed that making love was a very exclusive thing and should only be done with a husband. But during the last six months I have been having an affair. Let me explain. For the past year and a half my husband has been working nights till three in the morning, while I work days. We hardly ever see each other, and so our sex life is sparse. On top of that we moved from a small community on Cape Cod where I had lots of friends to a city outside Boston where I didn't know a soul. With no friends to visit at night, I started to feel very alone.

Last spring, after a very hard day at work, I decided to stop for a drink on the way home. I went to a place where my husband and I usually had dinner when we went out. I never dreamed I would be picked up. But I was sitting at the bar minding my own business when a guy sat down next to me and started talking to me. It was the day that President Carter tried to rescue the hostages from Iran, so there was a lot to talk about. He bought me a few drinks. We talked about the hostages. And then we wound up talking about everything under the sun, and our conversation drifted to getting high, and we went out to the car and smoked a joint. In the car we each told each other we were married. But we started kissing anyway. He was hot and horny and wanted to make love to me. And to my surprise, I wanted it too. I was ready for sex, after just five minutes of kissing, which surprised me because with my husband I often have to use additional lubrication. Anyway, my body was telling me yes, yes, yes, but my mind was racing and I felt so confused that I said no. But we agreed that I would think about it and meet him again a week later. And then, I couldn't wait. I called him right after the weekend and asked him to come up to my apartment, and we've been seeing each other ever since, about once every three weeks. No one has ever turned me on the way this man does. Our relationship is fantastic. But I love my husband, and I guess it will all end once he stops working nights . . .

A feeling of loneliness, whether it is because she really is alone or because she is psychologically removed from her husband, often seems to characterize the woman who decides to seek extramarital sex. Perhaps this is why among women, but not necessarily among men, affairs—rather than tumbles, rolls in the hay, or one-night stands—are the most hoped-for outcome of extramarital sex. Certainly committed affairs, not casual sex, were what unfaithful *Cosmo* women desired. But sometimes their extramarital partners had ideas of their own. A 25-year-old supermarket clerk from Maryland has been having an affair with a store customer who wants to keep things casual:

I met my lover two years ago, shortly after my husband and I moved to this new area. I got a job in the shopping center supermarket, but all my husband could get was the night shift at the plant. I met my lover when he was buying things at the store. He made some jokes with me, asked me how come he'd never seen me before, and when I said I was new and didn't know anyone in the neighborhood, he asked me where I lived, and since he lived right nearby he promised to stop over and talk with me after work sometime. He came over, and talked to me about the people on my road, and he was real friendly, and he understood about how lonely I was, and he took me over and showed me his house. He lives alone, about ten houses away from me. He made me laugh and feel good again after I'd been lonely for so long, and we talked about things I could never talk to my husband about. Eventually we went to bed at his place and it was as if I was sexually reborn. Sex with my husband hadn't been much for a long time. He never seemed very interested in sex, but when he started working the night shift till 12 P.M. he got worse. He didn't seem to have time for me or it, or want to make time. My lover was different. He asked me what I wanted sexually so he could please me, and after we made love he held and cuddled me. We both agreed to a no-strings-attached arrangement. You see, he didn't want to be the cause of any trouble between my husband and me, and besides he had a girlfriend he was going with. It was all right at first but now it's different. I sometimes think he regrets it all because I seem to want more of his time than he wants to give me. You see, I honestly believe I really love him. But he doesn't want me to leave my husband. Right now it's terrible. My husband just started working days again, so I can't even get away. The only time I even see my friend is in the store. And sometimes he has to shop with his girlfriend and I feel helpless because he's told me never to touch him in public or even to look at him because my feelings might show, and he wants to keep it light, like at the beginning, but I don't know how. I don't think I can stand it. Especially when he comes in with his girlfriend and they're standing in line together and he doesn't even look at me except if she's unloading the cart, and then he winks at me quick, or smiles till she straightens up.

The Maryland clerk is more worried about her lover's unfaithfulness to her than about hers to her husband. More often, the reverse was true, with the *Cosmo* women feeling deep concern about having betrayed their husbands, but incapable of living without infidelity. A 34-year-old Michigan woman who has had four affairs since marrying ten years ago is such a woman:

I don't believe I can ever be without a lover. I love my husband very much. I respect him and depend on him to catch me if I fall. He's my Rock of Gibraltar. When we first married, I couldn't even imagine what he saw in me. He was up on a pedestal and I adored him. Maybe I adored him too much. I was a doormat. One day, without any planning or conscious forethought, I left him. I'd met someone else, someone who looked up to *me*. I didn't have sex with this someone else, though. And after I left, my husband and I got back together again, and everything for the next seven years was great. My husband got even nicer. Less domineering. I stopped being a doormat. But then, for some inexplicable reason, I fell in love with my husband's best friend—just at the time when things were so good. And that affair lasted about a year, and then I had another, and another and another. Why? My husband is so good and so loving. I sometimes despise myself for deceiving him, but I don't see how I can change.

Perhaps this woman is still trying to "pay back" her husband for the years during which he treated her as a doormat. Although he has changed, and is now kind and loving, she is not yet ready to forgive him his earlier disregard of her. Instead, she continues to have affairs, while all the while feeling guilty.

The mechanics of adultery—whether they involve choosing a partner, or finding a secret place to meet, or handling painful feelings of jealousy about a lover, or guilt about a husband, or combinations thereof—can be overwhelming. A woman lawyer I once interviewed on the subject of her infidelities told me they were "damn hard work." She found them taxing, and sometimes suspected herself—and other adulterous women (such as, perhaps, the letter writer above)—of masochism, especially if, like herself, they were career women. She had been conducting an affair for some years with a fellow lawyer, but his career was firmly entrenched whereas hers was in the crucial phase and required extremely long hours and intense concentration on building her client list. In addition, she had young children at home. Her lover's children were grown. "He is filling up free time with me," she said, "whereas I am sandwiching him into a very crowded life."

She felt that the mechanics of an affair could make infidelity as much a trial as a triumph.

4. Motivations and Expectations

The most common motivation for infidelity was actual or perceived isolation. Sometimes the women felt their husbands had no time for them except time in bed; sexual communication was not enough when there was no other kind of communication. A 28-year-old from Kansas who has been having an affair for two years wrote, "My sex life with my husband was good, very good. But sex was about all we did together. We shared nothing but sex. He never wanted to talk to me about his work, or about mine, or go anywhere, or do anything. It got so that it was like going to bed with a stranger."

Some couples communicated well enough, but the women felt emotionally isolated because they no longer shared the values and goals that their spouse communicated. A 42-year-old mother of two from California felt that her husband, a film executive, "was consumed with the passion for success, whereas I was deeply interested in social causes." She started an affair with a man whose values were more to her liking:

> Nothing but money and power matters to my husband, but I am different. He's not a bad husband. He's a good provider, he's good in bed, and he's a terrific father to our kids. He's also very dependent on me, and says I keep him sane. I believe I do, and wouldn't want to hurt him in any way. But I might have gone nuts myself if I hadn't met my lover, a man who is creative, private, a humanitarian, and not blinded by the glitzy movie world.

But most of the time emotional isolation showed itself in vague stirrings of discontent, feelings that life was empty and meaningless. Most of the time the women couldn't pinpoint exactly what was wrong in their marriage. Typical was this 25-year-old from Georgia, the mother of a 3-year-old daughter:

> I've been married five years. About a year ago I woke up one morning and asked myself, "Is this all there is to life?" Then I thought, If the rest of my life is like this, I want no part of it. I pondered on this for a while and felt that what I needed was to know that I could be attractive to

someone besides my husband. I had to prove something to myself. I started an affair with my husband's best friend. I needed attention. And when I was getting it, I felt I was on the top of the world. So when that broke up, I started another affair, which has been going on about nine months now.

In situations like these, sexual dissatisfaction played only a minor or non-existent role in motivating infidelity. But of course there were also many women who had affairs simply as a result of sexual frustration. Dozens wrote letters similar to this one, sent in by a 40-year-old from Connecticut:

I have been married for many years. For most of those years, sex was just something I tolerated. Then, two years ago, I had an affair. It was the most enlightening experience of my life. I not only learned to enjoy sex, but I also found out I was multi-orgasmic. I would like to point out that my lovemaking with my lover is the conventional type of sex. No "way out" foreplay, just natural kissing, caressing, stroking. That is what makes it so heavenly. It's so natural! I feel like a woman for the first time in my life, and my only regret is that it took me so many years to make the discovery.

What was curious about women like this was how long they tolerated sexual dissatisfaction before attempting to resolve the problem through infidelity. A 60-year-old from Minnesota, mother of four children, has been married thirty-seven years to a man who has been "impotent since a few months following the birth of our last child twenty-five years ago." Three years ago this Minnesota woman, who had felt plagued for a quarter of a century by "very strong sexual desires," had her first affair, and since then she has had seventeen.

The first was a tennis pro—handsome, and only 25 years old. That was the beginning of many wonderful affairs, all with men who were much younger than me. I feel no guilt because of the many years I denied myself in the name of loyalty. My efforts to seduce my husband were always a complete failure, and made me feel humiliated, but I had been raised with strong moral principles and so I never looked at another man in all that time although I had very strong sexual desires and was quite attractive to men. It was only when my last child left home that I realized I would have to find a new life for myself or I'd go crazy. Now I live in constant excitement and anticipation of the pleasures in store for me. My lovers have all treated me very well, and because of them I have become interested not just in sexual things but in many new hobbies. My husband knows about my adventures, and allows me this freedom as long as I am discreet, for we live in a small community where I must protect my reputation.

A less common though nonetheless frequent motivation for infidelity was the urge to retaliate against an unfaithful partner. A 49-year-old business executive from California describes her get-even infidelity:

I have been having an affair for five years, ever since learning my husband had had one. Call it revenge if you wish. I guess it was. I had been raised strictly and had accepted the beliefs of my parents and my church. I would not have strayed except that my husband did. It was only when I found out about his infidelity that I decided to forget about the faithfulness routine and enjoy some of the temptations which are constantly available to me. As an executive, I have steady contacts with hundreds of men. So I pulled out all the stops and began to weed out the field. But believe me, there are very few really interesting men in the 45–55 age bracket. They are generally overweight, bald, slovenly, just plain dumb, or real phoneys. It took me a while to zero in on a man, but I did, and we have been lovers now—behind my husband's back—for five years. I've never let my husband know. He hasn't been hurt, the way he hurt me.

The business executive is content with her situation, but others who have had retaliatory affairs are not. A 30-year-old Virginia woman wrote:

I've been married nine years. I found out two years ago that my husband was having an affair. I was furious, but I didn't want to kick him out. So I figured, two can play at this game, and I started having an affair too. I picked an old boyfriend. But it hasn't been that great because after all, he was a guy I'd rejected in order to marry my husband. He was second best then and I guess I still feel he is.

Interestingly, behind all these motivations lies one other, a motivation common to all women when they are first unfaithful whether they have an affair for emotional closeness, sexual satisfaction or vengeance. I'm talking about the desire to preserve marriage. Traditionally women have affairs when it appears to them that, short of adultery, their married lives are intolerable and divorce is imminent. Traditionally adultery—while socially condemned—has been considered at least an alternative to divorce—though divorce has become increasingly acceptable. It is the rare woman who starts an extramarital affair with the conscious goal of breaking up her marriage.

But infidelity always carries the risk of divorce. Not just because a spouse may discover the infidelity and insist on ending the marriage (though that is always possible). Rather, infidelity carries the risk of divorce because sooner or later it makes the woman herself begin to question whether she really wants to stay in a marriage in which she is emotionally distant, sexually frustrated, or so angry that she puts vengeance above love. It's not possible to know how many of the unfaithful *Cosmo* women currently attempting to preserve their marriages will eventually divorce, but there is reason to believe that a good many will. I say this because my own research suggests it. In 1975, when I wrote *Playing Around,* I did in-depth interviews with 66 adulterous women. Of these, 21 (all of whom were then currently being unfaithful) said they were having affairs largely in the hope that infidelity would help preserve their marriages. In 1980, when I followed up on the marital histories of these twenty-one women, only three were still married. Not a very promising scorecard.

5. Secret vs. Open Infidelity

MAJOR FINDINGS:

The vast majority of the women—83 percent—kept their infidelities to themselves. Only 17 percent practiced open infidelity or had husbands who knew of their affairs.

For a time in the 1970s there was much talk about the advantages of "open" marriages, marriages in which sex with outside partners was sanctioned. The theory was that open marriages could prevent divorce. No one would have to break up a marriage in order to have sex with a new partner, and no one by having such sex would hurt his or her spouse—because infidelity had been agreed on, accepted in advance as being a *part* of marriage.

To many psychologists the theory seemed shallow. They had treated the victims of "open infidelity"—men and women who had outwardly accepted the theory because it sounded so reasonable, so logical. These men and women, however, had often suffered terribly with feelings of jealousy and sexual helplessness. Indeed, knowing about a spouse's affairs seemed to bring more pain than not knowing about them, even when such affairs were suspected. Psychologists also found that open infidelity did not particularly preserve marriages. Open marriages broke up just as regularly as traditional ones did. Today, based on the record, most psychologists seem to hold to the view that marriage is better served by keeping infidelity secret.

The *Cosmo* women emphatically share this view. A 34-year-old insurance agent from the northeast who tried open infidelity discovered that although her husband had given his permission for her to have outside sex, he really couldn't cope with the feelings of rejection it brought him:

> I am married to a very good man. He cares for me a great deal and the feeling is mutual. But he is thirteen years older than me, and although nine years ago, when we married, this didn't seem to make much difference, in recent years it began to. When we first married he was even more sexual than I was. We made love twice a day six days a week. Then he started slowing down, and now

we are averaging sex only about once every two weeks. Terrible! Because of this situation, which we have discussed openly, my husband indicated to me that he would understand it if I had to look for some sexual satisfaction elsewhere. However, when I started to do this, he had terrible feelings of rejection. He couldn't handle the thought of my really being unfaithful (although some years ago, when he was, I'd been able to handle it). I love him very much. I am a very independent, strong-minded and strong-willed person. And so although I do not like having to have secret affairs, I keep mine secret, as I know my husband's feelings would be crushed, no matter what he says, if he knew about them.

And a graduate student of science at a large midwestern university said:

I think fidelity is basically just not possible. I have been married for two years, and my marriage is just about perfect, and yet I strayed, and had an affair with a friend's husband. I don't think my husband has strayed, but since I know I wouldn't want to know about it if he had, I've made sure he doesn't know about me. I think people hurt each other beyond repair when they admit to sex outside their marriages, and so, okay, it happens, but you've both got to pretend it didn't happen or can't happen, not to the two of you, or else you'd be hurting each other and then what would be the point of staying married?

Some women who had been involved in open marriages claimed that their infidelities had not hurt their partners, but one, a 36-year-old woman from the state of Washington said:

Of course, you've got to play the game very carefully. Neither of you has to like an extramarital partner too much—that is, you have to not like the partner so much that you get goodies from knowing him as well as sleeping with him. You'd better not want to have a couple of drinks with him and talk, or see him when your husband doesn't have a ladyfriend to see. And how long can you keep up something like that? And why would you want

to? My husband and I had an open marriage for six years.
We each gave each other permission for sex with other
people. It worked out all right in the beginning. It was his
idea, because an old girlfriend of his had moved to our
city. She didn't like sex with her husband very much. My
husband started sleeping with her, and I got the other
husband, who was a big bore. Then they broke up and
moved away. I found a new lover, a single guy, before my
husband found one. He was jealous and depressed for a
while. Then he got a lover, another married woman.
Things were fine. Then mine said he couldn't stand seeing
me just once a week—which was the arrangement my
husband and I had agreed on. He said if he couldn't see
me more, he'd rather not see me at all. I wanted to keep
him. So I told my husband I had to sleep with him more
than once a week or I'd lose him. My husband said he
didn't care, I couldn't sleep with my lover more than once
a week because his couldn't sleep with him more than
once a week. I said okay, I won't sleep with him. I'll just
go out with him. Dinner and a movie. My husband said
no, you're just supposed to have sex, not a relationship.
I said I can't do that. He said well okay, you can see the
guy twice a week. But see him here. Have sex here. Don't
go out with him. I said, he doesn't want that. He said who
cares what he wants. I said I do. *He said you're cheating on me;
you were supposed to be having sex and now I find out you're having
a relationship.* [Author's italics.]

This situation, with its remarkable distinctions and redeploy-
ment of conventional language, speaks for itself.

6. Fidelity Among Couples Who Live Together

MAJOR FINDINGS:

Seventy percent of the women who were not married
but who lived with their lovers believed that fidelity
should be part of the living-together commitment.
Thirty percent did not.

There are innumerable legal and social rules governing marriage, all of which have evolved over the centuries and which, whether one likes them or not, serve to make marriage predictable and therefore secure. Living together is, literally, another story. Legal precedents to govern the arrangement are just beginning to emerge, and social rules are only in their infancy. The situation is sometimes chaotic, with one live-in partner believing that love carries the promise of economic responsibility, the other believing that only marriage entails such responsibility. Or one partner feeling that love requires fidelity, the other believing that only marriage does.

The *Cosmo* women, many of whom were unmarried but involved in long-standing live-in relationships, are, in a sense, pioneers exploring new social territories and carving out ethical positions that they can live with in relative comfort. It is interesting, then, to see that so many of them—70 percent—have adopted the ideal of fidelity. They do not feel free to have sex outside their relationship, nor consider their partners free to do so:

> Once a man and a woman agree to live together it is the same as if they were married. They're a couple. If they play around, it's going to end the relationship.
>
> —*a 25-year-old from Missouri*

> People shouldn't live together unless they're sure they can be faithful. It isn't easy to do this, but the rewards make up for the difficulties.
>
> —*a 26-year-old from California*

> My boyfriend and I made a pact when we got together. On the top of the list was that we would each be faithful. I wouldn't have moved in with him if he hadn't agreed.
>
> —*a 22-year-old from Massachusetts*

> If I wanted to be unfaithful to my lover, I'd move out. That's the whole point of living together, to try out whether you like each other enough to be faithful. If you do, you can get married. If you don't, then you may as well break up and look for someone it will work with.
>
> —*a 24-year-old from Wisconsin*

But 30 percent of the women who were living with their lovers did not believe in fidelity. Of them the great majority—three-fourths—characterized their outside sex chiefly as "a once-in-a-while occurrence." The others had sex outside their relationship more regularly—some having it on a continuing basis with one other person, a few having it on a frequent basis with several people. In other words, among women living with their lovers, infidelity was very uncommon, and when it occurred it was more likely to take the form of a one-night stand than a full-fledged affair.

So it would appear that infidelity is more of a problem among the married than among the living-together. The reason for this is obvious. Marriages tend to last longer than long-standing live-in relationships do, and it is usually only with time, and the erosion of sexual or emotional compatibility, that the longing to try out sex with a new lover strikes most people.

Interestingly, among women who lived with lovers and had had sex outside the relationship, there was a definite belief that such sex—and attitudes condoning it—were best kept secret. In this, the unfaithful living-together women were no different from the unfaithful married women. They tended to feel that fidelity was impossible, but they kept their convictions to themselves:

> I don't actively pursue other men, but once in a while a "distraction" comes along. I keep such affairs secret, as it serves no purpose to tell my lover. My affairs are purely recreational, and I wouldn't feel bad if my lover had sex like this either. It would be unrealistic to think there would never be another person in the world either of us would be attracted to, so as long as both of us have casual recreational sex, as opposed to *lovemaking* with someone else, it's okay.
>
> —*a 27-year-old from California*

> I was once badly hurt by a lover who had affairs and confessed them to me. I am of the opinion that one-night flings that I or my current live-in lover will never find out about are all right, because if they aren't found out about, they hurt no one. It's confessions that are a very bad idea. I haven't told my lover how I feel, though, as I think it would make him nervous about what I might do behind

his back, and I guess it would make me nervous about what he might do. So I just keep this to myself.

—a 26-year-old from New York

This tendency on the part of women who have sex outside a live-in relationship to be secretive about such sex suggests how powerful a hold the ideal of fidelity asserts over presumably non-traditional couples. Even those who don't quite believe in it would rather their attitudes went undiscussed and unnoticed. Apparently a majority of unfaithful live-in women recognize full well the threat that infidelity poses to a relationship's ultimate longevity.

7. The Fidelity of Married Men

MAJOR FINDINGS:

Sixty-one percent of the women had had an affair with a married man on at least one occasion. Twenty-nine percent had had an affair with a married man more than once.

In recent years there has been a marked shift in the way public opinion views the "other" woman, the woman who has sex with a married man. At one time she was considered the cause of marital stress. Now she is more often seen not as cause but effect. Increasingly it's believed that the man who seeks a sexual relationship outside his marriage is a man whose marriage is a deteriorated one. He and his wife, rather than the woman with whom he has sex, are the primary figures in his infidelity. The "other" woman is almost an accidental figure, one who bears relatively little responsibility for any ultimate break-up of the marriage.

This view has had the effect of making the "other" woman see herself as far less unsavory and unkind than she once did, and may to some extent account for the fact that more women today are less reluctant to have sex with married men and to admit having had it. In addition, the fact that divorce has become much more common has made single women more hopeful about their chances of ending up married to their married lovers.

Among the *Cosmo* women, nearly two-thirds had once or several times counted married men among their lovers. The experience was not necessarily a painful one. Indeed, 60 percent of the women described such relationships as "more rewarding than painful."

Happiest were those women who had chosen married lovers who wanted to leave their wives and remarry, rather than those who wanted just to shore up an existing marriage. Such a woman is the 34-year-old from Colorado, whose letter follows:

> Having an affair with a married man was something I'd sworn I'd never do. I had been raised as a Catholic and had had very strict ideas about right and wrong. But my two years with this man have been very wonderful. I'd been married for ten years. My husband was the first man I'd ever had sex with. We had a terrible marriage and we divorced. Then, after three years in which I had many lovers and finally came to enjoy sex, I met my married man. Our sex life is great—very satisfying to both of us. We engage in all sex practices, including oral sex. We even have a roadmap of Colorado with gold stars on it for wherever I gave him a blow job. And now my married man has gotten a divorce and we plan to wed early next year. In fact, we pick up our wedding rings tomorrow. Incidentally, we have pledged to be faithful to each other. Strange as it may seem we both feel very strongly about fidelity.

But not all women who have affairs with married men hope for marriage. Some career-oriented women particularly like such lovers because they do not, at the moment at least, desire a more permanent or demanding relationship. A 27-year-old management consultant from Virginia whose job entails a great deal of travel explains:

> Because I am career-oriented and not looking for marriage, I have often had affairs with married men. These affairs have been painful and frustrating at times, but when I look back on them and think of the men, I have to smile and say it was worth it. I wouldn't have missed

266 THE COSMO REPORT

getting to know those particular guys for all the world.
They have greatly enriched my understanding of men and
marriage, my sexuality, and my life. They—more than
any of my single lovers—were always the ones who were
most open with me, the ones who shared their vul-
nerabilities as well as their strengths.

And some women prefer married lovers because they feel they
tend to be more sexually experienced and emotionally caring than
single men. A 32-year-old boutique owner from Kentucky who is
divorced and having an affair with the husband of a friend praises
her married lover because unlike the single men she has been meeting he seems to have a greater ability to be physically and psychologically generous:

> The married man I am having an affair with helped me
> emotionally during the time of my divorce. One thing led
> to another and we became lovers. He never led me on in
> any way. And he is a perfect gentleman. He never runs
> down his wife, and he doesn't make promises he can't
> keep. He's totally honest with me, and I think that's why
> I care for him so much. He is also a gentle, considerate, and
> expert lover. I have not met any men, since I divorced last
> year, who have come up to him. The single men my age
> are emotional cripples, or sexual failures. It's no wonder
> a divorced woman has an affair with a married man. A
> married man is usually a man who likes women, and
> knows what a woman needs in all ways.

Still, 40 percent of the women found that having married lovers
was more painful than rewarding. Chiefly, they complained about
their partner's unavailability. Typical were such comments:

> I had three affairs with married men I worked with. Each
> time I was foolish enough to believe that they loved me.
> I always realized too late that all they wanted was sex, and
> that they never meant to leave their wives and children,
> no matter how unhappy they said they were. Worst of all
> was that they could never take me out. They were always
> worried about being seen.
>
> —*a 24-year-old legal secretary from Ohio*

I have been involved for seven months with a married man. He has taught me to appreciate all aspects of love-making, from holding hands to intercourse. But I would not advise another single girl like myself to have this kind of relationship. Although we love each other, all I can ever think about is that I wish he were single. And I'm always alone on weekends.

—a 21-year-old department store clerk from New Jersey

Before I was married three years ago I had an affair with a married man and I wouldn't do it again for all the gold wherever it's plentiful. I'm the kind of woman who wants an obligation. Oh sure, he had an obligation. But it wasn't to me. Besides, we were always sneaking around. He had to be home at a certain time. And he didn't ever want to leave his wife because they had a child and he felt guilty. I cared so much for him, yet I could never really have him.

—a 20-year-old housewife from Michigan

I am in love with a married man. He's not just a wonderful lover, but he's a hell of a wonderful man. He's everything I've always wanted. But he has a wife and three children. He told me about them before we ever went to bed. I had always lived by the rule that I would never get involved with a married man, but for some reason, when he told me all about his family, it didn't seem to turn me off. But now I'm in love with him and I don't know what will happen. He said his marriage, his love for his wife, was over long before he met me and that as soon as he could get a few technicalities straightened out he would leave. That's why I didn't feel guilty. But now I don't know whether he'll ever actually do it. All I do now is sit and wait to see him, and sit and wait to see if I am going to get hurt in the end, or get the happiness that is long overdue me.

—a 25-year-old secretary from New York

Having sex with married men was an experience that nearly two-thirds of the women had had, and of which number 60 percent described as more rewarding than painful. It was, nevertheless, an experience that only 25 percent would be likely to try again. As one put it, it would need to be a very unusual man before she would once again "settle for the flaws this kind of relationship just naturally has."

There is no doubt that the *Cosmo* women, while quite likely to have affairs with married men or to have affairs themselves while married or otherwise committed to lovers, were nonetheless made uneasy by infidelity. Their actions and their feelings were so often at loggerheads that it would appear that while adultery is quite common today, it continues to be a source of real and considerable emotional unease.

PART FOUR
Sexual Abuse

Chapter Eleven
Incest

1. Incest Fantasies and Realities

Daydreams about sex with blood relatives have been popularized as a consensual, harmless and exotic form of erotica ever since Victorian times when, as scholar Steven Marcus points out in *The Other Victorians*, incest began appearing in the middle of pornographic books "with about the same frequency as marriages occur at the end of English novels."

The realities of incest are another story. Incest—with the possible exception of brother-sister incest when the siblings are close in age—is a form of child abuse. In a study of incest conducted in the early 1970s in County Antrim, Northern Ireland, researchers found that the women studied—grown women who had for a time been sexual partners of their fathers—had been on the average only eight and a half years old when incestuous sexual activities were initiated. They had not been sexually seductive, not nymphets who were somehow irresistibly attractive. They had been board-flat, naive, skinny-armed children. Three-quarters of them sustained lifelong emotional scarring as a result of the incest, perpetual feelings of self-blame, social inadequacy and depression.

Yet in the rush to sexual liberation that characterized the 1970s a bizarre phenomenon occurred. Sexual radicals began spouting the view that the incest taboo was merely another social repression that needed exorcizing. Even some professional mental health workers began to take this view. At a national conference on child abuse held in Washington, D.C., a social worker declared that some incest could be not only a positive experience but a healthy form of sexual activity. And some psychologists took the detached view that the incest taboo was no longer necessary, since with the widespread use of birth control, genetic catastrophes resulting from intrafamily sexual relations were no longer to be feared.

Incest healthy? The taboo unnecessary? In 1973 I had occasion to interview the late Margaret Mead, the eminent anthropologist and a leading authority on taboos and totems. I will never forget Margaret Mead's reaction when I mentioned the position on incest that had begun creeping into fringe mental health literature. She fumed, she sizzled, she exploded: "People have the idiotic notion that incest became forbidden because the marriage of near-relatives might produce seven-toed, seven-fingered children. But actually the taboo was designed to protect the emotional well-being of the children within the household."

The stories of incest in this chapter are, for the most part, heartrending tales of the failure of some American families to protect the emotional well-being of their children.

They are also remarkably vivid and detailed. Those women who wrote to *Cosmopolitan* about incest wrote with a pencil sharpened by memory and emotion. Their stories are not mere summaries of experience but renditions of life, portraits of loneliness and grotesquerie in the midst of the American dream that at times have the power of short stories by a Sherwood Anderson or a Joyce Carol Oates.

2. The Frequency of Incest

MAJOR FINDINGS:

Eleven percent of the women had experienced incest. A little more than half of this incest had occurred between brothers and sisters. A little less than a third had occurred between fathers and daughters. The rest had involved uncles, grandfathers and other male relatives.

The incest figures yielded up by the *Cosmo* survey are especially important. No one really knows the extent of incest in America because most records are obtained only when incest is brought to the attention of legal or mental health authorities. This does not happen too often; incest is usually kept secret by fear or threat. Authorities have long assumed that reported cases are the mere tip of an iceberg. How massive that iceberg might be has defied knowledgeable speculation. I once questioned James Golden, a criminal-court officer for New York's Society for the Prevention of Cruelty to Children, about the extent of incest, and he said, "There's enough of it to make you realize there's plenty more that doesn't get reported, but this kind of thing, for obvious reasons, doesn't come out into the open too often."

With the *Cosmo* survey, meaningful speculation about the dimensions of the problem is now possible.

3. Father-Daughter Incest

MAJOR FINDINGS:

Three percent of the women had experienced father-daughter incest.

Father-daughter incest is immensely traumatic. *Cosmo* women who had had incest with a father remembered the experience, no matter how many years had gone by, with as much vividness and anguish as if it had occurred only yesterday. Here is an account sent in by a Colorado woman in her late twenties. She paints an unforgettable picture of what happened to her in an isolated, primitive farmhouse:

> I often have wished I was able to say my first time was a splendid event. You see, I was one of the numerous victims of rape and incest. My first time was at the naive age of eight.
>
> My family lived in an old, weather-beaten Victorian-style house in the country. It was a half-mile from the nearest neighbor. The cold wind blew drafts through the cracks unmercifully. There were none of the conveniences

of modern-day life in the place, no TV or phonograph, so my brothers and sisters and I would play Mother, May I? or other children's games for amusement, and dad would tell us fairy tales, or stories about our ancestors.

The night in mention was when my mother took a few of the kids to a church in town for an evening prayer meeting. My father was, trustingly, left to watch over the rest of us. How was a tiny child to perceive the events that would follow? There had always been only a purely healthy bond of love between us. But that night, after he'd told us stories and all the other children had drifted off onto the rug and fallen asleep, leaving only the two of us awake, my father suddenly was saying, "Daddy won't hurt you," and placing his hands on my being in very unfamiliar places and in strange ways.

Terror flooded my thoughts. I didn't understand why —only that this was utterly wrong. But he promised me a bridal doll if I kept this hush-hush, and I let him fondle me. That's all he did at first. Even so, I nearly blurted it out to my mother the following day. But something drew me back. I felt she would call me a liar and perhaps punish me severely.

Then as the years passed, he continued occasional episodes. By the time I realized what was really happening. I was a victim of circumstance, unable to find an effective manner of avoiding the whole situation. When I reached the young age of 13½ he decided it was his duty to be the one to take my virginity. He would not allow anyone else to have the privilege, he told me. A father should bring up his daughters properly, he said.

The very memory of that afternoon makes me cringe. My mother had gone to get groceries and the others were outside playing. He locked the door, claiming that the kids were running in and out too much during his football game. I had loads of homework to do so I was studying in my room. He called and asked me to get him a clean shirt out of the closet in my parents' room. Obediently I went to do so. He followed me, and as I reached for the fresh shirt he knocked me into a basket of mending and proceeded to rape me. I recall screaming and screaming as he broke my hymen. He put his hand over my mouth, muffling my cries of terror. It was so degrading, and afterwards I became a very closed-off and quiet teenager.

For a long time then he left me alone, barely speaking to me. But when I finally became of dating age, once more my life became a game of submission. Oh, the bribery and deceitful tricks he'd play. I would have to give in to his sexual demands just in order to stay overnight with a friend. Or to go to a dance at school. Or to be allowed to buy a new outfit for a special occasion. And then one night he raped me again, this time because, he said, I'd arrived home forty-five minutes late from a date. He felt my date had seduced me, he said, and said he was going to make sure.

His having sex with me continued for nearly two years until at last, to escape the situation, I accepted a proposal of marriage from a man I barely knew.

This woman, like the prototype of the women who had been studied in the Northern Ireland research project mentioned earlier, had been 8 when her father first molested her. Some of the *Cosmo* women—and again, they were like some of the Irish women—were even younger. An 18-year-old from Wyoming writes:

My father started playing with my body from before I can even remember. When I was 7 or 8, he broke my virginity.

And a 28-year-old factory worker from Texas:

I was sexually assaulted by my natural father at an early age, 3 or 4, I can't quite recall exactly. As I was so young, I cannot remember what he actually did. What I remember is him hugging and kissing me as we lay on a blanket at a lake, and that at first I loved it. He was my daddy and I loved him. Then I remember wondering why he was touching me in the way he was, and that I started feeling uneasy. I don't remember him taking my panties off, but I do remember him hurting me so that I screamed, and that later I felt something warm and sticky on the inside of my legs. I thought it was a bowel movement.

What kinds of families does incest occur in? What kinds of men would have sex with their daughters? Are they sociopathic, drifters whose entire lives reflect attitudes and behavior that the rest of us would find monstrous? Generally speaking, yes. According to social workers at The Society for The Prevention of Cruelty to Children, incestuous fathers are often characterized by severe alcoholism, social instability and a violently abusive temperament. They also say that the mothers in incest families are generally so terrorized by their husbands that they tend to give either actual assistance to the incest, or a covert assistance by blinding themselves to what is going on.

Incest often occurs in families with a lengthy history of brutality and tyranny—from one or both parents. A 28-year-old Louisiana woman came from such a family, and her story provides a near-classic portrait of an incestuous family, one for whom incest itself was only an aspect of many other forms of child abuse.

> I don't remember the first time my father had me fondle his genitals, but it was before I was 14 years old. Then when I was 14, he had intercourse with me, and it went on until I was 17. To understand it, you have to understand more of my background during this period in my life. I was physically abused by both my parents. I'm not complaining about a spanking. I was beaten, leaving marks on my body. My buttocks bled. I went to school with welts and bruises on my legs and buttocks. My mother used to take a loafer, a hard-heeled shoe, and beat me on the head with it. My father sometimes took a wooden cutting board and beat my fingers flat on the floor with the side edge of it. If three days went by and nobody beat me, I was overjoyed. But that didn't happen too often.
>
> I never enjoyed in the least the sexual things my father made me do. But you have to understand the fear I lived with during this period of my life. And you have to understand that I thought all fathers and daughters did the same things my father made me do. Nobody, nowhere, told me any differently. There was never a discussion about sex from my mother. Not even about menstruation. I learned about it from films at school. So even if I had known it was wrong to have sex with my father, there would have been nobody to tell. But the point I want to make for myself and others like me is that I just did not know any better. You think back to the relationship you had with your father at this age. He was just under God

on your list of those who knew the most about anything. He was always right in your eyes. For someone as ignorant as myself, there was never any questioning. I did what I was told to do, with the same frame of mind as if I'd been told to brush my teeth or wash the dishes. Incest was just something you did, because your father told you to.

Most people don't understand. Most people think of some little cutie, deliberately flaunting herself in front of her father, and teasing him, until he can't control his desire. If something sexual happens to a female, no matter what her age, no matter how against her will, the majority of people will say she asked for it by the way she walked or dressed. No matter what the circumstance the female is made to feel *she* did something wrong.

I speak from personal experience because when I was 17, my brother, two years younger than myself, got in trouble with the law. He was being sent to a juvenile detention home. A lawyer on the case figured out the incest between my father and me. How he did it I will never know. Anyway, I was brought before a grand jury and questioned. If I had been a year older I might have been sent to jail or prison, for something that was not in my control.

Well, it was my father that went to prison. I moved in with my grandmother—my father's mother—and lived there until I got married. Now, after all these years, I still have only one confidante with whom I can discuss my anger and hatred. That is an aunt by marriage. Nobody in my real family ever tried to help me. They just took it and buried it deep in the back of their minds. I've had to live with this alone. Here is my life before you to examine. I hope you can do something with it. I can't, except get depressed.

But if incest is often found in families in which members are brutal, brutalized, and economically disadvantaged, it also occurs in seemingly well-organized families, in middle-class homes marked by a front of social respectability. Here is an account from a 28-year-old woman now living in Missouri. Her family was well-to-do. Her father worked for the United States government in France. Her mother, like that of the Colorado woman whose story opened this section, was a churchgoer. Sex was a taboo subject in the household, and social propriety was at the top of the family's list of priorities. Small wonder when one reads:

> I was an incest victim from approximately 5 or 6 through the age of 11 or 12. My parents were very strict. There were five of us children and sex was never discussed in our presence. I was not allowed to date until I was out of high school. And yet my father sexually molested both me and my sister, who was a year older than me. It started when our family was living in France. I remember my father molesting us with his fingers, and having us stroke his penis, and getting on top of us and shifting his penis back and forth on our naked bodies for long periods of time. He told my sister and me that if we ever told anybody he would kill us, and throughout our childhood we kept silent.
>
> Fear was ingrained in us from the very beginning, so my father continued these things throughout our childhood. It went on until my sister started her period. Then he quit molesting both of us.
>
> But when my sister and I were 16 and 15 the truth came out. My sister was being disciplined because she had been caught messing around with a boyfriend at our house when my parents were out of town. My little brothers told. You know how little brothers are. My sister and I decided that if we were going to get in trouble for doing the same things my father had done to us, we were going to tell our mother. We did, and she confronted him with it. And he denied it all. She decided to believe him, or at least say she did. Maybe she too was brainwashed with fear of him. But although ever since she has blamed the wrong people for this horrible event, and has had more love for her daughters-in-law than for us her daughters, I do believe that there will be scars of this forever, both in myself, my sister, my father, and even my mother.

Do the scars of father-daughter incest last forever? Most of the women who described father-daughter incest to *Cosmopolitan* reported that their lives were in a shambles for years afterward. A 23-year-old woman from Connecticut said, "I tried to kill my father and, being unable to, then tried to kill myself." The factory worker from Texas said, "I have never been able to get close to a man. I seem purposely to keep my relationships of brief duration in order not to become too involved with anyone." The Missouri woman, whose mother refused to believe the incest between her father, her sister and herself, has had, she reports, over 200 lovers during the last ten years, been close to none of them, and needed constant psychological help. And a 15-year-old from New York City, for whom incest is not an experience shrouded in the mists of memory but one that is painfully fresh, describes the rage, resentment and despair that plague her daily:

> I would like to make you aware of a devastating problem I went through for two years, when I was 12 and 13. I spent those years in abject terror of being raped by my father. He made blatant passes at me, once in front of my mother. Afterwards, he would make jokes about sex with me, constantly, even in front of people, but they never believed the horrible reality behind his jokes. My mother did, but when I told her what was going on, she shocked me with her comment: "You know perfectly well that he beats me, so why should I care about you?" I completely broke down. She never tried to stop him from bursting into my bedroom unexpectedly. I still dress in the bathroom. Counselors didn't care. *They felt sorry for my father, saying he was sick.* [Author's italics.] Even a female psychiatrist didn't sympathize with me. She said I should move into a foster home. I spent many nights in a terror only victims of incest can understand. I was plagued by nightmares and often slept fully dressed. Nobody cared—nobody would help. The government doesn't want to hear about girls like me. If I ever had been raped I would have committed suicide. Even as it was, with just his sexual passes all the time, I did consider suicide. I must stress: I would *enjoy* being raped by ten men on the street compared to being raped *once* by my father. Only the support of my friends kept me from suicide. I am now 15 and my father has moved away, but resentment toward my mother and the "counselors" remains. A psychiatrist would gladly analyze my trauma now, but they did nothing, nothing at all to save me from danger before. Who knows how many girls, and even boys, there are like me or worse than me? I felt so helpless, so alone, and there was no one that would help me at all. I have no words to

describe the fear I went through, and the anger at a world
that didn't care. Even now, I will not engage in any sex,
even with boys my own age. When they hold me I have
an uncontrollable desire to escape, to fight, to run away.

Can an incest victim ever recover from the experience, ever
trust and love a man, ever establish a happy, healthy sexual relationship? As their letters show, most of the women who had experienced father-daughter incest were still foundering, even years
after the event.

But the Colorado woman whose letter was the first in this
section, and who married a man she hardly knew in order to escape
her father, was eventually able, despite tremendous odds and tremendous additional suffering, to view her life as a happy one. It
took years. Her marriage didn't help, for even once she had left
home her father continued to blackmail her for sex, threatening that
he would tell her husband about what they had done together. She
was 15, a married woman, but still a frightened child. She continued
to submit to her father's demands, hoping to keep the horror of their
relationship from her husband, a soldier. She rejoiced when her
husband was sent overseas and took her with him. She had two
young babies, but on a visit home, once again her father raped her.
This time a neighbor overheard her cries and told her mother, who
immediately confronted the father and forced him to move away.
This woman, now about to give birth to a third child, had at last
been rescued. But with the story out, a new disaster struck:

> His heart in tatters, my spouse asked me how I could have
> kept such a vile secret from him. My reply was that I was
> too ashamed and frightened to tell him. His knowing now
> had a tragic effect on our already flimsy relationship.
> When we'd watch TV, or even when we'd make love, he'd
> ask how sex had felt with my father, or why I'd done it;
> and on and on with questions. Then, later, all hell broke
> loose. He began to stay out late and come in staggering
> drunk and accuse me of infidelity and beat me, even in
> front of our three tiny babies, who screamed and
> screamed in fear. Finally I came to the realization that I did
> not deserve this punishment, that what I had done with
> my father wasn't my fault. And finally, slowly, I deter-
> mined to live alone and raise the babies myself. I moved

out. And I started a new job. Within months, I began to
gain confidence, and the day even came when I allowed
another man into my life. I emptied out my problem to
him right from the beginning and his only reply was, "I
love you and all of that doesn't change my love one iota."
This man and I have presently been married for three
years. Our love grows greater daily. Our friendship had
grown a hundredfold.

So even if you have experienced incest and rape by
your father, life can start afresh and memories of that
trauma can fade. Happiness can be found. You have to
know it wasn't your fault and that you didn't deserve
such punishment. No one does.

This woman at last found a confidant, a man to whom she
could reveal her secrets without fear of rejection. With this, both
her sexual and emotional life blossomed healthily at last.

A significant and too little understood aspect of father-daughter incest is that while it occurs between family members, it is
actually an expression of emotional estrangement. To have sex with
a daughter, a man needs to feel disconnected from his daughter.
Incestuous fathers, whether they are outwardly sociopathic or outwardly respectable, are usually men of extreme psychological re-
moteness. So while incest is defined as sex between family members
too close to marry legally, it can also be defined as sex between
family members who are capable of viewing one another as strangers.

All this, of course, is slight comfort to victims of incest.

4. Incest with Grandfathers, Stepfathers and Other Older Male Relatives

While father-daughter incest may be the most traumatic form of
incest, violating as it does that most necessary familial bond, the
trust between a parent and a child, other incest can also be exceedingly distressing and emotionally damaging. Women who have had
relations with uncles, grandfathers and even stepfathers often expe-

rience the same feelings of helplessness, abandonment and degrada-
tion that accompany father-daughter incest. Perhaps the only difference between the two experiences is that when the incestuous
older male is not a girl's father, she may feel freer about expressing
her rage and hatred—which in turn may protect her psyche to some
extent, allow her to come away from the event somewhat less emotionally wounded, more able to recover. But we are talking of a
distinction between a great wound and a greater one. The 26-year-
old Wisconsin farm girl whose letter follows could hardly be said
to have recovered easily from the experience of being raped by her
grandfather:

> I come from a family of six boys and two girls. I was the
> third eldest, my sister the youngest. Our family, especially
> my parents, were very close-mouthed about sex. They
> never told any of us the facts of life. I believe this played
> a part in the events that follow.
>
> In the summer of 1965, I was spending my school
> vacation with my grandparents, as I had done often be-
> fore, but this summer was different. My grandmother was
> spending a lot of the time with a sick relative and so I was
> often alone. One day my grandfather asked me to go with
> him to pick up my grandmother at the relative's house.
> We had gone only a short distance when he said he had
> to check one of his corn fields. He took me with him, but
> we never checked the corn. Instead, he took me into some
> woods next to the field and raped me. I was 11 years old.
>
> Afterwards he told me that if I ever told anyone, he'd
> do it to me again, and worse. Because I didn't want to run
> the risk of rape again, I decided to keep my terrible secret
> to myself.
>
> I never told anyone, not even my parents. Instead, I
> drew into myself and wondered how I could prevent my
> little sister from being raped by him someday. I became
> more withdrawn with time, and began to eat more and
> more, hoping I could make myself so homely that no man
> would ever again even want to touch me. For years the
> hate grew inside me and I became more introverted and
> a lot heavier. I had nightmares for years. I woke time after
> time in a cold sweat wishing I could confide in someone.
>
> By the time I was 20, I was more disturbed than ever.
> I would wake up knowing I had been somewhere but with

no memory of where. After many months of these blackouts I decided I needed help of some kind. Perhaps if I
could just tell someone about the rape I would feel better.

I saw the pastor of my church and told him, but I
didn't feel better. Then he gave me the name and number
of the local mental health office and suggested I go there.
I went, and after two years of professional help I finally
got rid of most of my pain and the blackouts. At that time,
I decided I would at last tell my parents.

After a long, tearful confession, the secret came out.
My father was upset, but extremely understanding. My
mother didn't look surprised. She just asked me why I
hadn't told them until then. Afterwards, when I described
their reactions to the psychiatrist, he asked me to find out
why my mother hadn't seemed surprised. So I asked her,
and she confessed that years ago, when she was a girl, my
grandfather had tried the same thing with her.

I was horrified, and full of anger to think that if she
had warned me I would not have had to experience all that
pain. Although I love my mother I will never be able to
forgive her. I often think it was not my grandfather but
her father who hurt me so.

Incest is a terrible experience. To be raped by your
own flesh and blood disturbs the mind much more than
being raped by a stranger. You don't have to face that
stranger year after year, day after day. Most people cloud
their minds with thoughts that it couldn't happen in their
families. But it could.

This girl, like so many victims of incest, felt that she might have
been spared some of her suffering had her mother been more open
with her, had there not been a veil of silence in her family to cover
up all sexual matters. She seems right. Many of the survey letters
about incest reveal it occurs most often in families that are sexually
secretive.

On the other hand, openness about sex, even a limited dialogue
between mother and child, can prevent incest, as shown in this
account of a Long Island, New York, woman:

My parents were divorced when I was little and my
brother and I used to go and visit my dad on weekends.
But my dad was often out, and when he was, his father,

my grandfather, used to baby-sit us. Sometimes at night
he would go under my dress and touch me, or put me in
his bed and say, "If you lick my penis like it's a lollipop,
I'll give you money." I was 7. I was scared, and I did what
he said. It took many weekends like this until I finally told
my mom. I didn't tell her about the lollipop thing, but just
that grandpa always tried to wipe my bottom after I went
to the toilet. That was enough. She went to court and we
never stayed overnight at my dad's again.

Incest with grandfathers is less common than with uncles. But
both are dwarfed by what is apparently becoming increasingly
prevalent in our society as divorce and remarriage rates go up—
incest between stepfathers and their stepdaughters.

Indeed, a majority of the letters on incest received by *Cosmopolitan* involved incest between young girls and their mothers' new
husbands. As with father-daughter incest, the relationships usually
began when the girls were quite young. They involved threats and
the fear of exposure. And they produced almost equal amounts of
tension and despair in the girls involved. The 14-year-old whose
letter follows is living with a burden of guilt and fear that would
make many an older woman panic:

When I was 6 I lived in an apartment building in Redwood
City. My mother had been divorced from my father about
one year earlier, and while we lived in the apartment
building she started seeing a new man. I'll call him Sam.
My mother had to work until 7:30 each night, so after a
while Sam used to pick me and my younger brother and
sister up from the baby-sitter and take us to dinner at A
& W or McDonald's and then keep us at his apartment till
my mother got home. Sometimes my brother would go
outside to play with the other kids, and my sister, who
was only 2, would tag along. Sam always asked me to stay
behind to help with the dishes, or anything else he could
find to use as an excuse. Then when we were alone he
would first tell me how beautiful I was and then he would
sexually molest me. He never actually raped me, he just
kissed and licked me. I was often forced to totally undress
and roll on top of him. At the age of 6, what was I to do?
I'd had a very strict upbringing and always obeyed my
elders.

The incidents with Sam kept up until I was 11 and he and my mother announced their engagement. When I heard they were going to get married I went to the room that I still shared with my little sister and I fainted on the floor. No one knew of this, which was fortunate. If my mother had found me, she might have demanded an explanation of some kind.

I have never wanted to tell her about Sam. She loves her new husband, and I do not wish to make her feel alone again. Anyway, since their marriage three years ago he has not touched. He never talks to me unless necessary. When he enters a room, I leave. But I am afraid. I am now 14. I have four more years to stay at home. I am not afraid for myself but for my little sister. If he did this once before, mightn't he do it again?

I am very pretty on the outside, but on the inside I have many scars. Some will heal and some may not. Of this letter, I make but one request. Please publish some information for the help of other women who may be suffering like I was. I will be forever grateful to you if you can help someone.

An 18-year-old from Texas had a similar experience, but one she could not protect her mother from:

From the time I was 12 years old until last year, when I moved away from home to get married, I had an incestuous relationship with my stepfather. He never used physical force with me but he used tremendous mental force. At times I felt almost as if I had been brainwashed. He told me that he loved me and that he would kill himself if I ever stopped allowing what was going on. He also told me that if I ever told anyone he would go to jail and my mother would hate me forever. At one time he had me so confused I felt the whole thing was my fault. Anyway, it went on for five years with me always trying to stop it, and him using threats to keep it going. Finally when he found out I was going to be married, he told my mother, to get even with me. There was a big confrontation, and he and my mother got a divorce. If that isn't a heavy guilt trip to lay on someone, I don't know what is. My mother believed my side of the story, at least, and has tried to

forget everything. Only I can't forget. I have horrible
nightmares all the time in which he is coming to get me.
Sometimes I can't even stand for my husband to touch me.
I feel that what happened has had an enormous influence
on my personality. It has made me a harder person. I've
built a wall around myself, and I find it very hard to share
myself with other people. I don't trust other people. I
haven't even told my husband what happened, because
I'm afraid he would not understand, and would blame me.

Nearly all the women who wrote to the *Cosmopolitan* survey
about incest asked that their experiences be made available to other
—especially young—women in the hope that somehow they might
help relieve the anguish of others.

One woman, who has made it her life's work to help incest
victims, wrote that "women need to share these experiences." She
is 30 and living in Oakland, California, and she was raped at the age
of 12 by her stepfather, as a result of which she became pregnant
and gave birth to a son before she herself was a teenager. Today she
works as a sexual trauma counselor. Her thoughtful words appro-
priately conclude this section: "Children are extremely easy prey
and they often blame themselves for incest. They imagine they 'did
something' to cause it. But we women used to feel the same way
about rape, and today we know forced sex is not our fault. It is time
society reached the same level of indignation and awareness about
incest."

5. Brother-Sister Incest

MAJOR FINDINGS:

Some 5 percent of the women had had incestuous
experiences with brothers.

Most studies of incest have shown that brother-sister incest is less
traumatic than other forms. Masters and Johnson have reported that
sex therapy patients who described brother-sister incest did so,
except in very rare circumstances, "by casual reference and without

reluctance," and that these patients' incestuous experiences rarely proved crucial to their sexual dysfunction. In the Northern Ireland incest project, only one of the fifteen women who had slept with a brother suffered "any morbid consequences or ill effects" from the experience.

What apparently makes brother-sister incest less emotionally disturbing than other forms is the smaller age-gap that usually exists in a brother-sister pair, as opposed to a father-daughter, stepfather-stepdaughter or uncle-niece pair. Brother-sister incest usually begins as a kind of sexual exploration between two individuals, neither of whom is particularly more sexually knowledgeable than the other.

This was true of most of the *Cosmo* women who had experienced brother-sister incest. Sometimes the brother initiated the sexual activity, sometimes they did it, but usually both were in full agreement about pursuing their explorations. A 24-year-old Florida woman wrote:

> I first learned about sex when I was 8. My brother was 5, and I wanted to have sex so that I'd know what it was like. We tried and failed, I guess because we were so young. We couldn't figure out how to get in the proper position, or even what to do once "it" was "in." Did you just lie there like that? Or what? For how long? After about forty-five minutes we gave up in disgust and got out the Play-Doh or something. After that we never had any sexual interest in each other, and what we'd done.

Similarly a 24-year-old from Illinois reported:

> I have had incest with my younger brother. It happened when we were teenagers. Most of the time he just stroked my breasts, but one time we got fully undressed and he fingered me, and I sucked on his erect penis. We both were high the time this happened. Afterwards we were kind of embarrassed, and it never happened again, but we continued to be close and to maintain a good relationship.

Even a 21-year-old college student from Michigan who became pregnant as a result of incest with her brother did not feel the incest in itself had had long range emotionally damaging effects, although she was frightened about having to have an abortion:

> My first time at intercourse was when I was 14, going on 15, and my partner was my 13-year-old brother. I remember the occasion very well because I got pregnant and had to have an abortion three-and-a-half months later. It was December 1973, and my brother and I were visiting our father and stepmother in Flint. It was their league night and they were out bowling. My brother and I were watching TV and we started talking about sex. "Have you done it yet?" "Have *you?*" That sort of thing. And then we decided we'd try it. We went down to the basement where there were two studio beds, and we took off our pajamas and proceeded. My brother asked me if I could get pregnant and I fiercely said, "No," thinking it was true. I'd heard you only got pregnant when you wanted a baby and I somehow thought that since I didn't want one, I wouldn't. I didn't know much about sex, as you can see. I got pregnant. And afterwards I didn't tell my mother because I was afraid. Finally she guessed, and confronted me. She kept accusing my boyfriend from school, until finally I felt I simply had to tell her the truth about who the father was. She went hysterical. I was sent to a psychiatrist, and taken out of school, and given an abortion. It had to be a saline job because I'd waited so long before telling my mother. Anyway, I don't think I had any harsh thoughts or feelings about my brother, or what we'd done. I was just real scared about the abortion. But after my mother's hysteria calmed down, she helped me out a lot. I was very glad to have her near me. And although for the next two years I developed a sort of mental block about sex, and wouldn't let any boy so much as hold my hand or kiss me, when I finally did start having sex again, I wanted to make up for lost time and I did it as often as I could talk my boyfriend into it.

But there are some circumstances under which brother-sister sex can be as distressing as other forms of incest. If there is a considerable age difference between the siblings, and the male is the aggressor, the female can feel victimized and psychically injured. Virginia Woolf stands out. Even when she was 59 years old, she still reminisced about how humiliated she had felt when, at age 6, her older half-brother, George Duckworth, would examine her by standing her up on a ledge. Her biographer-nephew Quentin Bell, who first revealed the details of the experience, felt the incest could be blamed for the writer's lifelong frigid sexual attitudes. "A first experience of loving or being loved," wrote Bell, "may be enchanting, desolating, embarrassing, or even boring, but it should not be disgusting. Eros came with a commotion of leathern wings, a figure of mawkish incestuous sexuality. Virginia felt that George had spoiled her life before it had fairly begun. Naturally shy in sexual matters, she was from this time terrified back into a posture of frozen and defensive panic."

The second circumstance is, of course, when the incest occurs not as a result of a mutual decision to explore one another sexually but when incestuous sex is forced sex. One of the *Cosmo* women, a 31-year-old high-school teacher, was raped by a brother taunted into having sex with her by his friends, and then was gang-raped by those friends:

> It was a few weeks before my 15th birthday. We lived on a farm on the outskirts of a small California town. My brother was 16. A bunch of us kids used to fool around a lot together and the boys would get turned on when we played cards or spin-the-bottle or post office, especially in the summertime when we girls would wear short-shorts and sit around cross-legged. One Saturday my brother and his friends coaxed me into going into an old shed with them, to play cards. When we got inside, they started kissing and pawing me, and I told them to bug off and tried to break away and run outside but they wouldn't let me. They stripped me and lay me back on a bale of straw. It was prickly and sharp, and they wouldn't even put something down on it to keep it from hurting. They just started pushing my brother forward to have sex with me. Apparently he'd bragged to them that I had let him lay me. But it wasn't true and when they discovered I was a virgin, they started taunting my brother and arguing over who was going to break my cherry. For some reason, none of the boys wanted to be the one to do it. For a minute I thought they would back out, but then my brother, his ego bruised by the taunts and ridicule of his friends,

climbed on. I screamed and yelled bloody murder, but it was fall, after harvest was over, and our folks were at a Farm Bureau meeting, and there weren't any workers around.

After my brother was finished with me, his friends took turns without any more arguing. I cried and cussed and screamed at them, and I threatened my brother. But later I never told. I was afraid that if our dad didn't kill him, he'd send him to prison, and despite what he had done to me, I couldn't bring myself to ruin his life. I've never told anyone else before this what he did. I just kept quiet about it. And although he could never make up to me for what he did, he has tried. He was really ashamed of himself, and I've more or less forgiven him. But things will never be the same between us. And I will never understand how a brother could do such a thing to his own sister.

How could a brother do such a thing to his own sister? This schoolteacher still wonders fifteen years after the event. Some social scientists have long wondered about the opposite. How is it that sex between brothers and sisters isn't more common? How does the incest taboo operate, even to the faltering extent that it does?

Many scholars have attempted to solve the workings of the taboo, generally without great success, but a few years ago a new, quite curious clue came along by way of a study about Israel's kibbutzim, conducted by Joseph Shepher of Haifa University. On kibbutzim, boy and girl age-mates are raised as brothers and sisters in peer groups that permit nudity and sexual play during early childhood. In adolescence, when it is acceptable to pick a sexual partner, no pressures are put on the pseudo-siblings to avoid one another. Yet, surprisingly, on one kibbutz that was closely monitored, no peer-group members engaged in any form of sexual activity with same-group partners once they turned adolescent. And, in an examination of the marriages entered into by 2,769 kibbutz peer-group members from numerous kibbutzim, only thirteen out of the entire lot proved to be between peer-group members. Then it was discovered that every one of these thirteen relationships involved people who at some point in the first six years of their lives had had their peer-group living interrupted for a time.

Shepher concluded as a result of this fascinating statistical information that there is a critical period between birth and age six during which exposure to other children "will define with whom one will not fall in love." Perhaps. More investigations will be needed. But this one certainly does suggest that while, as seen, incest arises in families that treat their members as strangers, it is usually avoided in those where even strangers are treated as family, where all females become sisters.

Chapter Twelve
Rape and Sexual Molestation

1. Change and Stasis

One of the most important accomplishments of the women's movement in the 1970s was to change, on deep, essential levels, the way society views victims of rape and sexual molestation. As recently as 1968 even Susan Brownmiller, who was eventually to write the landmark study of rape, *Against Our Will,* believed that rape victims were somehow different from other women. They brought sexual violence on themselves, was Brownmiller's pre-1970s view. And, indeed, that was the view of most men and many women. I can still recall a friend of mine, a noted psychiatrist, insisting that a young girl who had been brutally raped by some classmates in their schoolyard "must have been wearing a provocative dress," and how I nodded my head in agreement. We clearly had less than full sympathy for the girl's suffering, little knowledge of the ubiquitousness of sexual violence against women, and precious poor appreciation of the lack of provocation in that violence, the randomness of rape, the way it menaces not just attractive adolescents but children, toddlers and even 80-year-old grandmothers.

Our lack of awareness seems hard to believe today, with society's understanding of sexual violence against women so changed. And more than opinions and understanding have been changed. Our laws and our police procedures also have been altered, making it more possible to obtain convictions of rapists and somewhat easier for women to step forward and ask for such convictions.

Still, we have by no means eliminated or even reduced rape. As Brownmiller observed at the conclusion of *Against Our Will,* "Rape can be eradicated, not merely controlled or avoided on an individual basis, but the approach must be long-range and cooperative." Such an approach is yet to come, and rape and sexual molestation still menace American women.

At times the dimension of the problem seems staggering. One out of every four of the *Cosmo* women reported having had at least one experience of rape or sexual molestation. Many many more reported experience with a similar problem—being pressured into sex. Some of their brushes with violence and pressure are described in this chapter. But, interestingly, while forced sex was frequently mentioned by the *Cosmo* women, it was infrequently elaborated on. They noted their experiences but did not dwell on them—perhaps at once testimony to the awfulness of the experience and an underlying desire not to allow it to spoil healthy sex for them.

2. The Frequency of Rape and Sexual Molestation

MAJOR FINDINGS:

Twenty-six percent of the respondent women have been raped or sexually molested.

One out of every four of the women who took the survey had had at least one experience of rape or sexual molestation. While the figure at first sounds high, it may, in fact, represent the experience of a group of women more safe from sexual attack than are American women as a whole. The National Center on Child Abuse and Neglect estimates that one out of every four American girls is today sexually abused before the age of eighteen. In light of this figure, it is reasonable to conclude that considerably more than 26 percent of *all* American women may be victims of sexual violence.

Although all women are potential rape victims, most studies of rape and sexual molestation have shown that adolescent girls are in the greatest danger. Writes Susan Brownmiller, "Overall, the danger to women is greatest between the ages of 10 and 29. Teenage girls, simply by being teenage girls, run the greatest risk of any age group." The *Cosmo* survey would seem to affirm this. For the entire sample, 26 percent had been raped or molested, but among girls under 18, the figure was 30 percent.

The following letter from a San Bernardino, California, teenager suggests, with an immediacy that figures cannot, how vulnerable adolescent girls are:

> I'm 17, I live at home, and I have a job in a supermarket after school. The other day when I was walking out to my car after work a man jumped out at me and started pulling off my blouse and trying to get his hands between my legs. I screamed at the top of my voice and stuck my car keys in his face and hit his eye and I ran to my car and drove off quickly, but ever since I've seen him lurking in the parking lot and I'm afraid, so afraid, and I get chills just thinking about it.

This letter had a powerful impact on me. For all I knew, since writing to *Cosmopolitan* she had been caught and raped. Her letter effectively made the point that rape is not an abstract problem, but an outrageously real and immediate one for millions of American teenagers.

3. The Relationship of the Attacker to the Woman

MAJOR FINDINGS:

Thirty-three percent of the women who had been raped or molested were attacked by strangers. Forty-six percent were attacked by friends; 22 percent by relatives; 7 percent by husbands.

While sexual attack by a stranger is perhaps the most terrifying of all sexual violence to contemplate, the fact is that a great deal of quite frightening rape and sexual molestation occurs between a woman and someone known to her. A 23-year-old from Virginia was raped when she was 16 by a friend of her boyfriend:

> My boyfriend and I went out driving for the evening, along with a friend of his. The friend said he wanted to stop and visit another friend, so we dropped him off. Then my boyfriend and I walked into the woods, found a secluded spot, and made love. Before I'd gotten my clothes back on, the friend found us. He was drunk, and he jumped on me. My boyfriend tried to make him stop, but couldn't.

A 24-year-old from Florida was gang-raped by schoolmates:

> I was raped when I was 17 by five guys, all of whom I knew from school. They each took turns with me, while the others held me down. It was a nightmare, and the pain that it left me with will never go away.

A 23-year-old bookkeeper from California was raped when she was a teenager by a trusted family friend:

> I was raped at 14 by a friend of my parents. He took me out to a bar to celebrate my graduation, and gave me lots of attention and champagne which, as you can imagine, I found very flattering. He also gave me Quaaludes, telling me they were aspirin for the headache I'd have the next day. Then, on our way home, he made up a story about having to stop off at his apartment to pick up something. I went in with him, and inside he grabbed me, pulled off my slacks and raped me. It hurt like hell. I'd never had sex before. I didn't even know what to call what he'd done until I got home and told my mother about it.

And a woman from Tennessee was raped by her husband:

> I was 22. It was eighteen years ago. But I have never forgotten it. No woman ever forgets rape. I had just given birth to my first child and the rapist was my husband. I was sick in bed at the time and unable to escape him. He was drunk and demanding sex. He acted like a madman. He forced himself on me, and as a result I wasn't able to

take any birth-control precautions, and I became pregnant once again. It is very possible for a husband to rape his wife.

For these women, and all the others who described being raped or molested by men they knew, there were serious emotional after-effects—feeling fearful, degraded, and uncomfortable for years afterwards when having partner sex. But the after-effects of stranger-rape or molestation were even more devastating. Those who had been attacked by strangers were often unable to put the experience out of their minds for a single day, or hour, and some said they were subsequently unable even to *attempt* sex with their partners. A 27-year-old from California was typical:

> Last year I was raped by a stranger who threatened to cut my face if I didn't cooperate. It was the most terrifying experience you can imagine, and I haven't felt able to have sex ever since, even with my boyfriend.

This woman was not injured physically as a result of the rape. But there were other women who, as a result of stranger rape, had had their bodies maimed, their beauty stolen. It was so painful to read their letters, I ultimately decided not to reprint them. The brutal purposes to which the sex drive is sometimes put are daily emblazoned in the press and broadcast on radio and television.

It is enough to say—and emphasize—that, despite what sexual idealists have often predicted, forced sex has *not* withered away now that consensual sex has become more common.

4. A Related Problem: Being Pressured into Sex

MAJOR FINDINGS:

An overwhelming majority of the women—72 percent—felt that on at least one occasion they had been unpleasantly pressured into sex and had given in to it against their better judgment.

Some men deride women's complaints about sexual pressure. They insist that even when a woman shows reluctance about having sex, she really wants it; she is only pretending reluctance, for propriety's sake. Or they argue that women crave being pressured into sex, that they enjoy men's insistence and urgency.

This survey says both opinions are wrong. The *Cosmo* women pressured into sex found it an experience they neither wanted nor enjoyed. They gave in to it, despite their better judgment, often out of the fear that if they didn't capitulate they would be raped. And indeed, it was sometimes difficult to tell, when a woman described being pressured into sex, whether the experience might not after all have been called rape. Here, for example, is what happened to a Detroit woman, now only 20, when she was 14:

> I was very much in love with a boy, or thought I was, who was a year younger than me. He had bothered me for months to have sex with him, but I repeatedly refused. One day he finally lost patience and began slapping me and ordering me to submit, threatening to hurt me seriously if I did not. When I attempted to fight him off I was roughly thrown to the floor. He put his hand to my throat to prevent me from moving. And he used his other hand to undress me. I remember the sharp pain as he forced himself into me, and my telling him he was hurting me, and his not caring or stopping. It was my first time.

She calls the experience one of "sexual pressure." Many of us would call it rape.

Similarly, here is what happened to the legal secretary from California, whose sexual initiation was with "Pencil Dick." She had given up her virginity willingly, eager to consider herself a woman. But soon afterward she found that some boys she went to school with, learning through the grapevine about her new non-virginal state, assumed she would have sex with anyone at all. One boy began to haunt her:

> Word just started getting around. Then one boy, who'd been trying to win my affections for quite some time, asked me out for a date. We went out drinking, and as the evening progressed he became more and more belligerent. He kept accusing me of not liking him, and he showed a

dangerous jealousy I'd never like to encounter again. I got
so upset with his badgering that I asked him to take me
home. He was furious. He stopped his van one block from
my house, and proceeded to semi-rape me. He pulled me
into the back and vigorously tried to get my clothes off.
He had my pants down, and I was a wreck—crying and
screaming for him to get off me. Finally, I calmed him
down enough to get away, and the bruises and scratches
I sported were to be a constant reminder to stay away
from that particular male person.

Sexual pressure of this sort, exerted on women who are already
in late adolescence, is widespread, and obviously upsetting, but less
so than sexual pressure exerted during childhood or early adolescence. A 21-year-old from Maine said:

When I was a young teenager, I went camping with a
bunch of friends and I shared a camper with a boy I knew.
I woke up with my sleeping bag off me, my pants unzip-
pered, and my shirt and bra undone. He forcibly held me
down, pulled my pants off, and entered me. I did not
scream or yell. I did not want to make a scene and embar-
rass myself in front of the others. But the shame and the
humiliation that I felt and still feel while thinking of this
are so great that I wish I'd never even mentioned it.

And a woman from Pennsylvania who was pressured into sex
when she was only 14 by a 35-year-old married friend of her father's, says:

He forced me to suck on his penis. I was so repulsed—
mostly because he forced me—that I threw up. After that
I avoided him all the time. I felt he was a menace to my
life. Fortunately he didn't come around to see my father
so much after this had happened.

Beyond question or myth, the *Cosmo* women disliked being
pressured into sex, and all of them would likely agree with these
words of a 20-year-old student from Kansas: "Being pressured into
sex is an absolute turn-off. I like a loving, gentle man."

PART FIVE
The Sexual Revolution

Chapter Thirteen
Evaluating the Sexual Revolution

Evaluating the Sexual Revolution

MAJOR FINDINGS:

Forty-nine percent of the respondents felt that the sexual revolution had had a good effect on the lives of most women. Fifty-three percent felt that it had caused sex to be too casual or made it hard for them to find acceptable reasons to say no to a man sexually. (The figures add to more than 100 percent because 2 percent of the women straddled both sides of the question.)

As a group, the *Cosmo* women are perhaps the most sexually experienced women in western history. They tend to start their erotic lives young, have sex with a considerable number of partners, and practice a considerable variety of sexual techniques. They are comfortable about ackowledging masturbation and sexual fantasy, and the great majority of them believe that good sex is possible without love. These women have apparently reaped the sexual fruits planted by idealistic social reformers throughout the eighteenth, nineteenth and early twentieth centuries. But as the figures above show, by no means all the *Cosmo* women are happy about the harvest.

More than half of them are disappointed in or disillusioned with the sexual revolution.

Why? Is their dissatisfaction simply a result of the usual human

301

tendency to disparage whatever exists and long for the greener grass of whatever does not? Or are there, in fact, real and serious flaws in the sexual revolution, at least as it affects women? The *Cosmo* women who were dissatisfied with the sexual revolution seemed to feel there were. Many believed that, like the heirs to political revolutions, they had been betrayed. They had participated in the overthrow of one tyranny only to see another installed in its place. A 24-year-old schoolteacher from Pennsylvania was typical of this group:

> The sexual revolution is in reality a big sad joke that we women mindlessly allowed to be played on us. What we did when we freed ourselves physically was free men to live out their wildest fantasies of promiscuity and irresponsibility. Men never wanted to form commitments, but in the past they had to in order to obtain sex. Now that we women are no longer afraid of one-night stands, men don't have to commit themselves. Before the revolution, life offered the average women half a glass with which to slake her thirst. Now she's being doused with a fire hose.

Similarly, a 24-year-old aeronautics worker from Florida wrote:

> I have to say that the sexual revolution has made sex worse for me, not better. Yes, the men I meet know how to kiss, suck, touch and fondle, They know how to make me come. But they do it to satisfy their own egos, not because they want to give me pleasure. They don't really care about me, about women, just about sex and their egos. In the past a man used to have to offer a relationship in order to get sex. Tat for tit. But now, since so many women give sex so freely, the men offer nothing—and we women must accept this, even if we don't like it. Throughout the centuries, women have gotten the short end of the stick. We're still getting it. Only now it's a different stick.

The feeling that sexual freedom had benefited men more than women was the predominant underlying complaint against the sexual revolution. The dissatisfied women did not register this complaint out of a Victorian sensibility; they did not argue that sex was not as physically pleasurable to women as it was to men. Rather, they tended to feel that what women wanted from enjoyable sex was not what men wanted from it.

What women wanted, said the critics of the sexual revolution, was not necessarily love. Three-fourths of the *Cosmo* women, including a large number of those who disliked the sexual revolution, believed that good sex was possible without love. What they wanted, *needed,* said the critics, was some form of committed ongoing interchange, and men did not. They believed, for example, that men, unlike women, thoroughly enjoyed one-night stands.

I wonder about this distinction. If it were true, why would so many millions of men continue to opt, today, for living-together arrangements and even marriage? (Despite the sexual revolution and divorce rate, the latest census shows no decline in the American marriage rate.) Some men may have one-night stands—isolated sexual encounters after which they never call again—not so much because they like casual sex as because they decide, after an evening with a particular woman, that they don't care to pursue further intimacy with *her.* What woman doesn't have a friend who complained about having sex with some man who never called her again and then learned, six months or a year later, that he was about to marry someone else—thereby throwing cold water on her theory that he was a devotee of casual sex?

Of course, there *are* men who never form commitments, who never have sex with the same woman twice if they can help it. And although I suspect they are rarer than some imagine, to the woman who has been unable to link up with a lover willing to form an ongoing relationship with her, the sexual revolution can seem empty indeed. A 23-year-old from New York City writes:

> I'm always surprised when I hear from a man after we've spent the night in bed. You can't count on it. That's the way men are. And we women, myself included, have made fools of ourselves by going along with the sexual revolution. We've made it possible for them to have sex with us at the drop of a hat, and never feel enough responsibility to call up the next day and see how we are, or even *if* we are. There are nights I say goodbye to a lover to whom I've just given the greatest ecstasies in bed, and I think to myself, Here I am in my dangerous Greenwich

Village apartment, with its fire escapes and dingy stair-
cases. Maybe someone will break in and rape me during
the night. Or kill me. Will this guy I'm saying goodbye to
ever wonder about me in the morning? Will he wonder
enough to call and discover I don't answer the phone? Will
he notify the police? Probably not. That's the sexual revolution for you.

Some women who were dissatisfied with the sexual revolution
felt that a great deal of what they said and did sexually was insincere. They pretended to enjoyments they did not actually feel. A
22-year-old from Maine was typical:

> I feel 40, I've had so many lovers. I usually go to bed with
> men on the first date. All the guys I meet expect this. If
> you don't do it, you run the very high risk of never seeing
> them again. I try to convince myself I enjoy sex with a
> total, or semi-total, stranger. I do it because the guys I
> meet are convinced that they do. But I really detest it.
> Why can't things be the way they used to be before this
> sexual revolution? Why can't a woman get to know and
> like a guy first, and then have intercourse with him?

And a 19-year-old from Oregon who pretends to an enjoyment of
sadomasochistic sex with her lover, but who has never had an
orgasm during this kind of sex, writes:

> My feelings about the sexual revolution are that it is mov-
> ing too fast. People are too free about sex. But you have
> to act like you like it or you'll be sitting home all alone.

Those who approve of and admire the sexual revolution do not
feel they have been insincere about their pleasures. And, usually,
they are women who have had, at least from time to time, ongoing
committed relationships with men. A 22-year-old woman from
Oregon, whose route to orgasm was described in Chapter Five, is
typical: Although she had some ten lovers during college, many of
whom were one-night stands, she praises the sexual revolution
because it enabled her to experiment with men until she found the
one she has now, a man she is planning to marry at the end of the
year:

My earlier sexual experiences, while not very good, helped me over some insecurities and feelings of unattractiveness, and paved the way for me to enjoy my present boyfriend. I am all for the sexual revolution. There are some problems connected with it, but for the most part it seems to mature people faster and help them not to have fears about sexual feelings. Life seems a lot more natural this way.

The contrast between the feelings of this Oregon woman and those of the Oregon woman whose letter precedes hers suggests an all-important . . . if not surprising . . . fact about the sexual revolution: It is different things to different people. To one woman, the revolution may be in her having had premarital sex with one or two lovers. To another, it may be in her having had a dozen. To one woman, it means she can comfortably discuss with her husband the sexual techniques most likely to bring her to orgasm. To another, it's that the men who call her expect her to accompany them to orgies. There has been a sexual revolution, but when people say they are for it or against it, they are often speaking about very different phenomena.

So it is not enough to know that a woman approves of the sexual revolution for Reason X, or disapproves of it for Reason Y. For her reasons to be meaningful, one needs to know what experiences shaped her reasoning. Is her sexual revolution the same as yours or mine?

Chapter Fourteen
What Revolution?

What Revolution?

Because the erotic upheaval of the last few decades means different things to different people, it seemed that the most useful way to glimpse the scope and complexity of that upheaval would be to have some of the *Cosmo* women themselves describe what it is that they mean when they say the words "sexual revolution."

The first story comes from a 35-year-old woman from Texas. She enlisted in the army three years ago and is now stationed in a small town in Germany.

> My day here begins at 0500 hours. I dress in my uniform and spit-shined boots and leave for work. I am one of the fortunates who are allowed to maintain an apartment off-base. I report to the female barracks at 0545 to wake the rest of the women in my section. By 0600 I am down in the NCOIC's office for the day's briefing. By 0630 I and the other women in my section report for physical training, which includes a daily run of at least three miles, and sometimes five. Then we breakfast, shower and report for work call at 0830 hours. Our days are basically the same; usually we are in the field for a week, and then for the next week we work on our two-and-a-half and five-ton trucks. Every person here, male and female, pulls his own load.

306

Although most females in the civilian world would be extremely happy with the man-women ratio, which is approximately 100 men to 1 woman, it sometimes has extreme drawbacks. The male competitiveness seems to be exciting at first, but it gets boring after a while. Most of us women here don't believe a word the guys say to us, even when the approach is new.

I was brought up by very strict parents. I was not allowed even to date in high school. When I was 17 I was permitted, after much pleading, to visit a cousin in Louisiana. On my first weekend there I was raped by a friend of the family. I reported the rape to the police, and the chief of police called my father, who came immediately to pick me up. But although I had been beaten and bloodied, when I returned home my family treated me as if I was a whore. I left home soon after, never to return again.

Prior to enlisting in the army three years ago, I was married twice. And in those years, besides my two husbands, I had sex with only two other men. Since the army I have had fifteen lovers, some of them only one-night stands. On those occasions, all I wanted was to satisfy basic physical needs.

I love X-rated movies, and getting high. Marijuana stimulates my sexual appetites and releases all my inhibitions. I love to be tipsy and dance slowly and seductively with a man who is strong, dark and has a beautiful rear end. I like a lot of foreplay. I am most fond of oral sex. I have been fortunate lately to have had good lovers, men who see to my needs. This makes me give that much more of myself to them. I always climax at least once, and usually more often. I am a strong believer in fidelity, which is why I am divorced.

I am extremely thankful for the sexual revolution. It has changed me from an unhappy housewife/mother to a liberated free spirit. This is a wonderful era that we live in now. I don't agree with those women who say there is no longer any romance in sex. A woman of today who is smart and innovative can get any relationship to the exact place she wants it to be. I genuinely feel we have the most powerful weapon around, our mouths. We are capable of leading, deceiving, devouring and diverting. The world is ours to have.

A 22-year-old college student living in Florida never thought she would take money in exchange for sex, but when a man offered her a thousand dollars, she did. Her reasoning was that she had plenty of meaningless, casual sex just in the ordinary course of her life. So why not the casual sex of prostitution?

I don't really know where to begin, as I've never written down any of my thoughts about sex before, but I want to try. I feel I've been deeply affected by the sexual revolution and that I'm a pretty average person, so my views and experiences could be very useful.

I grew up in the midwest in a fairly conservative town where you weren't supposed to have sex unless you were seriously involved with your partner. So all through high school, since I never got serious about anyone, I never had sex.

By the time I graduated I was too curious about sex to go on waiting. I began frequenting the bars with my best girlfriend. We'd pick up guys, and pet with them, and eventually I got around to having sex with one of them.

Since that time I've had sex with eleven guys, seven of them in the last eight months. None of my relationships has amounted to what you could call a long-term loving relationship, even though that is what I want. Sex here, where I go to school, is always casual. Most of my friends are students, and we all party together, and couples are constantly changing and no one stays with anyone very long. It's easy come, easy go.

Last month I let a man pay me for sex. The man was about 50 years old, gross, fat, rich and lonely. My girl-friend and I were at the beach having drinks at a bar near a pool. The man started talking to us and offered me and my girlfriend each a thousand dollars in cash if we would have sex with him. My girlfriend refused, but I said okay. He shook my hand, and when he did, he put ten one-hundred-dollar bills into my palm. I went to his house and for an hour I played hooker. It wasn't as hard as I'd thought it would be. I'd thought I'd feel guilty but I didn't. I'm a self-supporting student and that one hour with him meant I could finish school without having to ask my parents for any more money. So while I'm not proud of what I did, I'd do it again. It was a lot of money for very

little work, and it wasn't the first time I'd slept with someone and felt there wasn't any meaning associated with sex.
Interestingly, I later told a couple of close girlfriends about
what happened, and instead of being shocked they said
they wished I'd introduce *them* to the man. They wanted
the money too. Their reactions sort of surprised me, but
I guess they feel the same way about sex as I do.

A lot of the time I don't know where to draw the line
sexually, or even if it should be drawn, and a lot of times
I wonder if I'm being too loose and free about everything.
So I don't know what I think of the sexual revolution. I
only know that I enjoy sex, would never give it up, but
hope that someday I will find a deeper meaning in it than
just physical sensation.

For a very different college student, a sophomore at a college
in Georgia, the sexual revolution has made her feel joyous, has
caused her to discover the intimacy of love that can accompany sex:

I grew up in a small southern town. I fooled around with
boys in high school but never did more than heavy petting. My parents believe that sex is bad and a girl all used
up once her maidenhead is gone. A week after I arrived on
my college campus, I met a boy I liked very much. He was
tender, caring, gentle, and very experienced. Three weeks
after I met him, we made love, and soon I moved to his
room. We are getting engaged this December.

I love sex. I'd never thought such absolute closeness
and sharing could exist. I had my first orgasm about a
week after my boyfriend and I started to make love. Wow.
I cried and everything. Since then, we have tried sex in all
ways, all places, all times. We have sex an average of twice
a day. By sex, I mean, we make love and both have orgasms, whether we are making love manually, orally, or
with intercourse. Our relationship is not based on sex but
sex is a healthy part of it.

The sexual revolution? Of course I'm pleased about
it. Although my parents would never agree, I believe that
sex is a sacred thing, a beautiful way for a man and
woman to merge with one another. I wouldn't force anyone to hold my views, or even try to persuade them that
my way is the best way. But it is right for me. And because

of the sexual revolution, I can do what's right for me, instead of what might have been right for my parents' generation.

A young woman only two years younger than the Georgia college student, a high-school senior from a suburb of New York City, was experiencing a quite different sexual revolution:

> I am 17 years old and will soon be graduating high school. I had intercourse for the first time when I was 15. I was forced into it by my boyfriend. I didn't get anything out of it, and I felt nothing for him. I broke off with him after a year, and flung myself into another meaningless relationship. Then I broke off that one too and had another boyfriend. Then I had a few others. Once I even went to an orgy, and though I enjoyed it at the time I regretted it afterward. It really confused me, and I didn't know what to think or do. I was pretty messed up then. I was even contemplating suicide. I think the problem was the drugs I did—angel dust, acid, mescaline, ups, downs, everything but heroin. I wonder if other girls have done this. Anyway, lately I've been doing a lot of thinking, and I feel that everything will be all right. I am seeing a 19-year-old boyfriend and he and I are pretty close. I can tell him what I think and feel. I would really like to get married within the next two years and I'm hoping we will work it out.

For the next woman, the sexual revolution is not at all melancholy, even though it consists, for her, chiefly of what other women might term unsatisfying casual sex. Twenty-five, she works in the movie industry and, footloose and fancy free, derives great enjoyment from her sexual independence:

> I live in Los Angeles, work as a location auditor for motion pictures, and have never been married. In my work I travel approximately eight months out of the year. I spend a great deal of time with predominantly male movie crews, and have learned a great deal about the sexual revolution from my experiences.
>
> When I am on the road, I definitely have sex more indiscriminately than I do when I am on my home turf. This is the norm for the rest of my nomadic fellow work-

ers too. The relationships that develop based on this on-the-road freedom are surprisingly satisfying. When no one feels that he or she is a potential mate, barriers come falling down. I have really gotten to know the men with whom I have had sex on the road, and we have been able to share memorable experiences. I like this.

At home, even subconsciously, I am always regarding men with an eye toward the future. My ideal would be to have the freedom I experience away from my home when I am at home, but so far I seem unable to attain this. I suppose my upbringing has kept me from exploring sexual freedom fully. But to do so is my goal.

A 22-year-old woman who is particularly interesting because she has been a *Playboy* centerfold—the object of countless men's desires and women's jealousies—has experienced a similar sexual revolution, although she hopes for a different outcome from her partner experimentation than the Los Angeles woman does. She wants an intimate, committed relationship. But this desire is only recent. When she was 15½ she fell in love and had sex. When the relationship broke up she felt so remorseful about not being virginal that for three years afterward she abstained from sex. Finally, at 19, she rebelled against her own and her family's traditional views:

> I moved to California and just let loose. I slept with about twenty-five or thirty people in about a year and a half. I made love in ways I'd never even dreamed of. It was a great learning experience. At this point I am ready to settle down with one partner. I would love to have an intimate relationship with romance and commitment. But I'm real pleased that sex these days is so uninhibited and that a woman in today's world is not labeled as a "whore" or "cheap" because she chooses to have more than one sexual partner. Women have the same needs and sexual desires as men do, and there's no reason why they should back off.

To the 30-year-old woman whose story follows, the sexual revolution was less a bed of roses than a "battleground":

> Since I answered the survey, everything in my life has changed. After three years of being single since a divorce

at age 27, after three years of being sexually liberated and having a large number and variety of lovers, several three-somes, and always no commitments, no tomorrows, I'm in love. And my lover is in love with me! I'm 30 years old, a good mother, a successful businesswoman and now, much to the shock of my friends, a one-man woman.

I am gladly leaving the battleground of the sexual revolution. I am gladly returning to being the square lit-tle Iowa girl my mama raised me to be. My friends said it couldn't be done, but I will be doing it. My lover and I have both known divorce, loneliness and lots of casual sex. Now we have commitments and tomorrows.

To a much older divorced woman, a 57-year-old grandmother, the sexual revolution has meant the opportunity to have—despite her age—quantities of lovers. She sounds not embattled but en-chanted:

I am divorced and have a great job as an inspector at a large hydraulic plant. I have a lovely apartment, a little Pinto, many friends and, right now, three steady lovers—aged 36, 33 and 28—although since my divorce I've had many, many more. I was married for twenty-three years and had five children. I was miserable, stuck in a small town where women were definitely second-class citizens. Men worked, drank in the bars with their buddies, came home to eat and sleep and, once a week, on Saturdays, to have sex. There were no good jobs for women. God, it was boring! One day I just walked out, leaving three children still at home. I had $200, no job and no place to live. It was a great struggle, but it was well worth it. Now I have my own money, and find life delightful and funny. Men like me because I am full of energy, honest, unpredictable, and make no demands. I have indulged in just about every-thing, except masturbation and lesbianism, which are just not for me. I wear blue jeans and keep my hair long. I love my life, and my feelings about the sexual revolution are: Hip, Hip, Hooray!

To a young Wisconsin woman, the sexual revolution has meant feeling old before her time:

> I lost my virginity when I was 11 years old, in 1971 (not against my will). I began to have a tremendous amount of sex with everyone, without birth control. When I was in eighth grade I remember my girlfriends and I bought a cake that had a big "50" on it to celebrate my fifty lovers! Yes, I kept a list and still do! (It's well over 200 now.) About ten on the list don't have any names, many just have first names. I can't remember what about a quarter of them looked like. And I don't care. In 1978 I got married. In 1979, after two affairs, I got a divorce. Now, after having lived with a man for two years while having relationships on the side, I live by myself.
>
> I have a very promising career in retail buying, but what concerns me is that at the age of 21 I seem to have become very burned out with sex. I never have an orgasm with a man anymore. I haven't had one in over three years. My idea of a good night of sex is taking a hot bath and getting into bed with my vibrator.
>
> Someday I would like to write a book on my experiences, thoughts and feelings. Maybe someone can fantasize and live through me without having to have experiences like mine themselves. Because yes, I do regret a lot of how I've lived my life.

But to a 41-year-old married woman from Connecticut the sexual revolution has meant feeling youthful.

> I got married at 29, having waited until I found a man I was sure I would be happy with. My husband and I enjoy great closeness, in and out of bed, both of us commuting to work together in the city, and each of us taking great joy in satisfying each other. We still, after twelve years together, make love three to four times a week, and each time it seems different, for we are always experimenting with new sexual techniques and trying to vary what we

do. I have two children, and a big house to take care of. Plus there's my job. But all my friends marvel at how young I look, and how energetic I am. I am convinced I have stayed young because of my happy, sexually exciting marriage.

To a 43-year-old mother of five, the sexual revolution has meant discovering the self-esteem that is so often a by-product of successful sex, and of which she was deprived for years:

> Here I am, a 43-year-old separated mother of three young adults, aged 16 to 20, quietly smiling to myself after reading your questionnaire, when just a few years ago I might have been shocked, or made angry by all the hints in it about people's wild sexual doings. I had a very deprived sexual life. I married my husband before having sex with him, and our first lovemaking occurred on our honeymoon. It was never good for either of us, but I at least kept quiet, whereas he made me feel it was all my fault. I never seemed to live up to his sexual expectations, and eventually he started having affairs. Then when I was 38 we divorced and I was thrown out into the roaring sexually-free seventies. I was terrified. And the first few years were awful. I was lonely and isolated. But then I met a man who taught me that I was a sexually responsive woman, not the frigid cold thing my husband said I was. He taught me to have confidence in myself. High time, when you consider how old I was. From this man on, it has all been uphill for me. I have been having a wonderful time. I love the sexual revolution.

And to a 26-year-old journalist from California who waited twenty-six years to have sex for the first time, the sexual revolution has meant being able to admit to and enjoy sexual feelings, even though she chose not to act on those feelings until she had established a firm, committed relationship:

> I was a virgin until this year. I spent my life believing that sex should be reserved for a marital or other strongly committed relationship. So I waited until I found the right person. This year I found him. Interestingly, my lover held

the same views I did, and he too was a virgin. I decided
I was ready for intercourse, with this man, because I was
fairly certain the relationship will lead to marriage, and I
am fairly certain we can make the marriage work. I am
glad the sexual revolution happened. Although I remained
a virgin until age 26, I was never uninterested in sex,
starting out at age 11 by reading *Valley of the Dolls,* and
continuing on through *The Sensuous Woman,* Xaviera Hol-
lander, *Thy Neighbor's Wife,* and many other such books. I
would hate to have lived in a time when women had to
pretend an absence of sexual feelings.

These twelve lives, plus the hundreds that have been touched
on previously in *The Cosmo Report,* suggest the difficulty of judging
a phenomenon as complex as the sexual revolution. Yet I am aware
that most of us are forever doing just that. We say, "It has made sex
meaningless," or "It has made sex more satisfying." We say, "It's
been bad," or "It's been good." We say, "It has added to the sum
of human happiness," or "It has brought nothing but despair in its
wake." And so forth, and so forth.

We are, of course, willy-nilly, judging how it has played itself
out in our own lives. If we believe that for society as a whole sex
has become "too casual," it is likely we ourselves who have become
"too casual"—after all, tens of thousands of women represented in
this book have not been casual about sex. If we believe that men
expect us always to say "yes" to a sexual encounter, it is likely we
ourselves who believe that a "yes" must be given—tens of thousands of women represented in this book do not automatically say
"yes." We ourselves can change our negative assessments of the
sexual revolution by making corrective changes in our own behavior.

There is no doubt that the sexual revolution has not been a
happy experience for all the women who participated in this study.
There is no doubt that it has been perplexing. But it is difficult to
imagine any woman living in today's sexual climate who would
choose to go back to Kinsey's time, with its stigmas against sexual
experimentation even in the marriage bed.

And so if the present sometimes seems unbearably turbulent,

perhaps the best policy of all would be to look not to the past, but to the future. The sexual revolution is, as demonstrated, not a monolithic phenomenon, nor is it a set of rules chiseled in stone. We can scrap parts, hold to others with all our dedication. It would seem the best question to ask ourselves (now that we know with a good degree of certainty the extent of the sexual revolution in America) is: Where can we take this sexual revolution, we who have inherited it?

APPENDIX

Table 1
AGE OF RESPONDENT

	TOTAL RESP.	AGE				
		UNDER 18	18–24	25–29	30–34	35 OR OLDER
Total Respondents	10000	225	4681	2664	1296	1125
Don't Know/No Answer	9	—	—	—	—	—
Total Answering	9991	225	4681	2664	1296	1125
	100.0	100.0	100.0	100.0	100.0	100.0
Under 18	225	225	—	—	—	—
	2.3	100.0	—	—	—	—
18 to 24	4681	—	4681	—	—	—
	46.9	—	100.0	—	—	—
25 to 29	2664	—	—	2664	—	—
	26.7	—	—	100.0	—	—
30 to 34	1296	—	—	—	1296	—
	13.0	—	—	—	100.0	—
35 or Over	1125	—	—	—	—	1125
	11.3	—	—	—	—	100.0

Table 2
SIZE OF RESPONDENT'S CITY/TOWN

	TOTAL RESP.	AGE				
		UNDER 18	18–24	25–29	30–34	35 OR OLDER
Total Respondents	10000	225	4681	2664	1296	1125
Don't Know/No Answer	189	4	103	45	19	17
Total Answering	9811	221	4578	2619	1277	1108
	100.0	100.0	100.0	100.0	100.0	100.0
City of More than 1 Million	1763	34	782	506	253	187
	18.0	15.4	17.1	19.3	19.8	16.9
City of 10,000 to 1 Million	4316	78	2037	1169	551	479
	44.0	35.3	44.5	44.6	43.1	43.2
City of Less than 10,000	810	23	427	212	88	60
	8.3	10.4	9.3	8.1	6.9	5.4
Suburb	1857	50	871	445	247	240
	18.9	22.6	19.0	17.0	19.3	21.7
Rural Area	1065	36	461	287	138	142
	10.9	16.3	10.1	11.0	10.8	12.8

Table 3
GEOGRAPHIC LOCATION OF RESPONDENT

	TOTAL RESP.	AGE				
		UNDER 18	18–24	25–29	30–34	35 OR OLDER
Total Respondents	10000	225	4681	2664	1296	1125
Don't Know/No Answer	67	3	31	10	13	8
Total Answering	9933	222	465	2654	1283	1117
	100.0	100.0	100.0	100.0	100.0	100.0
Northeast	2335	51	1189	580	266	246
	23.5	23.0	25.6	21.9	20.7	22.0
North Central	2248	46	1065	613	277	245
	22.6	20.7	22.9	23.1	21.6	21.9
South	2404	40	1107	651	330	275
	24.2	18.0	23.8	24.5	25.7	24.6
West	2560	77	1080	714	369	319
	25.8	34.7	23.2	26.9	28.8	28.6
Outside U.S.	386	8	209	96	41	32
	3.9	3.6	4.5	3.6	3.2	2.9

Table 4
MARITAL STATUS OF RESPONDENT

	TOTAL RESP.	AGE				
		UNDER 18	18–24	25–29	30–34	35 OR OLDER
Total Respondents	10000	225	4681	2664	1296	1125
Don't Know/No Answer	155	17	112	15	3	7
Total Answering	9845	208	4569	2649	1293	1118
	100.0	100.0	100.0	100.0	100.0	100.0
Living with Lover	1299	21	649	405	142	81
	13.2	10.1	14.2	15.3	11.0	7.2
Married	3032	8	964	1022	518	516
	30.8	3.8	21.1	38.6	40.1	46.2
Single and Living Alone or with a Platonic Roommate	4007	176	2709	815	223	83
	40.7	84.6	59.3	30.8	17.2	7.4
Separated	312	1	84	100	81	46
	3.2	.5	1.8	3.8	6.3	4.1
Divorced	1139	1	158	301	319	358
	11.6	.5	3.5	11.4	24.7	32.0
Widowed	56	1	5	6	10	34
	.6	.5	.1	.2	.8	3.0

Table 5
HOW LONG RESPONDENT HAS BEEN MARRIED OR LIVING WITH LOVER

	TOTAL RESP.	AGE				
		UNDER 18	18–24	25–29	30–34	35 OR OLDER
Married or Living with Lover	4331	29	1613	1427	660	597
Don't Know/No Answer	121	—	43	31	23	24
Total Answering	4210	29	1570	1396	637	573
	100.0	100.0	100.0	100.0	100.0	100.0
Less than 1 Year	857	17	490	237	73	39
	20.4	58.6	31.2	17.0	11.5	6.8
1 Year	427	6	234	112	47	27
	10.1	20.7	14.9	8.0	7.4	4.7
2 Years	623	3	351	179	50	40
	14.8	10.3	22.4	12.8	7.8	7.0
3 Years	448	1	213	160	48	25
	10.6	3.4	13.6	11.5	7.5	4.4
4 Years	309	—	107	146	38	18
	7.3	—	6.8	10.5	6.0	3.1
5 Years	266	2	84	129	36	14
	6.3	6.9	5.4	9.2	5.7	2.4
6 Years	200	—	45	119	26	10
	4.8	—	2.9	8.5	4.1	1.7
7 Years	153	—	17	99	23	14
	3.6	—	1.1	7.1	3.6	2.4
8 Years	128	—	8	85	28	7
	3.0	—	.5	6.1	4.4	1.2
9 Years	89	—	—	51	33	5
	2.1	—	—	3.7	5.2	.9
10 or More Years	710	—	21	79	235	374
	16.9	—	1.3	5.7	36.9	65.3
Mean	3.99	.86	1.97	3.95	5.98	7.54
Median	3.44	.85	2.17	4.07	7.02	10.23

Table 6
EDUCATION OF RESPONDENT

		AGE				
	TOTAL RESP.	UNDER 18	18–24	25–29	30–34	35 OR OLDER
Total Respondents	10000	225	4681	2664	1296	1125
Don't Know/No Answer	48	3	18	16	5	5
Total Answering	9952	222	4663	2648	1291	1120
	100.0	100.0	100.0	100.0	100.0	100.0
Elementary School or Less	15	3	4	—	4	4
	.2	1.4	.1	—	.3	.4
Some High School	478	99	206	74	39	60
	4.8	44.6	4.4	2.8	3.0	5.4
High School Graduate	2613	93	1310	605	329	273
	26.3	41.9	28.1	22.8	25.5	24.4
College	5151	27	2635	1337	622	526
	51.8	12.2	56.5	50.5	48.2	47.0
Some Graduate School or More	1695	—	508	632	297	257
	17.0	—	10.9	23.9	23.0	22.9

Table 7
OCCUPATION OF RESPONDENT

	TOTAL RESP.	AGE				
		UNDER 18	18–24	25–29	30–34	35 OR OLDER
Total Respondents	10000	225	4681	2664	1296	1125
Don't Know/No Answer	66	6	34	15	5	6
Total Answering	9934	219	4647	2649	1291	1119
	100.0	100.0	100.0	100.0	100.0	100.0
Creative Arts	496	15	239	131	56	55
	5.0	6.8	5.1	4.9	4.3	4.9
Management/Administrative	1360	8	459	415	231	245
	13.7	3.7	9.9	15.7	17.9	21.9
Professional/Technical	2248	9	833	783	346	276
	22.6	4.1	17.9	29.6	26.8	24.7
Secretary/Clerk	2582	33	1368	624	314	241
	26.0	15.1	29.4	23.6	24.3	21.5
Sales	764	33	374	174	95	85
	7.7	15.1	8.0	6.6	7.4	7.6
Homemaker	720	5	230	223	128	134
	7.2	2.3	4.9	8.4	9.9	12.0
Other	2005	118	1241	370	149	126
	20.2	53.9	26.7	14.0	11.5	11.3

Table 8
HOUSEHOLD EARNINGS PER YEAR OF ALL MEMBERS OF HOUSEHOLD COMBINED

	TOTAL RESP.	AGE				
		UNDER 18	18–24	25–29	30–34	35 OR OLDER
Total Respondents	10000	225	4681	2664	1296	1125
Don't Know/No Answer	182	9	105	32	20	16
Total Answering	9818	216	4576	2632	1276	1109
	100.0	100.0	100.0	100.0	100.0	100.0
Under $10,000	1379	40	832	297	117	92
	14.0	18.5	18.2	11.3	9.2	8.3
$10,000 to $14,999	2045	37	972	559	277	198
	20.8	17.1	21.2	21.2	21.7	17.9
$15,000 to $19,999	1679	36	769	478	222	172
	17.1	16.7	16.8	18.2	17.4	15.5
$20,000 to $24,999	1590	45	710	452	228	152
	16.2	20.8	15.5	17.2	17.9	13.7
$25,000 or More	3125	58	1293	846	432	495
	31.8	26.9	28.3	32.1	33.9	44.6

Table 9
RESPONDENT'S PERSONAL EARNINGS

	TOTAL RESP.	AGE				
		UNDER 18	18–24	25–29	30–34	35 OR OLDER
Total Respondents	10000	225	4681	2664	1296	1125
Don't Know/No Answer	54	1	26	11	5	11
Total Answering	9946	224	4655	2653	1291	1114
	100.0	100.0	100.0	100.0	100.0	100.0
None	924	46	434	207	119	117
	9.3	20.5	9.3	7.8	9.2	10.5
Under $10.000	4274	160	2595	866	353	297
	43.0	71.4	55.7	32.6	27.3	26.7
$10,000 to $14,999	2959	10	1243	975	430	297
	29.8	4.5	26.7	36.8	33.3	26.7
$15,000 to $19,999	1126	5	273	403	235	210
	11.3	2.2	5.9	15.2	18.2	18.9
$20,000 to $24,999	408	2	67	127	100	112
	4.1	.9	1.4	4.8	7.7	10.1
$25,000 or More	255	1	43	75	54	81
	2.6	.4	.9	2.8	4.2	7.3

328 THE COSMO REPORT

Table 10
HOW OLD WERE YOU WHEN YOU FIRST HAD SEX WITH A MAN?

	TOTAL RESP.	AGE				
		UNDER 18	18–24	25–29	30–34	35 OR OLDER
Total Respondents	10000	225	4681	2664	1296	1125
Don't Know/No Answer	5	1	1	2	1	—
Total Answering	9995	224	4680	2662	1295	1125
	100.0	100.0	100.0	100.0	100.0	100.0
Under 10	49	5	17	12	6	9
	.5	2.2	.4	.5	.5	.6
10 to 15	2080	139	1170	410	196	164
	20.8	62.1	25.0	15.4	15.1	14.6
16 to 20	6854	74	3260	1929	865	719
	68.6	33.0	69.7	72.5	66.8	63.9
21 to 25	905	—	200	292	207	205
	9.1	—	4.3	11.0	16.0	18.2
26 to 30	48	—	—	10	19	19
	.5	—	—	.4	1.5	1.7
31 or More	8	—	—	—	—	8
	.1	—	—	—	—	.7
Never Have	51	6	33	9	2	1
	.5	2.7	.7	.3	.2	.1

Table 11
DID YOU HAVE AN ORGASM THE FIRST TIME?

	TOTAL RESP.	AGE				
		UNDER 18	18–24	25–29	30–34	35 OR OLDER
Have Had Sex with a Man	9949	219	4648	2655	1294	1124
Don't Know/No Answer	52	2	23	10	5	12
Total Answering	9897	217	4625	2645	1289	1112
	100.0	100.0	100.0	100.0	100.0	100.0
Yes	988	37	440	259	141	111
	10.0	17.1	9.5	9.8	10.9	10.0
No	8909	180	4185	2386	1148	1001
	90.0	82.9	90.5	90.2	89.1	90.0

Table 12
HOW WOULD YOU DESCRIBE YOUR REACTION THE FIRST TIME?

	TOTAL RESP.	AGE				
		UNDER 18	18–24	25–29	30–34	35 OR OLDER
Have Had Sex with a Man	9949	219	4648	2655	1294	1124
Don't Know/No Answer	35	1	13	6	7	8
Total Answering	9914	218	4635	2649	1287	1116
	100.0	100.0	100.0	100.0	100.0	100.0
It Was a Thrilling Experience	1817	55	824	486	243	208
	18.3	25.2	17.8	18.3	18.9	18.6
It Was Moderately Pleasant	3024	63	1412	807	379	363
	30.5	28.9	30.5	30.5	29.4	32.5
Had No Particular Reaction	1576	32	783	409	193	159
	15.9	14.7	16.9	15.4	15.0	14.2
It Was Somewhat Disagreeable	1719	36	789	474	231	185
	17.3	16.5	17.0	17.9	17.9	16.6
It Was Painful and Upsetting	1778	32	827	473	241	201
	17.9	14.7	17.8	17.9	18.7	18.0

Table 13
HOW LONG HAD YOU KNOWN YOUR PARTNER?

	TOTAL RESP.	AGE				
		UNDER 18	18–24	25–29	30–34	35 OR OLDER
Have Had Sex with a Man	9949	219	4648	2655	1294	1124
Don't Know/No Answer	24	1	10	4	6	3
Total Answering	9925	218	4638	2651	1288	1121
	100.0	100.0	100.0	100.0	100.0	100.0
Less than a Week	630	26	355	154	57	37
	6.3	11.9	7.7	5.8	4.4	3.3
At Least a Week but Less than a Few Months	1466	47	758	378	158	125
	14.8	21.6	16.3	14.3	12.3	11.2
A Few Months	3472	76	1670	894	453	375
	35.0	34.9	36.0	33.7	35.2	33.5
Almost a Year or Longer	4357	69	1855	1225	620	584
	43.9	31.7	40.0	46.2	48.1	52.1

Table 14
WHO WAS YOUR PARTNER?

	TOTAL RESP.	AGE				
		UNDER 18	18–24	25–29	30–34	35 OR OLDER
Have Had Sex with a Man	9949	219	4648	2655	1294	1124
Don't Know/No Answer	83	3	46	19	6	9
Total Answering	9866	216	4602	2636	1288	1115
	100.0	100.0	100.0	100.0	100.0	100.0
Husband	505	1	72	89	120	222
	5.1	.5	1.6	3.4	9.3	19.9
Fiance	617	6	180	193	111	127
	6.3	2.8	3.9	7.3	8.6	11.4
Steady Boyfriend	6265	121	3025	1729	787	598
	63.5	56.0	65.7	65.6	61.1	53.6
Casual Acquaintance	1569	50	849	385	183	101
	15.9	23.1	18.4	14.6	14.2	9.1
Other	910	38	476	240	87	67
	9.2	17.6	10.3	9.1	6.8	6.0

Table 15
WITH ABOUT HOW MANY MEN HAVE YOU MADE LOVE?

	TOTAL RESP.	AGE				
		UNDER 18	18–24	25–29	30–34	35 OR OLDER
Have Had Sex with a Man	9949	219	4648	2655	1294	1124
Don't Know/No Answer	88	4	31	24	15	14
Total Answering	9861	215	4617	2631	1279	1110
	100.0	100.0	100.0	100.0	100.0	100.0
Only One	950	56	585	167	59	83
	9.6	26.0	12.7	6.3	4.6	7.5
2 to 5	2741	88	1480	622	274	273
	27.8	40.9	32.1	23.6	21.4	24.6
6 to 10	2223	27	1096	601	283	214
	22.5	12.6	23.7	22.8	22.1	19.3
11 To 25	2489	27	1026	766	370	298
	25.2	12.6	22.2	29.1	28.9	26.8
More than 25	1458	17	430	475	293	242
	14.8	7.9	9.3	18.1	22.9	21.8
Median	8.79	4.34	7.11	10.38	11.89	10.65

Table 16
HOW OFTEN DO YOU USUALLY MAKE LOVE?

	TOTAL RESP.	AGE				
		UNDER 18	18–24	25–29	30–34	35 OR OLDER
Have Had Sex with a Man	9949	219	4648	2655	1294	1124
Don't Know/No Answer	62	4	27	16	5	10
Total Answering	9887	215	4621	2639	1289	1114
	100.0	100.0	100.0	100.0	100.0	100.0
At Least Once a Day	777	25	422	178	88	66
	7.9	11.6	9.1	6.7	6.7	5.9
Three to Five Times a Week	3523	59	1734	975	414	338
	35.6	27.4	37.5	36.9	32.1	30.3
Once or Twice a Week	3194	59	1352	882	467	429
	32.3	27.4	29.3	33.4	36.2	38.5
Once or Twice a Month	1513	37	696	397	209	174
	15.3	17.2	15.1	15.0	16.2	15.6
Less than Once a Month	880	35	417	207	113	107
	8.9	16.3	9.0	7.8	8.8	9.6

MARITAL STATUS				SEX LIFE	
LIVE WITH LOVER	MAR-RIED	SINGLE AND LIVE ALONE	SEP./ DIV./ WIDOW	SATIS-FAC-TORY	NOT SATIS-FAC-TORY
1299	3032	3960	1507	6876	3005
2	8	35	14	27	33
1297	3024	3925	1493	6849	2972
100.0	100.0	100.0	100.0	100.0	100.0
272	203	208	83	707	64
21.0	6.7	5.3	5.6	10.3	2.2
649	1243	1151	438	3098	407
50.0	41.1	29.3	29.3	45.2	13.7
298	1174	1159	516	2238	932
23.0	38.8	29.5	34.6	32.7	31.4
67	310	817	295	618	884
5.2	10.3	20.8	19.8	9.0	29.7
11	94	590	161	188	685
.8	3.1	15.0	10.8	2.7	23.0

Table 17
WOULD YOU LIKE TO MAKE LOVE MORE FREQUENTLY OR LESS?

	TOTAL RESP.	AGE				
		UNDER 18	18–24	25–29	30–34	35 OR OLDER
Have Had Sex with a Man	9949	219	4648	2655	1294	1124
Don't Know/No Answer	30	1	10	10	3	6
Total Answering	9919	218	4638	2645	1291	1118
	100.0	100.0	100.0	100.0	100.0	100.0
More	6239	146	2831	1661	874	723
	62.9	67.0	61.0	62.8	67.7	64.7
Less	144	6	62	40	20	16
	1.5	2.8	1.3	1.5	1.5	1.4
About the Same	3536	66	1745	944	397	379
	35.6	30.3	37.6	35.7	30.8	33.9

MARITAL STATUS				SEX LIFE		FREQUENCY OF LOVE-MAKING				
LIVE WITH LOVER	MAR-RIED	SINGLE AND LIVE ALONE	SEP./DIV./WIDOW	SATIS-FAC-TORY	NOT SATIS-FAC-TORY	AT LEAST ONCE A DAY	3–5 TIMES A WEEK	ONCE/TWICE A WEEK	ONCE/TWICE A MONTH	LESS THAN ONCE/MONTH
1299	3032	3960	1507	6876	3005	777	3523	3194	1513	880
2	11	12	5	17	12	1	9	6	—	5
1297	3021	3948	1502	6859	2993	776	3514	3188	1513	875
100.0	100.0	100.0	100.0	100.0	100.0	100.0	100.0	100.0	100.0	100.0
589	1610	2827	1107	3598	2593	255	1493	2264	1393	793
45.4	53.3	71.6	73.7	52.5	86.6	32.9	42.5	71.0	92.1	90.6
26	68	43	7	96	45	30	67	19	12	15
2.0	2.3	1.1	.5	1.4	1.5	3.9	1.9	.6	.8	1.7
682	1343	1078	388	3165	355	491	1954	905	108	67
52.6	44.5	27.3	25.8	46.1	11.9	63.3	55.6	28.4	7.1	7.7

Table 18
AT WHAT TIME OF DAY DO YOU PREFER TO MAKE LOVE?

	TOTAL RESP.	AGE				
		UNDER 18	18–24	25–29	30–34	35 OR OLDER
Have Had Sex with a Man	9949	219	4648	2655	1294	1124
Don't Know/No Answer	130	3	46	31	24	26
Total Answering	9819	216	4602	2624	1270	1098
	100.0	100.0	100.0	100.0	100.0	100.0
In the Morning	2303	39	1041	612	297	312
	23.5	18.1	22.6	23.3	23.4	28.4
During the Day	2396	48	995	673	339	341
	24.4	22.2	21.6	25.6	26.7	31.1
At Night	6925	166	3341	1778	890	743
	70.5	76.9	72.6	67.8	70.1	67.7

Table 19
WHICH IS YOUR FAVORITE POSITION TO MAKE LOVE?

	TOTAL RESP.	AGE				
		UNDER 18	18–24	25–29	30–34	35 OR OLDER
Have Had Sex with a Man	9949	219	4648	2655	1294	1124
Don't Know/No Answer	97	3	41	14	19	20
Total Answering	9852	216	4607	2641	1275	1104
	100.0	100.0	100.0	100.0	100.0	100.0
Male Dominant/Female Underneath	6053	136	2873	1558	772	708
	61.4	63.0	62.4	59.0	60.5	64.1
Female Dominant/Male Underneath	2546	46	1214	688	316	278
	25.8	21.3	26.4	26.1	24.8	25.2
Side by Side	802	17	313	224	118	128
	8.1	7.9	6.8	8.5	9.3	11.6
Posterior	819	18	326	264	127	83
	8.3	8.3	7.1	10.0	10.0	7.5
Standing	164	8	70	36	19	30
	1.7	3.7	1.5	1.4	1.5	2.7
Other	514	13	226	137	55	81
	5.2	6.0	4.9	5.2	4.3	7.3

Table 20
WHAT IS YOUR FAVORITE SETTING TO MAKE LOVE —ASIDE FROM IN BED?

	TOTAL RESP.	AGE				
		UNDER 18	18–24	25–29	30–34	35 OR OLDER
Have Had Sex with a Man	9949	219	4648	2655	1294	1124
Don't Know/No Answer	63	2	28	17	4	12
Total Answering	9886	217	4620	2638	1290	1112
	100.0	100.0	100.0	100.0	100.0	100.0
Couch	1762	27	687	498	291	256
	17.8	12.4	14.9	18.9	22.6	23.0
Floor	3350	50	1448	928	492	428
	33.9	23.0	31.3	35.2	38.1	38.5
Beach	1734	59	923	432	169	150
	17.5	27.2	20.0	16.4	13.1	13.5
Grass	1274	29	666	334	143	100
	12.9	13.4	14.4	12.7	11.1	9.0
Car	407	19	157	86	57	88
	4.1	8.8	3.4	3.3	4.4	7.9
Shower or Bath	1569	47	800	396	180	146
	15.9	21.7	17.3	15.0	14.0	13.1
Other	473	9	209	139	66	49
	4.8	4.1	4.5	5.3	5.1	4.4
No Other Setting	197	3	94	47	19	34
	2.0	1.4	2.0	1.8	1.5	3.1

MARITAL STATUS			
LIVE WITH LOVER	MAR- RIED	SINGLE AND LIVE ALONE	SEP./ DIV./ WIDOW
1299	3032	3960	1507
10	16	25	11
1289	3016	3935	1496
100.0	100.0	100.0	100.0
254	585	562	337
19.7	19.4	14.8	22.5
385	1064	1318	529
29.9	35.3	33.5	35.4
252	425	807	220
19.6	14.1	20.5	14.7
175	373	536	165
13.6	12.4	13.6	11.0
48	169	130	52
3.7	5.6	3.3	3.5
207	429	689	224
16.1	14.2	17.5	15.0
75	150	162	77
5.8	5.0	4.1	5.1
20	76	79	21
1.6	2.5	2.0	1.4

Table 21
WHAT DO YOU FIND PLEASANT ACCOMPANIMENTS OR PRELIMINARIES TO SEX?

	TOTAL RESP.	AGE				
		UNDER 18	18–24	25–29	30–34	35 OR OLDER
Have Had Sex with a Man	9949	219	4648	2655	1294	1124
Don't Know/No Answer	63	2	34	10	4	13
Total Answering	9886	217	4614	2645	1290	1111
	100.0	100.0	100.0	100.0	100.0	100.0
Food	1680	24	724	473	243	216
	17.0	11.1	15.7	17.9	18.8	19.4
Drink	6480	131	2986	1764	882	711
	65.5	60.4	64.7	66.7	68.4	64.0
Music	7722	172	3605	2053	1015	870
	78.1	79.3	78.1	77.6	78.7	78.3
Smells (Perfume, Body Odor, Etc.)	5632	88	2573	1523	787	657
	57.0	40.6	55.8	57.6	61.0	59.1
Drugs (Pot, "Uppers," Etc.)	2912	76	1510	824	326	171
	29.5	35.0	32.7	31.2	25.3	15.4
Sexy Talk	4805	104	2185	1318	637	558
	48.6	47.9	47.4	49.8	49.4	50.2
Pornography	2121	37	838	659	336	249
	21.5	17.1	18.2	24.9	26.0	22.4
Other	780	26	361	203	108	82
	7.9	12.0	7.8	7.7	8.4	7.4

MARITAL STATUS			
LIVE WITH LOVER	MAR- RIED	SINGLE AND LIVE ALONE	SEP./ DIV./ WIDOW
1299	3032	3960	1507
3	24	29	6
1296	3008	3931	1501
100.0	100.0	100.0	100.0
206	429	729	293
15.9	14.3	18.5	19.5
803	1826	2688	1059
62.0	60.7	68.4	70.6
951	2213	3199	1243
73.4	73.6	81.4	82.8
719	1697	2211	929
55.5	56.4	56.2	61.9
520	712	1238	392
40.1	23.7	31.5	26.1
676	1470	1850	732
52.2	48.9	47.1	48.8
346	797	646	307
26.7	26.5	16.4	20.5
117	196	340	112
9.0	6.5	8.6	7.5

Table 22
HOW DO YOU LIKE TO MAKE LOVE?

	TOTAL RESP.	AGE				
		UNDER 18	18–24	25–29	30–34	35 OR OLDER
Have Had Sex with a Man	9949	219	4648	2655	1294	1124
Don't Know/No Answer	43	2	14	10	7	10
Total Answering	9906	217	4634	2645	1287	1114
	100.0	100.0	100.0	100.0	100.0	100.0
In Daylight or Bright Light	878	14	339	248	122	155
	8.9	6.5	7.3	9.4	9.5	13.9
With the Lights on Dimly	8192	169	3859	2187	1054	916
	82.7	77.9	83.3	82.7	81.9	82.2
In the Dark	1742	48	781	434	250	227
	17.6	22.1	16.9	16.4	19.4	20.4

Table 23
HOW LONG DO YOU USUALLY LIKE FOREPLAY TO LAST?

	TOTAL RESP.	AGE				
		UNDER 18	18–24	25–29	30–34	35 OR OLDER
Have Had Sex with a Man	9949	219	4648	2655	1294	1124
Don't Know/No Answer	45	1	23	6	4	11
Total Answering	9904	218	4625	2649	1290	1113
	100.0	100.0	100.0	100.0	100.0	100.0
Less than 5 Minutes	201	5	80	46	35	34
	2.0	2.3	1.7	1.7	2.7	3.1
5 to 15 Minutes	3574	62	1561	993	473	483
	36.1	28.4	33.8	37.5	36.7	43.4
Up to Half an Hour	4783	111	2294	1275	619	479
	48.3	50.9	49.6	48.1	48.0	43.0
Up to an Hour or More	1346	40	690	335	163	117
	13.6	18.3	14.9	12.6	12.6	10.5

MARITAL STATUS			
LIVE WITH LOVER	MAR-RIED	SINGLE AND LIVE ALONE	SEP./ DIV./ WIDOW
1299	3032	3960	1507
4	13	17	9
1295	3019	3943	1498
100.0	100.0	100.0	100.0
150	291	290	143
11.6	9.6	7.4	9.5
1095	2456	3257	1260
84.6	81.4	82.6	84.1
214	545	696	253
16.5	18.1	17.7	16.9

MARITAL STATUS			
LIVE WITH LOVER	MAR-RIED	SINGLE AND LIVE ALONE	SEP./ DIV./ WIDOW
1299	3032	3960	1507
5	11	16	12
1294	3021	3944	1495
100.0	100.0	100.0	100.0
36	79	52	29
2.8	2.6	1.3	1.9
523	1329	1200	472
40.4	44.0	30.4	31.6
591	1343	2010	767
45.7	44.5	51.0	51.3
144	270	682	227
11.1	8.9	17.3	15.2

Table 24
HOW LONG DO YOU USUALLY TAKE TO REACH ORGASM AFTER THE ONSET OF FOREPLAY?

	TOTAL RESP.	AGE				
		UNDER 18	18–24	25–29	30–34	35 OR OLDER
Have Had Sex with a Man	9949	219	4648	2655	1294	1124
Don't Know/No Answer	223	4	134	32	27	26
Total Answering	9726	215	4514	2623	1267	1098
	100.0	100.0	100.0	100.0	100.0	100.0
Less than 5 Minutes	1018	32	435	240	149	160
	10.5	14.9	9.6	9.1	11.8	14.6
5 to 10 Minutes	3423	81	1550	938	462	389
	35.2	37.7	34.3	35.8	36.5	35.4
Up to 20 Minutes	3079	70	1466	855	380	306
	31.7	32.6	32.5	32.6	30.0	27.9
Up to Half an Hour	1685	22	818	449	205	189
	17.3	10.2	18.1	17.1	16.2	17.2
Up to an Hour or More	521	10	245	141	71	54
	5.4	4.7	5.4	5.4	5.6	4.9

MARITAL STATUS			
LIVE WITH LOVER	MAR- RIED	SINGLE AND LIVE ALONE	SEP./ DIV./ WIDOW
1299	3032	3960	1507
27	50	111	32
1272	2982	3849	1475
100.0	100.0	100.0	100.0
141	382	318	155
11.1	12.8	8.3	10.5
473	1116	1303	476
37.2	37.4	33.9	32.3
421	930	1226	465
33.1	31.2	31.9	31.5
194	438	740	289
15.3	14.7	19.2	19.6
43	116	262	90
3.4	3.9	6.8	6.1

Table 25
WHEN MAKING LOVE, WHAT DO YOU LIKE?

	TOTAL RESP.	AGE				
		UNDER 18	18–24	25–29	30–34	35 OR OLDER
Have Had Sex with a Man	9949	219	4648	2655	1294	1124
Don't Know/No Answer	579	8	184	163	101	123
Total Answering	9370	211	4464	2492	1193	1001
	100.0	100.0	100.0	100.0	100.0	100.0
Have Your Man Undress You	8854	199	4240	2341	1110	957
	94.5	94.3	95.0	93.9	93.0	95.6
Pinch, Bite, Slap Him	681	21	309	177	107	67
	7.3	10.0	6.9	7.1	9.0	6.7
Be Pinched, Bitten, Slapped	775	16	355	218	121	65
	8.3	7.6	8.0	8.7	10.1	6.5
Have Someone Beat You	68	4	34	14	10	6
	.7	1.9	.8	.6	.8	.6
Pretend to Fight Physically with the Man or Try to Get Away	1949	56	964	560	227	140
	20.8	26.5	21.6	22.5	19.0	14.0

MARITAL STATUS			
LIVE WITH LOVER	MAR- RIED	SINGLE AND LIVE ALONE	SEP./ DIV./ WIDOW
1299	3032	3960	1507
69	242	168	93
1230	2790	3792	1414
100.0	100.0	100.0	100.0
1138	2627	3618	1337
92.5	94.2	95.4	94.6
97	166	298	106
7.9	5.9	7.9	7.5
139	200	286	134
11.3	7.2	7.5	9.5
13	17	23	12
1.1	.6	.6	.8
271	565	805	276
22.0	20.3	21.2	19.5

Table 26
HOW FREQUENTLY DO YOU HAVE AN ORGASM?

	TOTAL RESP.	AGE				
		UNDER 18	18–24	25–29	30–34	35 OR OLDER
Have Had Sex with a Man	9949	219	4648	2655	1294	1124
Don't Know/No Answer	114	4	66	20	15	9
Total Answering	9835	215	4582	2635	1279	1115
	100.0	100.0	100.0	100.0	100.0	100.0
Always	2001	40	846	567	260	287
	20.3	18.6	18.5	21.5	20.3	25.7
Usually	4843	102	2174	1329	666	568
	49.2	47.4	47.4	50.4	52.1	50.9
Sometimes	2038	47	1002	533	259	195
	20.7	21.9	21.9	20.2	20.3	17.5
Seldom	816	22	469	188	80	55
	8.3	10.2	10.2	7.1	6.3	4.9
Never	137	4	91	18	14	10
	1.4	1.9	2.0	.7	1.1	.9

MARITAL STATUS			
LIVE WITH LOVER	MAR- RIED	SINGLE AND LIVE ALONE	SEP./ DIV./ WIDOW
1299	3032	3960	1507
7	21	67	16
1292	3011	3893	1491
100.0	100.0	100.0	100.0
325	732	594	32
25.2	24.3	15.3	21.5
650	1521	1878	729
50.3	50.5	48.2	48.9
223	549	909	316
17.3	18.2	23.3	21.2
83	190	421	111
6.4	6.3	10.8	7.4
11	19	91	14
.9	.6	2.3	.9

Table 27
DO YOU HAVE MULTIPLE ORGASMS?

	TOTAL RESP.	AGE				
		UNDER 18	18–24	25–29	30–34	35 OR OLDER
Have Had Sex with a Man and Have Orgasms	9812	215	4557	2637	1280	1114
Don't Know/No Answer	55	3	28	10	8	6
Total Answering	9757	212	4529	2627	1272	1108
	100.0	100.0	100.0	100.0	100.0	100.0
Always	964	21	348	253	169	173
	9.9	9.9	7.7	9.6	13.3	15.6
Sometimes	6553	122	2982	1846	852	744
	67.2	57.5	65.8	70.3	67.0	67.1
Never	2240	69	1199	528	251	191
	23.0	32.5	26.5	20.1	19.7	17.2

MARITAL STATUS			
LIVE WITH LOVER	MAR- RIED	SINGLE AND LIVE ALONE	SEP./ DIV./ WIDOW
1288	3013	3869	1493
8	16	26	5
1280	2997	3843	1488
100.0	100.0	100.0	100.0
150	302	290	209
11.7	10.1	7.5	14.0
885	1992	2561	1020
69.1	66.5	66.6	68.5
245	703	992	259
19.1	23.5	25.8	17.4

Table 28
WHAT IS THE GREATEST NUMBER OF ORGASMS YOU HAVE HAD IN ONE LOVE-MAKING SESSION?

	TOTAL RESP.	AGE				
		UNDER 18	18–24	25–29	30–34	35 OR OLDER
Have Had Sex with a Man and Have Orgasms	9812	215	4557	2637	1280	1114
Don't Know/No Answer	78	2	42	15	10	8
Total Answering	9734	213	4515	2622	1270	1106
	100.0	100.0	100.0	100.0	100.0	100.0
1	1442	55	775	331	156	124
	14.8	25.8	17.2	12.6	12.3	11.2
2 to 5	6412	125	3040	1765	791	685
	65.9	58.7	67.3	67.3	62.3	61.9
6 to 10	1303	19	504	355	218	206
	13.4	8.9	11.2	13.5	17.2	18.6
11 or More	577	14	196	171	105	91
	5.9	6.6	4.3	6.5	8.3	8.2

MARITAL STATUS			
LIVE WITH LOVER	MAR- RIED	SINGLE AND LIVE ALONE	SEP./ DIV./ WIDOW
1288	3013	3869	1493
6	17	45	9
1282	2996	3824	1484
100.0	100.0	100.0	100.0
149	447	662	159
11.6	14.9	17.3	10.7
854	1999	2525	931
66.6	66.7	66.0	62.7
195	382	435	272
15.2	12.8	11.4	18.3
84	168	202	122
6.6	5.6	5.3	8.2

Table 29
DO YOUR ORGASMS VARY IN INTENSITY?

		AGE				
	TOTAL RESP.	UNDER 18	18–24	25–29	30–34	35 OR OLDER
Have Had Sex with a Man and Have Orgasms	9812	215	4557	2637	1280	1114
Don't Know/No Answer	25	2	13	2	6	2
Total Answering	9787	213	4544	2635	1274	1112
	100.0	100.0	100.0	100.0	100.0	100.0
Often	3926	61	1692	1092	550	526
	40.1	28.6	37.2	41.4	43.2	47.3
Sometimes	5533	141	2662	1464	696	566
	56.5	66.2	58.6	55.6	54.6	50.9
Never	328	11	190	79	28	20
	3.4	5.2	4.2	3.0	2.2	1.8

Table 30
HOW ARE YOUR ORGASMS USUALLY ACHIEVED?

		AGE				
	TOTAL RESP.	UNDER 18	18–24	25–29	30–34	35 OR OLDER
Have Had Sex with a Man and Have Orgasms	9812	215	4557	2637	1280	1114
Don't Know/No Answer	96	6	34	20	22	14
Total Answering	9716	209	4523	2617	1258	1100
	100.0	100.0	100.0	100.0	100.0	100.0
Vaginal Entry	3299	96	1438	851	453	459
	34.0	45.9	31.8	32.5	36.0	41.7
Clitoral Manipulation	6894	121	3260	1889	881	735
	71.0	57.9	72.1	72.2	70.0	66.8
Other Stimulation	857	18	360	227	133	119
	8.8	8.6	8.0	8.7	10.6	10.8

MARITAL STATUS			
LIVE WITH LOVER	MAR- RIED	SINGLE AND LIVE ALONE	SEP./ DIV./ WIDOW
1288	3013	3869	1493
1	6	11	6
1287	3007	3858	1487
100.0	100.0	100.0	100.0
543	1191	1501	655
42.2	39.6	38.9	44.0
706	1715	2211	796
54.9	57.0	57.3	53.5
38	101	146	36
3.0	3.4	3.8	2.4

MARITAL STATUS			
LIVE WITH LOVER	MAR- RIED	SINGLE AND LIVE ALONE	SEP./ DIV./ WIDOW
1288	3013	3869	1493
14	25	36	17
1274	2988	3833	1476
100.0	100.0	100.0	100.0
455	992	1244	553
35.7	33.2	32.5	37.5
915	2129	2753	1003
71.8	71.3	71.8	68.0
122	260	295	162
9.6	8.7	7.7	11.0

Table 31
IN WHICH OF THE FOLLOWING DO YOU REGULARLY PARTICIPATE?

	TOTAL RESP.	AGE				
		UNDER 18	18–24	25–29	30–34	35 OR OLDER
Have Had Sex with a Man	9949	219	4648	2655	1294	1124
Don't Know/No Answer	1287	43	663	263	146	172
Total Answering	8662	176	3985	2392	1148	952
	100.0	100.0	100.0	100.0	100.0	100.0
Cunnilingus	7307	151	3303	2016	998	832
	84.4	85.8	82.9	84.3	86.9	87.4
Fellatio	7282	138	3271	2073	992	800
	84.1	78.4	82.1	86.7	86.4	84.0
Anal Sex	1109	24	461	312	178	133
	12.8	13.6	11.6	13.0	15.5	14.0
Fetishes	604	21	308	164	73	37
	7.0	11.9	7.7	6.9	6.4	3.9
Flagellation or Other Sadomasochistic Behavior	162	8	91	26	25	11
	1.9	4.5	2.3	1.1	2.2	1.2

MARITAL STATUS			
LIVE WITH LOVER	MAR- RIED	SINGLE AND LIVE ALONE	SEP./ DIV./ WIDOW
1299	3032	3960	1507
144	438	505	174
1155	2594	3455	1333
100.0	100.0	100.0	100.0
951	2188	2909	1162
82.3	84.3	84.2	87.2
998	2137	2909	1144
86.4	82.4	84.2	85.8
186	332	392	183
16.1	12.8	11.3	13.7
120	154	256	63
10.4	5.9	7.4	4.7
31	43	62	23
2.7	1.7	1.8	1.7

Table 32
WHAT AREAS OF YOUR BODY OTHER THAN THE CLITORIS RESPOND EROTICALLY TO STIMULATION?

	TOTAL RESP.	AGE				
		UNDER 18	18–24	25–29	30–34	35 OR OLDER
Have Had Sex with a Man	9949	219	4648	2655	1294	1124
Don't Know/No Answer	30	1	12	10	5	2
Total Answering	9919	218	4636	2645	1289	1122
	100.0	100.0	100.0	100.0	100.0	100.0
Mouth	6461	122	2900	1717	920	795
	65.1	56.0	62.6	64.9	71.4	70.9
Ears	5670	120	2861	1472	678	536
	57.2	55.0	61.7	55.7	52.6	47.8
Breast, Nipples	8730	189	4072	2327	1136	998
	88.0	86.7	87.8	88.0	88.1	88.9
Anus	2651	37	1076	806	400	331
	26.7	17.0	23.2	30.5	31.0	29.5
Other	2518	66	1201	723	308	219
	25.4	30.3	25.9	27.3	23.9	19.5
None	81	3	36	26	6	10
	.8	1.4	.8	1.0	.5	.9

MARITAL STATUS			
LIVE WITH LOVER	MAR- RIED	SINGLE AND LIVE ALONE	SEP./ DIV./ WIDOW
1299	3032	3960	1507
3	11	13	3
1296	3021	3947	1504
100.0	100.0	100.0	100.0
840	1876	2567	1080
64.8	62.1	65.0	71.8
726	1522	2467	877
56.0	50.4	62.5	58.3
1149	2655	3451	1337
88.7	87.9	87.4	88.9
399	855	902	459
30.8	28.3	22.9	30.5
365	677	1081	362
28.2	22.4	27.4	24.1
8	30	32	9
.6	1.0	.8	.6

Table 33
HOW OLD WERE YOU WHEN YOU FIRST MASTUR-BATED?

	TOTAL RESP.	AGE				
		UNDER 18	18–24	25–29	30–34	35 OR OLDER
Total Respondents	10000	225	4681	2664	1296	1125
Don't Know/No Answer	114	7	54	28	13	12
Total Answering	9886	218	4627	2636	1283	1113
	100.0	100.0	100.0	100.0	100.0	100.0
Younger than 5	477	24	224	121	55	52
	4.8	11.0	4.8	4.6	4.3	4.7
5 to 9	1706	68	809	419	211	197
	17.3	31.2	17.5	15.9	16.4	17.7
10 to 15	3162	80	1616	780	368	316
	32.0	36.7	34.9	29.6	28.7	28.4
16 to 20	2094	22	1100	580	229	161
	21.2	10.1	23.8	22.0	17.8	14.5
Over 20	1403	—	264	506	326	306
	14.2	—	5.7	19.2	25.4	27.5
Never Have	1044	24	614	230	94	81
	10.6	11.0	13.3	8.7	7.3	7.3

Table 34
DO YOU STILL MASTURBATE?

	TOTAL RESP.	AGE				
		UNDER 18	18–24	25–29	30–34	35 OR OLDER
Have Ever Masturbated	8956	201	4067	2434	1202	1044
Don't Know/No Answer	59	3	35	11	5	5
Total Answering	8897	198	4032	2423	1197	1039
	100.0	100.0	100.0	100.0	100.0	100.0
Yes	4767	88	1968	1410	742	555
	53.6	44.4	48.8	58.2	62.0	53.4
Yes, but Only in the Absence of a Sexual Partner	3298	83	1594	826	374	417
	37.1	41.9	39.5	34.1	31.2	40.1
No	832	27	470	187	81	67
	9.4	13.6	11.7	7.7	6.8	6.4

MARITAL STATUS			
LIVE WITH LOVER	MAR- RIED	SINGLE AND LIVE ALONE	SEP./ DIV./ WIDOW
1162	2710	3556	1391
4	18	24	4
1158	2692	3532	1387
100.0	100.0	100.0	100.0
632	1491	1832	747
54.6	55.4	54.9	53.9
405	912	1390	542
35.0	33.9	39.4	39.1
121	289	310	98
10.4	10.7	8.8	7.1

Table 35
HOW OFTEN DO YOU MASTURBATE?

	TOTAL RESP.	AGE				
		UNDER 18	18–24	25–29	30–34	35 OR OLDER
Still Masturbate	8065	171	3562	2236	1116	972
Don't Know/No Answer	73	2	25	27	8	11
Total Answering	7992	169	3537	2209	1108	961
	100.0	100.0	100.0	100.0	100.0	100.0
Every Day	281	14	145	68	39	15
	3.5	8.3	4.1	3.1	3.5	1.6
Several Times a Week	1960	37	887	525	293	216
	24.5	21.9	25.1	23.8	26.4	22.5
Several Times a Month	2971	39	1242	840	449	396
	37.2	23.1	35.1	38.0	40.5	41.2
Rarely	2780	79	1263	776	327	334
	34.8	46.7	35.7	35.1	29.5	34.8

MARITAL STATUS			
LIVE WITH LOVER	MAR- RIED	SINGLE AND LIVE ALONE	SEP./ DIV./ WIDOW
1037	2403	3222	1289
9	22	32	10
1028	2381	3190	1279
100.0	100.0	100.0	100.0
29	54	161	33
2.8	2.3	5.0	2.6
223	440	917	344
21.7	18.5	28.7	26.9
362	931	1132	513
35.2	39.1	35.5	40.1
414	956	980	389
40.3	40.2	30.7	30.4

Table 36
WHEN YOU MASTURBATE, WHAT MEANS DO YOU USE?

	TOTAL RESP.	AGE				
		UNDER 18	18–24	25–29	30–34	35 OR OLDER
Still Masturbate	8065	171	3562	2236	1116	972
Don't Know/No Answer	93	4	44	25	12	8
Total Answering	7972	167	3518	2211	1104	964
	100.0	100.0	100.0	100.0	100.0	100.0
Hand	6713	135	3022	1885	909	755
	84.2	80.8	85.9	85.3	82.3	78.3
Vibrator	2115	31	693	618	420	353
	26.5	18.6	19.7	28.0	38.0	36.6
Water Spray	2254	58	1076	609	277	232
	28.3	34.7	30.6	27.5	25.1	24.1
Other	563	18	251	134	75	84
	7.1	10.8	7.1	6.1	6.8	8.7

MARITAL STATUS			
LIVE WITH LOVER	MAR- RIED	SINGLE AND LIVE ALONE	SEP./ DIV./ WIDOW
1037	2403	3222	1289
7	30	45	8
1030	2373	3177	1281
100.0	100.0	100.0	100.0
865	1967	2721	1065
84.0	82.9	85.6	83.1
305	715	659	414
29.6	30.1	20.7	32.3
309	649	936	339
30.0	27.3	29.5	26.5
73	166	236	77
7.1	7.0	7.4	6.0

Table 37
WHEN DO YOU HAVE SEXUAL FANTASIES?

	TOTAL RESP.	AGE				
		UNDER 18	18–24	25–29	30–34	35 OR OLDER
Total Respondents	10000	225	4681	2664	1296	1125
Don't Know/No Answer	54	—	24	12	9	9
Total Answering	9946	225	4657	2652	1287	1116
	100.0	100.0	100.0	100.0	100.0	100.0
During Intercourse	3576	62	1453	1051	549	459
	36.0	27.6	31.2	39.6	42.7	41.1
While Masturbating	5762	114	2459	1625	857	701
	57.9	50.7	52.8	61.3	66.6	62.8
Other Times When Not Active Sexually	6070	146	2931	1627	764	595
	61.0	64.9	62.9	61.3	59.4	53.3
In Dreams	6080	150	2957	1657	773	539
	61.1	66.7	63.5	62.5	60.1	48.3
Never	251	2	110	50	31	57
	2.5	.9	2.4	1.9	2.4	5.1

MARITAL STATUS			
LIVE WITH LOVER	MAR-RIED	SINGLE AND LIVE ALONE	SEP./ DIV./ WIDOW
1299	3032	4007	1507
7	18	24	4
1292	3014	3983	1503
100.0	100.0	100.0	100.0
511	1379	1121	532
39.6	45.8	28.1	35.4
751	1702	2274	954
58.1	56.5	57.1	63.5
749	1656	2683	889
58.0	54.9	67.4	59.1
748	1874	2542	813
57.9	62.2	63.8	54.1
31	82	88	47
2.4	2.7	2.2	3.1

Table 38
WHICH OF THE FOLLOWING DO YOUR FANTASIES INVOLVE?

	TOTAL RESP.	AGE				
		UNDER 18	18–24	25–29	30–34	35 OR OLDER
Have Sexual Fantasies	9749	223	4571	2614	1265	1068
Don't Know/No Answer	52	—	22	7	10	13
Total Answering	9697	223	4549	2607	1255	1055
	100.0	100.0	100.0	100.0	100.0	100.0
Your Partner	6871	181	3395	1775	834	679
	70.9	81.2	74.6	68.1	66.5	64.4
Someone Else You Know	6536	144	3041	1760	889	698
	67.4	64.6	66.8	67.5	70.8	66.2
A Celebrity	1638	55	828	471	181	102
	16.9	24.7	18.2	18.1	14.4	9.7
A Stranger	3669	71	1635	1088	499	375
	37.8	31.8	35.9	41.7	39.8	35.5
Animals	506	11	171	148	94	82
	5.2	4.9	3.8	5.7	7.5	7.8
Other	389	8	171	116	49	45
	4.0	3.6	3.8	4.4	3.9	4.3

MARITAL STATUS			
LIVE WITH LOVER	MAR- RIED	SINGLE AND LIVE ALONE	SEP./ DIV./ WIDOW
1268	2950	3919	1460
4	19	19	9
1264	2931	3900	1451
100.0	100.0	100.0	100.0
940	1850	2956	1017
74.4	63.1	75.8	70.1
741	2042	2680	978
58.6	69.7	68.7	67.4
195	443	780	193
15.4	15.1	20.0	13.3
488	1106	1481	542
38.6	37.7	38.0	37.4
80	162	164	92
6.3	5.5	4.2	6.3
67	105	151	62
5.3	3.6	3.9	4.3

Table 39
HAVE YOU EVER FELT UNPLEASANTLY PRESSURED INTO SEX AND FINALLY GAVE IN AGAINST YOUR BETTER JUDGMENT?

	TOTAL RESP.	AGE				
		UNDER 18	18–24	25–29	30–34	35 OR OLDER
Total Respondents	10000	225	4681	2664	1296	1125
Don't Know/No Answer	50	2	19	13	8	8
Total Answering	9950	223	4662	2651	1288	1117
	100.0	100.0	100.0	100.0	100.0	100.0
Yes	7144	136	3279	1923	982	817
	71.8	61.0	70.3	72.5	76.2	73.1
No	2806	87	1383	728	306	300
	28.2	39.0	29.7	27.5	23.8	26.9

Table 40
HAVE YOU EVER BEEN RAPED OR SEXUALLY MO-LESTED?

	TOTAL RESP.	AGE				
		UNDER 18	18–24	25–29	30–34	35 OR OLDER
Total Respondents	10000	225	4681	2664	1296	1125
Don't Know/No Answer	58	6	22	14	7	9
Total Answering	9942	219	4659	2650	1289	1116
	100.0	100.0	100.0	100.0	100.0	100.0
Yes	2583	66	1106	700	382	324
	26.0	30.1	23.7	26.4	29.6	29.0
No	7359	153	3553	1950	907	792
	74.0	69.9	76.3	73.6	70.4	71.0

Table 41
BY WHOM HAVE YOU BEEN RAPED OR SEXUALLY MOLESTED?

	TOTAL RESP.	AGE				
		UNDER 18	18–24	25–29	30–34	35 OR OLDER
Have Been Raped or Sexually Molested	2583	66	1106	700	382	324
Don't Know/No Answer	65	1	26	17	14	7
Total Answering	2518	65	1080	683	368	317
	100.0	100.0	100.0	100.0	100.0	100.0
Husband	184	—	33	52	43	56
	7.3	—	3.1	7.6	11.7	17.7
A Relative	558	11	229	155	88	74
	22.2	16.9	21.2	22.7	23.9	23.3
A Friend	1155	30	534	304	152	132
	45.9	46.2	49.4	44.5	41.3	41.6
A Stranger	839	29	354	237	130	87
	33.3	44.6	32.8	34.7	35.3	27.4

Table 42
HAVE YOU EVER HAD A LESBIAN EXPERIENCE?

	TOTAL RESP.	AGE				
		UNDER 18	18–24	25–29	30–34	35 OR OLDER
Total Respondents	10000	225	4681	2664	1296	1125
Don't Know/No Answer	44	3	22	6	7	6
Total Answering	9956	222	4659	2658	1289	1119
	100.0	100.0	100.0	100.0	100.0	100.0
Yes	2088	65	933	562	295	232
	21.0	29.3	20.0	21.1	22.9	20.7
No	7868	157	3726	2096	994	887
	79.0	70.7	80.0	78.9	77.1	79.3

MARITAL STATUS			
LIVE WITH LOVER	MAR- RIED	SINGLE AND LIVE ALONE	SEP./ DIV./ WIDOW
1299	3032	4007	1507
4	14	18	7
1295	3018	3989	1500
100.0	100.0	100.0	100.0
350	613	785	310
27.0	20.3	19.7	20.7
945	2405	3204	1190
73.0	79.7	80.3	79.3

Table 43
HOW OLD WERE YOU WHEN YOU HAD A LESBIAN EXPERIENCE?

	TOTAL RESP.	AGE				
		UNDER 18	18–24	25–29	30–34	35 OR OLDER
Ever Had a Lesbian Experience	2088	65	933	562	295	232
Don't Know/No Answer	83	2	42	18	9	12
Total Answering	2005	63	891	544	286	220
	100.0	100.0	100.0	100.0	100.0	100.0
Under 10	424	32	223	104	32	33
	21.1	50.8	25.0	19.1	11.2	15.0
10 to 15	698	23	337	180	83	75
	34.8	36.5	37.8	33.1	29.0	34.1
15 to 20	345	8	229	69	21	17
	17.2	12.7	25.7	12.7	7.3	7.7
21 to 25	329	—	102	148	57	22
	16.4	—	11.4	27.2	19.9	10.0
26 or Older	209	—	—	43	93	73
	10.4	—	—	7.9	32.5	33.2

	MARITAL STATUS		
LIVE WITH LOVER	MAR- RIED	SINGLE AND LIVE ALONE	SEP./ DIV./ WIDOW
350	613	785	310
8	26	31	14
342	587	754	296
100.0	100.0	100.0	100.0
60	112	193	51
17.5	19.1	25.6	17.2
113	232	248	97
33.0	39.5	32.9	32.8
73	82	150	32
21.3	14.0	19.9	10.8
63	92	127	45
18.4	15.7	16.8	15.2
33	69	36	71
9.6	11.8	4.8	24.0

Table 44
DO YOU STILL HAVE LESBIAN RELATIONSHIPS?

	TOTAL RESP.	AGE				
		UNDER 18	18–24	25–29	30–34	35 OR OLDER
Ever Had a Lesbian Experience	2088	65	933	562	295	232
Don't Know/No Answer	65	2	36	9	8	10
Total Answering	2023	63	897	553	287	222
	100.0	100.0	100.0	100.0	100.0	100.0
Occasionally	274	11	112	77	46	28
	13.5	17.5	12.5	13.9	16.0	12.6
Regularly	63	2	26	20	7	8
	3.1	3.2	2.9	3.6	2.4	3.6
Exclusively	46	1	26	8	5	6
	2.3	1.6	2.9	1.4	1.7	2.7
Never	1640	49	733	448	229	180
	81.1	77.8	81.7	81.0	79.8	81.1

Table 45
HAVE YOU EVER HAD AN INCESTUOUS EXPERIENCE?

	TOTAL RESP.	AGE				
		UNDER 18	18–24	25–29	30–34	35 OR OLDER
Total Respondents	10000	225	4681	2664	1296	1125
Don't Know/No Answer	200	5	101	52	15	27
Total Answering	9800	220	4580	2612	1281	1098
	100.0	100.0	100.0	100.0	100.0	100.0
Yes	1051	34	457	280	155	124
	10.7	15.5	10.0	10.7	12.1	11.3
No	8749	186	4123	2332	1126	974
	89.3	84.5	90.0	89.3	87.9	88.7

MARITAL STATUS

LIVE WITH LOVER	MAR-RIED	SINGLE AND LIVE ALONE	SEP./DIV./WIDOW
350	613	785	310
3	18	28	14
347	595	757	296
100.0	100.0	100.0	100.0
57	76	103	34
16.4	12.8	13.6	11.5
11	20	23	7
3.2	3.4	3.0	2.4
16	6	18	6
4.6	1.0	2.4	2.0
263	493	613	249
75.8	82.9	81.0	84.1

MARITAL STATUS

LIVE WITH LOVER	MAR-RIED	SINGLE AND LIVE ALONE	SEP./DIV./WIDOW
1299	3032	4007	1507
27	62	82	24
1272	2970	3925	1483
100.0	100.0	100.0	100.0
159	318	375	182
12.5	10.7	9.6	12.3
1113	2652	3550	1301
87.5	89.3	90.4	87.7

Table 46
WITH WHOM DID YOU HAVE AN INCESTUOUS EXPERIENCE?

	TOTAL RESP.	AGE				
		UNDER 18	18–24	25–29	30–34	35 OR OLDER
Ever Had an Incestuous Experience	1051	34	457	280	155	124
Don't Know/No Answer	145	4	63	41	23	14
Total Answering	906	30	394	239	132	110
	100.0	100.0	100.0	100.0	100.0	100.0
Father	283	10	106	87	42	37
	31.2	33.3	26.9	36.4	31.8	33.6
Brother	471	12	219	117	66	57
	52.0	40.0	55.6	49.0	50.0	51.8
Uncle	196	9	81	56	29	21
	21.6	30.0	20.6	23.4	22.0	19.1

MARITAL STATUS			
LIVE WITH LOVER	MAR- RIED	SINGLE AND LIVE ALONE	SEP./ DIV./ WIDOW
159	318	375	182
22	36	52	35
137	282	323	147
100.0	100.0	100.0	100.0
42	107	87	45
30.7	37.9	26.9	30.6
63	134	187	78
46.0	47.5	57.9	53.1
37	56	65	32
27.0	19.9	20.1	21.8

Table 47
HAVE YOU EVER BEEN TO AN ORGY, SEX CLUB OR PARTNER-SWAPPING PARTY?

	TOTAL RESP.	AGE				
		UNDER 18	18–24	25–29	30–34	35 OR OLDER
Total Respondents	10000	225	4681	2664	1296	1125
Don't Know/No Answer	205	3	107	40	19	36
Total Answering	9795	222	4574	2624	1277	1089
	100.0	100.0	100.0	100.0	100.0	100.0
Often	105	4	45	26	13	17
	1.1	1.8	1.0	1.0	1.0	1.6
Occasionally	410	12	139	105	85	68
	4.2	5.4	3.0	4.0	6.7	6.2
One Time Only	1105	26	467	341	171	99
	11.3	11.7	10.2	13.0	13.4	9.1
Never	8175	180	3923	2152	1008	905
	83.5	81.1	85.8	82.0	78.9	83.1

MARITAL STATUS			
LIVE WITH LOVER	MAR- RIED	SINGLE AND LIVE ALONE	SEP./ DIV./ WIDOW
312	481	566	244
13	26	32	18
299	455	534	226
100.0	100.0	100.0	100.0
240	326	383	164
80.3	71.6	71.7	72.6
59	129	151	62
19.7	28.4	28.3	27.4

Table 48
DID YOU PARTICIPATE IN AN ORGY, SEX CLUB OR PARTNER-SWAPPING PARTY?

	TOTAL RESP.	AGE				
		UNDER 18	18–24	25–29	30–34	35 OR OLDER
Ever Been to an Orgy, Sex Club, Etc.	1620	42	651	472	269	184
Don't Know/No Answer	91	1	43	23	12	12
Total Answering	1529	41	608	449	257	172
	100.0	100.0	100.0	100.0	100.0	100.0
Yes	1126	36	450	325	189	124
	73.6	87.8	74.0	72.4	73.5	72.1
No	403	5	158	124	68	48
	26.4	12.2	26.0	27.6	26.5	27.9

MARITAL STATUS			
LIVE WITH LOVER	MAR- RIED	SINGLE AND LIVE ALONE	SEP./ DIV./ WIDOW
1299	3032	4007	1507
19	62	87	28
1280	2970	3920	1479
100.0	100.0	100.0	100.0
18	34	39	12
1.4	1.1	1.0	.8
86	126	122	72
6.7	4.2	3.1	4.9
208	321	405	160
16.3	10.8	10.3	10.8
968	2489	3354	1235
75.6	83.8	85.6	83.5

Table 49
HAVE YOU HAD SEX WITH MORE THAN ONE PERSON AT THE SAME TIME?

	TOTAL RESP.	AGE				
		UNDER 18	18–24	25–29	30–34	35 OR OLDER
Total Respondents	10000	225	4681	2664	1296	1125
Don't Know/No Answer	160	3	69	43	14	31
Total Answering	9840	222	4612	2621	1282	1094
	100.0	100.0	100.0	100.0	100.0	100.0
Often	44	2	16	10	10	6
	.4	.9	.3	.4	.8	.5
Occasionally	612	12	239	165	107	89
	6.2	5.4	5.2	6.3	8.3	8.1
One Time Only	1226	27	524	376	188	109
	12.5	12.2	11.4	14.3	14.7	10.0
Never	7958	181	3833	2070	977	890
	80.9	81.5	83.1	79.0	76.2	81.4

MARITAL STATUS			
LIVE WITH LOVER	MAR-RIED	SINGLE AND LIVE ALONE	SEP./ DIV./ WIDOW
1299	3032	4007	1507
15	68	47	25
1284	2964	3960	1482
100.0	100.0	100.0	100.0
9	7	14	12
.7	.2	.4	.8
123	172	208	101
9.6	5.8	5.3	6.8
223	303	488	205
17.4	10.2	12.3	13.8
929	2482	3250	1164
72.4	83.7	82.1	78.5

Table 50
WHO WERE THE PARTNERS? (WHEN MORE THAN ONE AT THE SAME TIME)

	TOTAL RESP.	AGE				
		UNDER 18	18–24	25–29	30–34	35 OR OLDER
Had Sex With More than 1 Person at the Same Time	1882	41	779	551	305	204
Don't Know/No Answer	17	1	5	7	2	2
Total Answering	1865 100.0	40 100.0	774 100.0	544 100.0	303 100.0	202 100.0
A Man and a Woman	778 41.7	12 30.0	298 38.5	223 41.0	142 46.9	103 51.0
Two or More Men	1098 58.9	25 62.5	488 63.0	306 56.3	173 57.1	104 51.5
Two or More Women	65 3.5	— —	24 3.1	22 4.0	14 4.6	5 2.5
Some Other Combination of Men and Women	215 11.5	7 17.5	76 9.8	72 13.2	31 10.2	29 14.4

Table 51
IS GOOD SEX POSSIBLE WITHOUT LOVE?

	TOTAL RESP.	AGE				
		UNDER 18	18–24	25–29	30–34	35 OR OLDER
Total Respondents	10000	225	4681	2664	1296	1125
Don't Know/No Answer	76	2	36	15	11	12
Total Answering	9924 100.0	223 100.0	4645 100.0	2649 100.0	1285 100.0	1113 100.0
Yes	7352 74.1	142 63.7	3305 71.2	2038 76.9	1018 79.2	845 75.9
No	2572 25.9	81 36.3	1340 28.8	611 23.1	267 20.8	268 24.1

MARITAL STATUS			
LIVE WITH LOVER	MAR-RIED	SINGLE AND LIVE ALONE	SEP./ DIV./ WIDOW
355	482	710	318
3	5	6	3
352	477	704	315
100.0	100.0	100.0	100.0
148	199	268	154
42.0	41.7	38.1	48.9
200	269	447	172
56.8	56.4	63.5	54.6
17	14	25	9
4.8	2.9	3.6	2.9
55	61	68	30
15.6	12.8	9.7	9.5

MARITAL STATUS			
LIVE WITH LOVER	MAR-RIED	SINGLE AND LIVE ALONE	SEP./ DIV./ WIDOW
1299	3032	4007	1507
10	25	30	11
1289	3007	3977	1496
100.0	100.0	100.0	100.0
939	2184	2937	1195
72.8	72.6	73.8	79.9
350	823	1040	301
27.2	27.4	26.2	20.1

Table 52
IF YOU ARE SINGLE AND ENGAGED IN A LONG-STANDING AFFAIR, DO YOU FEEL FREE TO HAVE SEX OUTSIDE THE RELATIONSHIP?

	TOTAL RESP.	AGE				
		UNDER 18	18–24	25–29	30–34	35 OR OLDER
Single and Living With Lover	1299	21	549	405	142	81
Don't Know/No Answer	29	—	16	8	2	2
Total Answering	1270	21	633	397	140	79
	100.0	100.0	100.0	100.0	100.0	100.0
Yes	376	10	158	123	44	41
	29.6	47.6	25.0	31.0	31.4	51.9
No	894	11	475	274	96	38
	70.4	52.4	75.0	69.0	68.6	48.1

Table 53
HOW DO YOU DESCRIBE YOUR EXPERIENCE WITH HAVING SEX OUTSIDE A LONG-STANDING RELATIONSHIP?

	TOTAL RESP.	AGE				
		UNDER 18	18–24	25–29	30–34	35 OR OLDER
Feel Free to Have Sex Outside Relationship	376	10	158	123	44	41
Don't Know/No Answer	19	—	10	6	2	1
Total Answering	357 100.0	10 100.0	148 100.0	117 100.0	42 100.0	40 100.0
A Once-in-a-While Occurrence	267 74.8	4 40.0	115 77.7	85 72.6	36 85.7	27 67.5
On a Continuing Basis with One Other Person	61 17.1	4 40.0	23 15.5	18 15.4	6 14.3	10 25.0
Frequent, Almost Regular Events with New People and/or One or More Old Friends	29 8.1	2 20.0	10 6.8	14 12.0	— —	3 7.5

Table 54
IF MARRIED, HAVE YOU HAD AN AFFAIR OUTSIDE MARRIAGE?

	TOTAL RESP.	AGE				
		UNDER 18	18–24	25–29	30–34	35 OR OLDER
Married	3032	8	964	1022	518	516
Don't Know/No Answer	535	2	227	171	67	68
Total Answering	2497	6	737	851	451	448
	100.0	100.0	100.0	100.0	100.0	100.0
Yes	1342	—	301	450	280	310
	53.7	—	40.8	52.9	62.1	69.2
No	1155	6	436	401	171	138
	46.3	100.0	59.2	47.1	37.9	30.8

Table 55
HOW DO YOU DESCRIBE YOUR EXPERIENCE WITH AN EXTRAMARITAL AFFAIR?

	TOTAL RESP.	AGE				
		UNDER 18	18–24	25–29	30–34	35 OR OLDER
Have Had Extramarital Affair	1342	—	301	450	280	310
Don't Know/No Answer	27	—	8	8	5	6
Total Answering	1315	—	293	442	275	304
	100.0	—	100.0	100.0	100.0	100.0
It Helped Your Marriage	440	—	95	149	91	105
	33.5	—	32.4	33.7	33.1	34.5
It Hurt Your Marriage	340	—	69	110	80	81
	25.9	—	23.5	24.9	29.1	26.6
It Had No Effect on Your Marriage	550	—	131	189	107	122
	41.8	—	44.7	42.8	38.9	40.1

Table 56
DID YOUR HUSBAND KNOW YOU WERE HAVING AN AFFAIR?

	TOTAL RESP.	AGE				
		UNDER 18	18–24	25–29	30–34	35 OR OLDER
Have Had Extramarital Affair	1342	—	301	450	280	310
Don't Know/No Answer	22	—	8	5	5	4
Total Answering	1320 100.0	— —	293 100.0	445 100.0	275 100.0	306 100.0
Yes	225 17.0	— —	54 18.4	63 14.2	58 21.1	50 16.3
No	807 61.1	— —	192 65.5	285 64.0	153 55.6	176 57.5
He Suspected but Never Knew for Sure	301 22.8	— —	51 17.4	102 22.9	66 24.0	82 26.8

Table 57

WHAT IS YOUR FEELING ABOUT YOUR PARTNER OR HUSBAND HAVING OTHER SEXUAL CONTACTS?

	TOTAL RESP.	AGE				
		UNDER 18	18–24	25–29	30–34	35 OR OLDER
Total Respondents	10000	225	4681	2664	1296	1125
Don't Know/No Answer	610	14	254	141	105	95
Total Answering	9390	211	4427	2523	1191	1030
	100.0	100.0	100.0	100.0	100.0	100.0
Think He Should and Would Not Mind Particularly	1848	46	755	513	286	247
	19.7	21.8	17.1	20.3	24.0	24.0
Wish He Wouldn't	7542	165	3672	2010	905	783
	80.3	78.2	82.9	79.7	76.0	76.0

MARITAL STATUS			
LIVE WITH LOVER	MAR- RIED	SINGLE AND LIVE ALONE	SEP./ DIV./ WIDOW
1299	3032	4007	1507
47	136	278	137
1252	2896	3729	1370
100.0	100.0	100.0	100.0
159	606	730	328
12.7	20.9	19.6	23.9
1093	2290	2999	1042
87.3	79.1	80.4	76.1

Table 58
HAVE YOU EVER SLEPT WITH A MAN ON THE FIRST DATE?

	TOTAL RESP.	AGE				
		UNDER 18	18–24	25–29	30–34	35 OR OLDER
Total Respondents	10000	225	4681	2664	1296	1125
Don't Know/No Answer	40	—	19	8	3	10
Total Answering	9960	225	4662	2656	1293	1115
	100.0	100.0	100.0	100.0	100.0	100.0
Frequently	1317	23	528	397	213	155
	13.2	10.2	11.3	14.9	16.5	13.9
Occasionally	2286	21	910	729	367	257
	23.0	9.3	19.5	27.4	28.4	23.0
Only Once or Twice	3214	75	1611	825	384	315
	32.3	33.3	34.6	31.1	29.7	28.3
Never	3143	106	1613	705	329	388
	31.6	47.1	34.6	26.5	25.4	34.8

Table 59
HAVE YOU EVER GONE TO BED WITH MORE THAN ONE MAN IN THE SAME DAY?

	TOTAL RESP.	AGE				
		UNDER 18	18–24	25–29	30–34	35 OR OLDER
Total Respondents	10000	225	4681	2664	1296	1125
Don't Know/No Answer	37	—	16	11	5	5
Total Answering	9963	225	4665	2653	1291	1120
	100.0	100.0	100.0	100.0	100.0	100.0
Frequently	149	3	52	40	23	31
	1.5	1.3	1.1	1.5	1.8	2.8
Occasionally	1246	16	381	378	234	236
	12.5	7.1	8.2	14.2	18.1	21.1
Only Once or Twice	3323	52	1311	1021	538	398
	33.4	23.1	28.1	38.5	41.7	35.5
Never	5245	154	2921	1214	496	455
	52.6	68.4	62.6	45.8	38.4	40.6

Table 60
HAVE YOU MADE LOVE ON YOUR LUNCH HOUR?

	TOTAL RESP.	AGE				
		UNDER 18	18–24	25–29	30–34	35 OR OLDER
Total Respondents	10000	225	4681	2664	1296	1125
Don't Know/No Answer	47	—	22	9	6	10
Total Answering	9953	225	4659	2655	1290	1115
	100.0	100.0	100.0	100.0	100.0	100.0
Frequently	533	8	193	149	82	101
	5.4	3.6	4.1	5.6	6.4	9.1
Occasionally	2584	30	989	769	420	373
	26.0	13.3	21.2	29.0	32.6	33.5
Only Once or Twice	2351	54	1080	649	319	246
	23.6	24.0	23.2	24.4	24.7	22.1
Never	4485	133	2397	1088	469	395
	45.1	59.1	51.4	41.0	36.4	35.4

MARITAL STATUS			
LIVE WITH LOVER	MAR- RIED	SINGLE AND LIVE ALONE	SEP./ DIV./ WIDOW
1299	3032	4007	1507
6	18	13	7
1293	3014	3994	1500
100.0	100.0	100.0	100.0
79	196	149	106
6.1	6.5	3.7	7.1
404	901	787	470
31.2	29.9	19.7	31.3
320	713	917	363
24.7	23.7	23.0	24.2
490	1204	2141	561
37.9	39.9	53.6	37.4

Table 61
HAVE YOU EVER HAD AN AFFAIR WITH A MARRIED MAN?

	TOTAL RESP.	AGE				
		UNDER 18	18–24	25–29	30–34	35 OR OLDER
Total Respondents	10000	225	4681	2664	1296	1125
Don't Know/No Answer	42	2	23	10	3	4
Total Answering	9958	223	4658	2654	1293	1121
	100.0	100.0	100.0	100.0	100.0	100.0
YES. ONLY ONCE	3112	57	1392	924	416	320
	31.3	25.6	29.9	34.8	32.2	28.5
YES. MORE THAN ONCE	2887	27	805	850	605	598
	29.0	12.1	17.3	32.0	46.8	53.3
NO	3959	139	2461	880	272	203
	39.8	62.3	52.8	33.2	21.0	18.1

Table 62
HOW DO YOU FEEL ABOUT YOUR EXPERIENCE WITH A MARRIED MAN?

	TOTAL RESP.	AGE				
		UNDER 18	18–24	25–29	30–34	35 OR OLDER
Have Had an Affair with a Married Man	5999	84	2197	1774	1021	918
Don't Know/No Answer	98	4	34	34	17	9
Total Answering	5901	80	2163	1740	1004	909
	100.0	100.0	100.0	100.0	100.0	100.0
More Rewarding than Painful	3595	47	1303	1025	607	611
	60.9	58.8	60.2	58.9	60.5	67.2
More Painful than Rewarding	2314	33	864	715	401	298
	39.2	41.3	39.9	41.1	39.9	32.8

MARITAL STATUS			
LIVE WITH LOVER	MAR- RIED	SINGLE AND LIVE ALONE	SEP./ DIV./ WIDOW
1299	3032	4007	1507
6	13	17	3
1293	3019	3990	1504
100.0	100.0	100.0	100.0
434	949	1198	491
33.6	31.4	30.0	32.6
412	800	932	719
31.9	26.5	23.4	47.8
447	1270	1860	294
34.6	42.1	46.6	19.5

MARITAL STATUS			
LIVE WITH LOVER	MAR- RIED	SINGLE AND LIVE ALONE	SEP./ DIV./ WIDOW
846	1749	2130	1210
13	31	39	14
833	1718	2091	1196
100.0	100.0	100.0	100.0
496	1086	1242	732
59.5	63.2	59.4	61.2
339	633	853	465
40.7	36.8	40.8	38.9

Table 63
DO YOU ENJOY MAKING LOVE?

	TOTAL RESP.	AGE				
		UNDER 18	18–24	25–29	30–34	35 OR OLDER
Total Respondents	10000	225	4681	2664	1296	1125
Don't Know/No Answer	38	2	21	10	3	2
Total Answering	9962	223	4660	2654	1293	1123
	100.0	100.0	100.0	100.0	100.0	100.0
Always	5366	137	2636	1342	641	604
	53.9	61.4	56.6	50.6	49.6	53.8
Usually	4297	78	1881	1229	617	489
	43.1	35.0	40.4	46.3	47.7	43.5
Occasionally	274	5	128	79	34	28
	2.8	2.2	2.7	3.0	2.6	2.5
Never	25	3	15	4	1	2
	.3	1.3	.3	.2	.1	.2

MARITAL STATUS			
LIVE WITH LOVER	MAR- RIED	SINGLE AND LIVE ALONE	SEP./ DIV./ WIDOW
1299	3032	4007	1507
—	5	29	1
1299	3027	3978	1506
100.0	100.0	100.0	100.0
738	1450	2230	861
56.8	47.9	56.1	57.2
534	1460	1625	617
41.1	48.2	40.8	41.0
26	114	102	28
2.0	3.8	2.6	1.9
1	3	21	—
.1	.1	.5	—

Table 64
WHAT DO YOU THINK ABOUT THE SEXUAL REVOLUTION?

	TOTAL RESP.	AGE				
		UNDER 18	18–24	25–29	30–34	35 OR OLDER
Total Respondents	10000	225	4681	2664	1296	1125
Don't Know/No Answer	239	2	100	62	44	31
Total Answering	9761	223	4581	2602	1252	1094
	100.0	100.0	100.0	100.0	100.0	100.0
The Sexual Revolution Has:	3385	77	1627	813	441	423
Caused Sex to Be Too Casual. You Still Feel Sex Should Be Saved for a "Meaningful" Relationship	34.7	34.5	35.5	31.2	35.2	38.7
Made It Hard for You to Find Acceptable Reasons to Say No to a Man Sexually	1810	52	1044	452	158	100
	18.5	23.3	22.8	17.4	12.6	9.1
Had a Good Effect on Most of Us	4740	100	2003	1363	675	597
	48.6	44.8	43.7	52.4	53.9	54.6
Other Comments	715	16	344	197	94	63
	7.3	7.2	7.5	7.6	7.5	5.8

INDEX